MODES OF RELIGIOSITY

COGNITIVE SCIENCE OF RELIGION SERIES

Series Editors: Harvey Whitehouse
and Luther H. Martin

The Cognitive Science of Religion Series publishes research into the cognitive foundations of religious thinking and behavior and their consequences for social morphology. The emphasis of the series is on scientific approaches to the study of religion within the framework of the cognitive sciences, including experimental, clinical, or laboratory studies, but works drawing upon ethnographic, linguistic, archaeological, or historical research are welcome, as are critical appraisals of research in these areas. In addition to providing a forum for presenting new empirical evidence and major theoretical innovations, the series publishes concise overviews of issues in the field suitable for students and general readers. The series is published in cooperation with the Institute for Cognition and Culture at Queen's University Belfast.

TITLES IN THE SERIES:

Modes of Religiosity: A Cognitive Theory of Religious Transmission
By Harvey Whitehouse

Magic, Miracles, and Religion: A Scientist's Perspective
By Ilkka Pyysiäinen

Why Would Anyone Believe in God?
By Justin L. Barrett

Ritual and Memory: Toward a Comparative Anthropology of Religion
Edited by Harvey Whitehouse and James Laidlaw

Theorizing Religions Past: Archaeology, History, and Cognition
Edited by Harvey Whitehouse and Luther H. Martin

How the Bible Works: An Anthropological Study of Evangelical Biblicism
By Brian E. Malley

FORTHCOMING TITLES:

Mind and Religion: Psychological and Cognitive Foundations of Religion
Edited by Harvey Whitehouse and Robert N. McCauley

The Evolution of Religion
By Harvey Whitehouse

God from the Machine
By William Sims Bainbridge

MODES OF RELIGIOSITY

A Cognitive Theory of
Religious Transmission

BY
HARVEY WHITEHOUSE

ALTAMIRA PRESS
A Division of Rowman & Littlefield Publishers, Inc.
Walnut Creek • Lanham • New York • Toronto • Oxford

Library
University of Texas
at San Antonio

AltaMira Press
A division of Rowman & Littlefield Publishers, Inc.
1630 North Main Street, #367
Walnut Creek, CA 94596
www.altamirapress.com

Rowman & Littlefield Publishers, Inc.
A wholly owned subsidiary of The Rowman & Littlefield Publishing Group, Inc.
4501 Forbes Boulevard, Suite 200
Lanham, MD 20706

PO Box 317
Oxford
OX2 9RU, UK

British Library Cataloguing in Publication Information Available

Library of Congress Cataloging-in-Publication Data

Whitehouse, Harvey.
    Modes of religiosity : a cognitive theory of religious transmission /
by Harvey Whitehouse.
        p. cm.
Includes bibliographical references (p.   ).
    ISBN 0-7591-0614-2 (cloth) — ISBN 0-7591-0615-0 (paper)
    1. Religion. I. Title.
    BL48.W36 2004
    200—dc22   2003022519

Printed in the United States of America

♾ TM The paper used in this publication meets the minimum requirements of American National Standard for Information Sciences—Permanence of Paper for Printed Library Materials, ANSI/NISO Z39.48-1992.

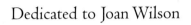

Dedicated to Joan Wilson

CONTENTS

ILLUSTRATIONS

Figures

Tables

Preface

MORE THAN ANY OF MY PREVIOUS PUBLICATIONS, this book is the outcome of long-term and intensive discussions with colleagues, students, and friends. Much of that dialogue has been informal and ongoing. With regard to my closest collaborators, Justin Barrett, James Laidlaw, and Luther Martin, I cannot begin to measure my debts. All three read entire drafts of the manuscript and provided detailed and searching comments. Bob McCauley commented at length on my chapter 2 summary of his book with Tom Lawson, *Bringing Ritual to Mind* (2002), but he did not (by choice) read any drafts of my chapter 8 criticisms of it. I therefore await (with some trepidation) a more public response to that. Others, too, have provided immensely valuable feedback on large parts of the evolving text. I am especially indebted to Pascal Boyer, Robert Hinde, Deb Kelemen, Kimmo Ketola, Brian Malley, Ilkka Pyysiäinen, Bekah Richert, Benson Saler, Tom Sjöblom, Jason Slone, Emma Stewart, Todd Tremlin, and Ted Vial. Boyer's influence on me has been especially important, partly because our conversations have been developing over an exceptionally long time, but mainly because of his intellectual brilliance and generosity. Other old friends have, as always, influenced my thinking at various times, including Veikko Anttonen, Pascale Bonnemère, Mark Burnett, Richard English, Jeppe Sinding Jensen, Tom Lawson, Jorun Rugkåsa, Carlo Severi, and Jesper Sørensen.

While writing this book, I benefited from three main kinds of formal feedback. First, from 2000 to 2003 I was the recipient of a British Academy Networks grant, which (together with significant additional support from the Templeton Foundation, the Universities of Cambridge and Vermont, and the Emory University Conferences Subvention Fund) covered the costs of a series of conferences on modes of religiosity in Cambridge, Burlington, and Atlanta. The papers presented at these conferences—and the discussions that arose from them—inevitably shaped my thinking during the production of the present book. AltaMira will publish many of these conference papers in their Cognitive Science of Religion series, and others will appear soon in special issues of *Method and Theory in the Study of Religion*, *Historical Reflections/Reflections Historiques*, and *Journal of Cognition and Culture*, as well as in other venues. It has been tempting to address or incorporate (suitably attributed) many of the new ideas raised in these forthcoming publications. I have tried to curtail that urge as far as possible, however, so as to avoid "stealing the thunder" of my collaborators and to allow the process of intellectual advancement to unfold in print in much the same order as it emerged at successive conferences. Nevertheless, the benefits to me, however, of having gone through that process while writing have, inevitably, been considerable. Second, my earlier book *Arguments and Icons* (Oxford University Press, 2000) was the focus of a review forum published by *Journal of Ritual Studies* in 2002. The years in which those reviews were being written (2001 to 2002) coincided fortuitously not only with the British Academy conferences in Cambridge and Burlington, but also with much of the writing of the present book. In consequence, I am deeply grateful to the JRS reviewers: Fredrik Barth, Pascal Boyer, Michael Houseman, Bob McCauley, Brian Malley, Luther Martin, Tom Sjöblom, and Garry Trompf. I would also like to thank the JRS editors, Pamela Stewart and Andrew Strathern, for making the page proofs of the review forum available to conference participants at the Universities of Cambridge and Vermont. Third, over the last couple of years I received substantial feedback from staff and students at the London School of Economics, the School of Oriental and African Studies, the University of Turku, Virginia Wesleyan College, the University of Michigan, King's College (Cambridge), Queen's University Belfast, and the CNRS (Paris and Marseille), as well as at lectures I was invited to present at the University of Helsinki, University College London, the University of Vermont, and the British Association Annual Festival of Science (Glasgow). I also learned a lot from participating at conferences in Durban and Houston and especially at two conference sessions last year on modes of religiosity in Toronto, organized by the North American Association for the Study of Religion. Although the contributors to all these events are too numerous to list, I would like to record my gratitude to all the organizers and participants for the valuable feedback they provided.

Two forms of institutional support aided me during the final—at times desperate—push to prepare the manuscript for production. The first was a British Academy Research Readership, which began one month before the text was due for submission. The second took the form of a financial contribution from the Faculty of Humanities at the Queen's University Belfast to support research assistance for two weeks from Noga Kadman.

I would like to thank Brill, Cambridge University Press, and Continuum Press for permission to reprint revised versions of previously published papers, as follows. Chapter 1 contains revised portions of my article "Transmissive Frequency, Ritual, and Exegesis" in *Journal of Cognition and Culture* 2: 167–181, published by Brill (2001). Chapter 4 is largely based on my article "Modes of Religiosity: A Cognitive Explanation of the Sociopolitical Dynamics of Religion" in *Method and Theory in the Study of Religion* 14: 293–315, published by Brill (2002). Chapters 5 and 6 incorporate an amalgam of two of my previously published articles: "Implicit and Explicit Knowledge in the Domain of Ritual" in Veikko Anttonen and Ilkka Pyysiäinen's (eds.) *Current Approaches in the Cognitive Science of Religion*, published by Continuum (2002), and "Religious Reflexivity and Transmissive Frequency" in *Social Anthropology/Anthropologie Sociale* 10: 91–103, published by Cambridge University Press (2002b). Inevitably, those papers incurred separate debts of their own, not only in the process of publication, but also through their early development as conference papers. I would like particularly to thank Ilkka Pyysiäinen and Veikko Anttonen for hosting the conference on cognitive approaches to religion on the beautiful Finnish island of Seili, and Christian Højberg for organizing a highly instructive workshop on religious reflexivity in Copenhagen.

Given the diversity and quality of all these inputs, the present book should, no doubt, be better than it is. To those whose advice I have misunderstood or overlooked, I apologize. To those who have successfully transmitted their criticisms and suggestions, I thank you.

September 2003

Introduction

THIS BOOK SETS OUT A TESTABLE THEORY of how religions are created, reproduced, and transformed. Parts of this theory have been published in two recent monographs, one focusing on a single religious tradition (Whitehouse 1995), and the other seeking to generalize the theory to a wider range of cases (Whitehouse 2000a). Both of these books focused primarily on the consequences of particular psychological processes for patterns of religious dissemination and political association. This was in keeping with the fact that both studies drew mainly on ethnographic evidence. This book, by contrast, concentrates more heavily on the underlying psychological processes themselves. The kinds of theories and evidence examined are, consequently, rather different. The central tenets of the theory advanced in my earlier books will not be abandoned in what follows, but the theory's cognitive foundations will be substantially enriched and extended. My further aim is to distinguish clearly between what we can now say with confidence on the subject of religious transmission and what we still need to find out.

What Is "Religion"?

The everyday meaning of the word "religion" is not all that easy to pin down. Few people subscribe to a formal definition of religion, which they then apply systematically to the world around them. More commonly, people decide if something is an instance of religion on the basis of a range of exemplary features. None of these features is necessary for the attribution of the label, but almost any combination is sufficient. Moreover, it is not at all clear that exemplars of the category religion used by, say, middle-class Americans would match those widely recognized by people in, say, rural Japan or South India. Some traditional societies do not entertain the concept of having *a* religion at all, although certain of their activities may strike the visiting tourist as self-evidently "religious." If people's everyday notions of what constitutes religion are both loose and diverse, then what are students of religion really studying?

Some scholars believe that the concept of religion is a recent invention of imperialist colonial empires, used as a means of justifying expansionary and exploitative interests.[1] It is certainly the case that the contrasts commonly drawn between the religious and the secular—for instance, in modern liberal democracies—are the product of a unique history, in the course of which it has taken a rather astonishing variety of guises (Asad 1993). But just because folk notions of religion are somewhat variable and have been put into the service of all kinds of dubious imperialist projects, it does not follow that we should give up on the search for scientific theories of religion. A scientific theory of religion must tell us what, for the purposes of that theory, constitutes religion. Whatever-it-is should ideally be widespread, not only in the contemporary world, but also throughout most of what we know about the human past; the properties of whatever-it-is should be clearly distinguishable from properties of whatever-it-is-not; and its existence should be explainable with reference to general capacities of our species, activated under generally specifiable conditions.

Edward Tylor's (1871, 424) "minimum definition" of religion as "the belief in Spiritual Beings" has long invited the riposte that Buddhism does not postulate such entities. Nevertheless, this is rather a weak criticism, insofar as the vast majority of Buddhists do indeed express and act upon beliefs in various kinds of spiritual beings, even if that is contrary or superfluous to the teachings of many of the tradition's more learned practitioners and theologians. In actual fact, concepts of supernatural agency[2] seem to lurk in the imaginations of humans everywhere. For the present purposes, let us simply say that religion consists of any set of shared beliefs and actions appealing to supernatural agency.

Such a definition has the merits of parsimony, but also masks some rather thorny problems. The question of what constitutes supernatural agency and why such a concept is so widespread in human populations has recently attracted some persuasive answers from cognitive scientists (set out in chapter 2). This body of scholarship proposes that simple concepts of supernatural agency (e.g., notions of ghosts or witches) fit rather closely with certain evolved features of human cognitive architecture. It is this close fit that makes such concepts easy to form and remember and that sometimes makes them especially salient as we struggle to make sense of our experiences. This line of argument has proven to be empirically productive and sits comfortably with a wider body of current theories about the way human minds operate. But it does not explain all the facts before us. We also know that people may display belligerent skepticism with regard to the alleged operations of supernatural agency. They may dismiss claims (even their own spontaneous intuitions) about supernatural intervention or consider, a priori, certain kinds of claims to be more plausible than others. Moreover, a marked tendency of many religious traditions is to uphold extremely complex (elaborate and hard-to-conceptualize) notions of supernatural agency and to scorn simpler (nonstandard or proscribed) versions. One of the goals of this book is to explain how and why this happens. Under what conditions does religious thinking harden into systems of doctrine or give rise to epiphanic revelations? How is such knowledge transmitted or otherwise reproduced? What are the consequences of this for the structure and scale of religious communities?

A set of closely related problems surrounds the nature of ritual. The performance of more or less widely standardized rituals appears to be a cross-culturally recurrent human trait. Moreover, ritualization has important implications for the way religious concepts are generated and transmitted, as we shall see.

What Is "Ritual"?

People do not regard ritual actions as exclusively technical procedures. If you ask me how to get from A to B, and I draw you a map in the sand, then you will assume that my acts of inscription are intended to highlight salient features of the landscape that will guide you on your way. Of course, you might suspect that I'm trying to deceive you. But, either way, you'll assume that my actions have some relevant technical motivation. When actions become ritualized, this state of affairs is significantly altered (Sperber 1975). If somebody insists that the act of drawing in the sand must be carried out in certain peculiar ways—not with any old implement or body part (such as a stick or an index finger) but only with some special object, such as a bone that must be held between the teeth—then we know that this is no ordinary action. In part, what makes this action different is the fact that it incorporates elements that lack any adequate technical relevance. The anthropologist Edmund Leach described these elements as "aesthetic frills" (1954). As his phrase implied, there are certain similarities here between ritual and art. If my map in the sand were to be adorned by clouds and rainbows, which have no relevance to the task of guiding you from A to B, then you would be justified in interpreting this as some sort of artistic embellishment. (Of course, it might not be good art, but it would be art, nonetheless.)

What both ritual and art have in common is their incorporation of elements that are superfluous to any practical aim and, thus, are irreducible to technical motivations. As such, both ritual and art are potentially puzzling forms of behavior. We may well ask why bones have to be held between the teeth or why clouds and rainbows are included in the map (rather than other equally superfluous images or designs). In art forms for which individual authorship matters, we tend to think that the artist's choices of style, color, composition, and subject matter are all driven by complex intentions located inside his or her mind. And even over and above the technical skill or virtuosity displayed in the artwork, we might consider these intentions to be the real measure of an artist's genius or originality. But in ritual actions, intention is quite a different matter. The bone must be held between the teeth, not because I wish to express something of my own choosing, but because that's the way it should be—or always has been—done. Whether historically accurate or not, our representations of rituals accord them a past (however indefinite). In this way, the intentional states that give rise to rituals are not seen as being located inside us but, rather, are accorded to a procession of shadowy predecessors, primordial ancestors, or gods (Humphrey and Laidlaw 1994, Sjöblom 2000, Pyysiäinen 2001, Bloch 2004). Herein lies a crucial difference between art and ritual. The intentional states behind ritual actions, unlike works of art, are assumed to be located at least partly outside the mind of the actor.

Still, you may ask, why is this important? The answer is because rituals, in ways that both resemble and differ from works of art, invite *exegesis*. Since rituals are actions that lack intrinsic meanings, in terms of both what they intend and what they accomplish, they open the floodgates to an indefinite flow of possible interpretations or symbolic motivations. Sometimes exegesis gushes forth; sometimes it is channeled and regulated as a network of canals; and sometimes it dries up. One of the aims of this book is to help explain all of that.

Ritual and Religious Revelation

Any experience that is reasonably shocking, emotionally arousing, and personally consequential will be hard to forget and is likely to set off many chains of seemingly unanswerable questions. Why did this happen to me? What does it all mean? What consequences should follow from it? Traumatic ritual episodes furnish an especially fertile breeding ground for possible answers to these kinds of questions. As noted in the preceding, rituals are special sorts of actions, insofar as they are open to many exegetical interpretations and layers of interpretation. When never-to-be-forgotten ordeals are ritualized, the temptation to speculate about their significance and meaning never goes away. Every trigger of these painful memories is also a plea for interpretation, and every interpretation remains provisional until some kind of coherent corpus of knowledge eventually matures and hardens. All these moments of insight may be described as "revelatory," although some moments of revelation have more wide-ranging and long-lasting conceptual ramifications than others. One insight, like a pinprick of light, might seem shallow or inconsequential and is then forgotten. Another, like a giant beacon, might seem to illuminate the entire cosmological landscape—and this epiphany is remembered forever. Yet many other degrees of luminescence are experienced as time passes. This is one way in which revelations may be said to originate in ritualization. But there are others.

Consider cases in which the corpus of religious knowledge is transmitted in words as a more or less standardized "orthodoxy." The learning of this knowledge might seem to require exactly the same techniques as used in schools and universities— learners are required to rehearse the information through listening to sermons and lectures, reading core texts, being subjected to regular tests (whether formally or informally), and so on. Yet there are also differences between religious and nonreligious forms of education, and this is where ritual once again becomes important.

Whether or not one is being trained in the principles of art criticism, evolutionary biology, or religious doctrine, it is clearly important to one's teachers not only that the principles themselves are transmitted intact but also that the learner has grasped these principles at a structural level and has not merely encoded sets of superficial properties. The graduate must not only be able to trot out memorized knowledge but must also be able to apply that knowledge to indefinitely many new situations. In the case of art criticism and evolutionary biology, however, the application of expert knowledge can (and should) foster curiosity, thereby encouraging the formation of new questions, whether interpretive or theoretical. Producing questions and provisional answers of this kind might involve a more or less fleeting sense of revelation. For experienced adherents to a religious orthodoxy, however, new questions and new answers are few and far between. This is not because those adherents are less imaginative. At least part of the reason for low rates of innovation in religious orthodoxies (given the numbers of "experts" out there) is that their techniques of transmission are so heavily ritualized.

When you have acquired the desired level of expertise as a lawyer, a scientist, an artist, or a critic (or as any other kind of trained, nonreligious specialist), you stop having to go to classes. You might have to attend refresher courses and keep up with new developments in your chosen field. But once the basic requisite knowledge has been learned, you get your certificate, and off you go. For adherents to a religious orthodoxy, the situation is very different. Long after you have mastered the relevant teachings, you are required to continue listening to endless repetitions of that information through processes of ritualized public oratory.

The effects of routinization on religious thinking are complex. To begin with, carrying out the same ritual procedures day in and day out (or week in and week out) results in habituation. When people end up performing rituals largely as a matter of automated habit, they are far less likely to reflect explicitly upon the possible symbolic meanings of these rituals. So, in one respect at least, routinization suppresses revelation. Much the same may be said of religious speech. Audiences can obviously become habituated to doctrinal repetition and can simply switch off.

But verbal repetition can also ensure the stable reproduction of a substantial corpus of knowledge. The interpretative framework becomes frozen (one might say rigid or dogmatic), so that the process of revelation is no longer a matter of creative invention, but of creative application of previously stipulated principles. So elaborate can these standardized principles become in conditions of routinized transmission that there might seem to be no experience, whether trivial or momentous, that cannot be readily accorded a standard religious interpretation. Revelation in these circumstances can feel deeply meaningful and, in its own way, creative. But it operates within a closed system of ideas in which there is little scope for widespread innovation. Successful innovators (those who are not cast out or executed as heretics) are rare, although their importance in the history of religious orthodoxies is undeniable. For most adherents to traditions of this kind, however, revelation is not a matter of invention. Rather, it is a process of applying special kinds of knowledge to situations for which the analogical connections seem to have been anticipated in advance. To understand this odd state of affairs, we need to understand the nature of routinized ritualization.

When a particular body of ideas is repeated far beyond the point of redundancy, the speech itself ceases to be reducible to technical motivations—that is, seen as merely a means of communication. It also ceases to be anchored to the presumed intentional states of the speaker. The more formulaic the speech becomes, the less certain we can be about the origins of its meaning (cf. Bloch 2004). Is it the priest or the guru who is speaking, or is it the thousand priests or gurus who came before them? The corpus of doctrinal knowledge seems to originate somewhere other than in the intentional states of those who taught it and those who remember it. When these heavily reiterated connections are triggered, they seem to have an external and unknowable source. Thus, when we encounter a new situation to which our standardized religious schemas seem to apply, though the analogical mapping is our own creation, we don't experience it that way. Rather, we implicitly assume that the source problem and its solution come from outside us, and, therefore, so do the connection to the target problem and its solution. It is as if the implicitly unknowable source of the religious teachings somehow anticipated the situations we encounter. We might have been taught to describe that source as the Holy Spirit, the Prophet, or Something Else. But part of the reason this seems so believable is because we have no deep intuitions capable of specifying an alternative source.

Outline of the Volume

This book is divided into three parts. Its argument is built upon the foundations of a number of other theories set out in part I concerning relatively intuitive religious thinking. The more complex and nuanced concepts of religious people with which this book is primarily concerned are generated against a backdrop of cognitively simpler implicit knowledge about the world. We need to understand that backdrop before we can grasp ways of thinking that persistently subvert or confound it.

Some first principles for our project are set out in chapter I. The first is that religious traditions are *materially constrained*—that is, they are not composed of infinitely plastic kinds of concepts and practices. They are subject to psychological and ecological constraints, and it is these constraints that must provide the starting points for any explanation of religion. The second is that religious phenomena are *selected*—that is, religion is not the sum of all mental events, actions, and artifacts created by religious people. Rather, it consists of those private and public representations that have become widely distributed as recognizably similar tokens of the same thing: a ritual, a prayer, a holy book, a temple, a myth, and so on. Though these are the representations that survive countless cycles of transmission, they are only a tiny proportion of all the representations that enter the minds of human beings. And so, the challenge of explaining religion is, first and foremost, one of identifying particular mechanisms that drive the selection of culturally widespread representations in preference to all the other representations that fleetingly occur in any population. The third is that the selection of religious phenomena is *context dependent*. We might imagine the human mind as a kind of filter. Of all the representations that enter the filter, only a fraction of them pass through it. If all minds constitute the same kind of filter, then the representations that make it would all be roughly similar. We could call the similar representations "culture," and a particular portion of those representations "religion." The only problem is that the human mind provides not one but many kinds of filters. And, to complicate matters, its filters are not just static artifact-like structures but organically developing ones. The development and activation of filtration mechanisms need to be understood not only in terms of properties located inside minds but also in terms of properties of the contexts in which mental processes unfold. The fourth is that religious transmission is motivated by explicit concepts. This is certainly not the case in all kinds of cultural transmission. Implicit motivations direct a great deal of human behavior. But since we humans (I) are aware of most of what we do but not why we do it and (2) are inveterate fabricators of stories, much of culture consists of relatively standard post hoc rationalizations of why we do what we do. By contrast, some religious concepts run against the grain of more intuitive kinds of thinking, pushing behavior in directions that are contrary to our "natural" impulses and inclinations. Obedience to religious imperatives is often a matter of overriding—rather than rationalizing—implicit decision making. Chapters 2 and 3 address these issues at greater length.

With these foundations in place, part 2 of the book sets out a detailed account of the psychological underpinnings of contrasting modes of religiosity. Chapter 4 outlines some of the key features that distinguish doctrinal and imagistic modes of religiosity, respectively, as alternative *attractor positions*, around which religious traditions tend to coalesce. The mechanisms driving selection are psychological, involving different modalities of memory and exegetical learning, as well as varying levels of arousal, familiarity, and consequentiality at encoding. These variables, in turn, have far-reaching consequences for the social morphology of religious traditions, producing either large-scale, inclusive, highly standardized, centrally regulated, diffusely cohesive religious traditions (doctrinal mode) or small-scale, exclusive, ideologically heterogeneous, uncentralized, intensely cohesive religious traditions (imagistic mode). The factors that kick-start one mode rather than the other are not yet known in detail. This is a matter for archaeology to resolve, since all instances of independent invention of modes of religiosity predate historical records. Pascal Boyer (2001a) proposes that the emergence of elaborate theology depends upon the prior establishment of literate guilds. The theory of modes of religiosity proposes, by contrast, that complex religious cosmologies are much more ancient than the invention of literacy and professionalized priesthoods and that writing systems swiftly followed—rather than triggered—the emergence of the doctrinal mode of religiosity. Once established, however, modes of religiosity came to constitute extremely robust models for religious transmission, capable of interacting in complex ways (since both modes commonly occur within religious traditions and are not necessarily confined to separate populations of adherents).

Chapters 5 and 6 explore in much closer detail the psychological mechanisms involved in the formation of modes of religiosity. Chapter 5 focuses on the complex ramifications of religious routinization in the doctrinal mode. In conditions of very frequent repetition, knowledge of how to carry out particular rituals correctly is handled substantially by implicit systems of memory. Procedural competence is, therefore, somewhat disconnected from people's explicit concepts of why rituals take the forms that they do. This produces a deflation in the volume and intensity of creative reflection on matters of ritual meaning or exegesis. When people do reflect spontaneously on these issues—for instance, in response to some external pressure or inducement—the concepts they generate are characteristically simple and provisional. At the same time, however, routinization provides excellent conditions for the transmission of much more complex "official" religious concepts, including not only authoritative exegetical knowledge but also the intricacies of orthodox doctrine. High-frequency repetition is conducive to conditions of doctrinal learning, but often greatly exceeds that which is needed for maintenance and consolidation of the corpus in memory after it has been thoroughly learned. Redundant repetition may not only produce tedium and lowered motivation, but it is also capable of inspiring special kinds of revelation, insofar as the contents of ritualized speech can be readily attributed to sacred sources. When this happens, the worshipper may fancy himself or herself a conduit for "higher" ideas and values—a process that is, in its own way, revelatory and motivating, even if it has the external appearance of mental rigidity or dogmatism.

By contrast, chapter 6 focuses on the psychological ramifications of low-frequency, high-arousal ritual episodes. In many cases, such episodes vividly endure in memory. This may help to ensure that ritual procedures are recalled accurately at future performances. But whether or not that is the case, this pattern of remembering has major consequences for the highly creative elaboration of ritual meanings, a process that is described here as "spontaneous exegetical reflection." Drawing on some of the same psychological theories discussed in chapter 5, it is suggested that explicit memories for rituals that are surprising, moving, and personally consequential trigger especially rich patterns of analogical thinking that can only gradually give rise to a body of complex exegetical or cosmological knowledge. Moreover, that knowledge, having been acquired, is personal and idiosyncratic and cannot be taught directly to other religious adherents in the absence of routinized methods of training and instruction.

Cognitively costly aspects of religion are driven and sustained by powerful motivational systems. We know that such systems exist, for they are evidenced by all kinds of expressions of religious enthusiasm, ranging from evangelism and missionization to crusades and holy wars. Chapter 7 attempts to explain both the excesses of religious fanaticism and the equally widespread incidence of tedium and lowered motivation in religious traditions. Again using Boyer's brilliant scholarship (2001) as both an inspiration and a foil, this chapter suggests that religious extremism is an expression of some of the most fundamental features of modes of religiosity. In the doctrinal mode, extremism often takes the form of hardened dogmatism and rigidity of thought. Nevertheless, the levels of risk-taking and sacrifice countenanced by real religious fanatics are most effectively fostered by imagistic-mode dynamics. The imagistic mode is an extremely robust model for religious transmission and can usually only be curtailed or eliminated through either overwhelming external pressure or catastrophic depletion or displacement of the populations sustaining it. By contrast, the doctrinal mode is always delicately balanced between the competing demands of popular consent and priestly control. If the doctrinal orthodoxy is excessively routinized and policed, it runs the risk of triggering tedium and demoralization. If the burdens of repetition are reduced too much, however, the laity may develop its own, more cognitively optimal versions of authoritative teachings. Excessive routinization may give rise to sporadic outbursts of imagistic splintering, whereas underpolicing may encourage periodic movements of renewal and reformation. Either way, the disintegration of the orthodoxy or the flagging of motivational levels in the doctrinal mode or both can be reinvigorated. At its most stable and robust, however, the doctrinal mode provides highly valued and salient forms of ritualized discourse that serve to maintain elevated levels of commitment and an ongoing sense of revelation.

In the third part of this volume, the main predictions of the theory of modes of religiosity are reviewed and sharpened. Chapter 8 examines a set of theoretical challenges advanced by Robert McCauley and Thomas Lawson (2002), who have developed a closely related theory of the relationship between ritual, memory, and transmissive frequency. According to their ritual form hypothesis, the theory of modes of religiosity is, at best, incomplete, since it fails to specify the independent variable driving differences in the frequency of ritual transmission. McCauley and Lawson argue that this independent variable is ritual form. Chapter 8 examines in some detail this hypothesis and the associated critique of the modes theory. Much of this chapter is devoted to a countercritique, providing a valuable opportunity to clarify certain key aspects of the theory of modes of religiosity and to avert potential misunderstandings. But there is a more important reason for attending closely to the claims of the ritual form hypothesis—namely, that it provides highly original and persuasive insights into the intuitive dynamics of rituals.

Chapter 9 focuses on the kinds of evidence needed to test the predictions of the theory of modes of religiosity. Unlike most other cognitive theories of religion, the theory advanced here accords equal importance to both implicit processing (as studied primarily by psychologists and other cognitive scientists) and bodies of explicit knowledge (as studied by anthropologists, historians, classicists, archaeologists, and others). The process of testing my hypotheses must, therefore, draw on the findings and expertise of a number of disciplines. Work of that kind is currently being undertaken collaboratively and is due to be published in separate books (Whitehouse and Laidlaw 2004, Whitehouse and Martin 2004, Whitehouse and McCauley, forthcoming). This book marks the beginning of a substantially new program of research rather than the end of it.

Notes

1. For particularly edifying discussions of this topic, see Chidester 1996, Smith 1998, Fitzgerald 2000, Wiebe 2000, and McCutcheon 2001.

2. The distinction between natural and supernatural agency is examined in the next chapter (see also Boyer 2001a). For the present discussion, natural agents are those that think like ordinary agents (e.g., can only report reliably on past or present experiences, and are unable to access directly other people's intentions), that have ordinary biological properties (e.g., cannot transform themselves into other species or defy the aging process), and

that obey all normal physical expectations (e.g., cannot pass through solid objects or be in two places at one time). Supernatural agents are those that somehow supersede these natural constraints—for instance, by being able to read one's mind, live forever, or pass through walls. Some supernatural agents can do lots of miraculous things, whereas others are more limited in their special abilities. But they are all "super" in the sense that they are presumed capable of overcoming the intuitively expectable limitations of normal agents.

COGNITION AND RELIGIOUS TRANSMISSION

I

First Principles for Explaining Religion and Ritual

ANY STORY ABOUT THE ACTIONS, meanings, and feelings involved in religion and ritual deals with extremely complex subject matter. Only by carving up this subject matter at the joints can we hope to lay bare the mechanisms that shape religious thinking and ultimately explain patterns of spread, cohesion, and social organization in religious communities. To get this task underway, we need a strategy based on robust principles. Four principles may be proposed at the outset: (1) religious traditions are materially constrained, (2) religious phenomena are selected, (3) the selection of religious phenomena is context dependent, and (4) religious transmission is partly motivated by explicit religious concepts.

Religious Traditions Are Materially Constrained

Many aspects of culture are materially constrained. For instance, it is obvious that economic systems of production, exchange, barter, and consumption are constrained by states of technological development and that patterns of kinship and marriage are constrained by the nature of sexual reproduction and infant dependency in our species. The precise nature of the constraints is a matter of contention, but the claim that constraints exist is scarcely debatable. By contrast, it is quite common for religion to be envisaged as relatively free from material constraints. We now have a vast profusion of labels to characterize various aspects of religious thinking, such as revitalist, messianic, prophetic, nativistic, cargoist, salvationist, millenarian, separatist, revolutionary, activist, syncretic, independent, and so on. From these sorts of catalogs it might seem that there are as many diverse strands to religious thinking as to the untethered human imagination. Typologies of religious phenomena, of course, often have their origins in the concerns of religious communities themselves and in the discourses of politicians and bureaucrats. Rather than forming a basis for explanation, however, it is precisely these concerns and discourses that need to be explained. It may matter a great deal to colonial authorities whether a particular religious movement is millenarian, nationalistic, and revolutionary, rather than congregationalist, passivist, and ecumenical. But for the purposes of a scientific theory of religion—that is to say, a theory of the causes of religious phenomena and the variations among them—we require a rather different method of carving up our subject matter.

We must look for direct material constraints on religion, no less significant than the technological and reproductive constraints on economic and kinship organization. Such constraints on religion do exist, and at least some of these are derived from human cognition. Indeed, patterns of mental activity, rooted in the biology of brain functions and their developmental contexts, have direct effects on the elaboration of all domains of human culture, not only the religious. As long ago as the 1960s, it was shown that the variety of kinship systems is constrained as much by the limitations of short-term memory for genealogical categories as it is by the so-called facts of life mentioned previously (D'Andrade 1995, 42–44). More recent work in psychology on cheater-detection, altruism, cooperation, theory of mind, and other aspects of cognition is showing with increasing precision that the structure of mental processing, at least as much as exterior technologies, constrains the patterns of economic and political activity found within our species (Sperber 1975, 1996; Hirschfeld 1996; Bloch 1998; Whitehouse 2001a; Astuti 2001). And so it is with religion. Our cosmologies, eschatologies, ethics, ritual exegeses, and so on, are all firmly constrained by what we can encode, process, and recall (Lawson and McCauley 1990; Guthrie 1993; Boyer 1994b, 2001a; Hinde 1999; Barrett 2000; Pyysiäinen 2001, Atran 2002). Only once we begin to understand these restraints can we begin to disassemble and explain the constituents of religion.

Religion, like any cultural domain, is a distributed phenomenon. That is to say, it inheres not merely in the thoughts and feelings of an individual devotee but also in the recognizably similar or complementary thoughts and feelings of a population of religious adherents. Indeed, some of those thoughts and feelings presuppose that religion is distributed. For instance, the doctrine that only ordained priests can perform efficacious rites of baptism presupposes that religion encompasses different categories of participants, such as priests and candidates for baptism. Moreover, if specialist knowledge is possessed by different categories of officiants, the reproduction of the religious tradition will depend on cooperation. The problem of explaining religion is therefore a problem of explaining a particular type of distributed cognition (cf. Hutchins 1995).

As a general rule of thumb, recognized religious experts are people who have invested more energy and labor in mastering the complexities of religious knowledge than ordinary worshippers, novices, or apprentices.[1] When confronted with a conceptually thorny religious problem, religious experts are therefore in a better position than most to grasp the problem, to formulate solutions, and to recall and articulate relatively stable outputs in line with what they understand to be the authoritative position. Relatively inexperienced persons within the religious tradition are more or less conscious of this state of affairs and look to the specialists for guidance. That is not to say, however, that they are incapable of formulating solutions of their own to religious puzzles. We shall see that a number of variables come into play that regulate the rate and volume of independent reflection on religious mysteries but that produce tendencies only at a population level. Personal reflection and innovation will always be taking place at all levels of a religious tradition, albeit to varying degrees. In the case of relatively inexperienced and "lay" adherents to a religion, reflexive outputs may often be constrained more by commonsense principles than by the kind of complex theoretical knowledge available to experts. At least under certain conditions, as we shall see in the course of this book, popular religious thinking will err in the direction of simpler, more "naturalized" concepts (often to the great annoyance of religious experts and authorities). These are just some of the cognitive constraints with which the transmission of religious thought and action must contend.

Religious Phenomena Are Selected

According to cognitive anthropologist Dan Sperber (1996), the challenge of explaining culture is really to explain the spread and persistence of cultural representations in much the same way as some medical researchers seek to explain the spread and persistence of diseases. The latter project falls to the medical field known as epidemiology. What we require, then, is an "epidemiology of representations" (Sperber 1985). Two main strategies currently exist for the epidemiological study of cultural selection. One comes from the new field of memetics, which envisages units of culture as "replicators" capable of achieving varying degrees of distribution (Aunger 2000). The other comes from cognitive science and seeks to identify ways in which distinctively human methods of processing information tend to favor particular kinds of cultural outputs (Barrett 2000).

Originating in a set of radical proposals advanced by the biologist Richard Dawkins (1982), memetics has come to embrace a great variety of competing arguments. There is no consensus, as yet at least, on such basic questions as what constitutes a "meme," whether an agreed definition is necessary in the first place, and even whether memes are located in minds or in the environments that surround them (or both). Not only are there diverse notions of what memes are and where they can be found, but there is no agreement on the general aim of memetics: is it to explain something, to describe it more precisely, to provide an inspiring metaphor for the analysis of some other process, or what?

By contrast, Sperber's epidemiological approach to cultural transmission has generated a more coherent body of theory and evidence. The main strategy adopted by Sperber and the cognitivist school has been to look to universal biases in cognitive systems as a way of accounting for patterns of cultural recurrence. In other words, the aim has been to explain the relatively low mutation of particular representational forms in terms of invariable features of cognitive architecture. Sperber has often drawn an analogy between this enterprise and the central insight of Chomskean linguistics—namely, that humans are endowed with "a genetically determined preparedness to interpret . . . [linguistic] data in a domain-specific way and to generalize from it to the grammar of the language, going well beyond the information given" (Sperber 2000, 172). Similarly, Sperber and others have argued that humans are predisposed to organize a range of cultural data in ways at least partly dictated by genetically prespecified mechanisms.

These arguments have been applied to the study of religion most prominently by Pascal Boyer, who suggests that the selection of religious concepts is influenced by a number of regular features of cognitive organization. According to this view, certain concepts of supernatural agency are intrinsically easier to generate, encode, store, and recall than are a range of alternatives. The more memorable concepts correspond to the catalog of supernatural representations actually found in the world's cultures, whereas hypothetical concepts predicted to fall below this cognitive optimum are found to be rare or nonexistent in real-world conditions. This hypothesis has extensive psychological and ethnographic empirical support, discussed at greater length in the next chapter.

Given its heterogeneity, it is hardly surprising that memetics has generated at least some approaches that have little in common with the concerns of the cognitivist school. For instance, certain explicitly behaviorist versions of memetics (e.g., Blackmore 1999) argue that the causes of meme-replication can be studied entirely without reference to mental processes. Nevertheless, memetics does encompass approaches that overlap substantially with those of the cognitive scientists. This is not always obvious to scholars in both camps.

According to Boyer, memeticists commit four cardinal sins in their selectionist accounts of cultural transmission (2001a, 75–78). First, they assume that memes, as cultural concepts, are copied from one mind to the next. Second, they assume that all the information necessary for this copying is socially transmitted. Third, they assume that cultural concepts as memes are shared among populations. Fourth, memeticists assume that all cultural concepts are communicated and learned in the same way, as if there were some sort of general cognitive mechanism for acquiring cultural knowledge of all kinds. As a general critique of memetics, Boyer's observations would seem to be well placed; but at least some memeticists clearly recognize the four sins just mentioned and are determined to commit none of them. The recent work of Robert Boyd and Peter Richerson (2000) provides an instructive case in point.

Although Dawkins's (1982) original analogy between genes and memes suggested that memes are somehow "downloaded" from one mind to another, Boyd and Richerson do not assume the presence of replicators in brains—only the presence of similar outputs of mental processing (2000, 155–156). Like Boyer, Boyd and Richerson assume that the transmission of cultural concepts is a process of triggering rather than of replication (cf. Sperber 2000). Person A does not download any concept from person B; rather, because the perceptual and cognitive equipment of both persons is similar or complementary, person B is capable of triggering activity in the mind of person A in a way that causes the latter to generate outputs that resemble those of the former. Boyd and Richerson's more recent accounts of these processes not only are consistent with Boyer's but also present the possibility of building on it in interesting ways.

Boyer's work focuses on the presence of similar cognitive equipment among carriers of culture. It is thanks to the presence of genetically prespecified—and therefore universal cognitive architecture—that the same cues that trigger a certain concept in person A can trigger much the same concept in person B. Not only do Boyd and Richerson recognize the possibility that the triggering of similar patterns of processing can produce similar outputs, but they also consider another equally interesting possibility—that the triggering of different patterns of cognitive processing can produce similar outputs. Boyd and Richerson (2000, 156) present an extended example of this (Bynon 1977), relating to the transmission of phonemes. Their example envisages two cultural classes marked by differences in the pronunciation of words beginning with *wh*. In this hypothetical scenario, the dominant class pronounces *wh* words with a voiced *w*, making it indistinguishable from all other words starting with *w*. The oppressed class, by contrast, pronounces all *wh* words as an unvoiced *w*, indicating the presence of separate mental categories for words starting with *wh* and words starting with a *w+vowel*. In this example, members of the oppressed class seek to shed the unvoiced *w*, and, in consequence, their children learn to pronounce only the voiced *w*. What we then have are two generations in which a particular public representation, or meme, is widespread—namely, the voiced *w*. And yet, this very same meme is reproduced by different but complementary patterns of processing in respective generations. The elderly still have mental categories distinguishing voiced and unvoiced *w*'s, whereas younger people have only a single category of *w*'s—but there is no statistically significant variance across generations in the *outputs* (i.e., the observable pronunciation).

The second sin identified by Boyer is the assumption that the spread of memes is an exclusively social process. Boyd and Richerson, however, positively cite Boyer's (1994b) argument that much of what people know about their cultural concepts does not need to be transmitted at all, since it is derived from genetically prespecified cognitive architecture (Boyd and Richerson 2000, 148). The point made by Boyd and Richerson, however, is that the role of innate cognitive capacities in cultural transmission could only form a limited part of explanations for cultural distributions—limited, that is, in the sense that most culture is established cumulatively over generations and relies on observational learning rather than on information stored and transmitted genetically (Boyd and Richerson 2000, 150–152).

Boyer's third criticism of memetics concerns the assumption that identical concepts are distributed among populations. As Boyer points out, people seldom have exactly the same concepts. The task of selectionist models is not to show how concepts spread though successful replication; rather, it is to show how variations in concepts are not random but tend to cluster around identifiable attractor positions (Sperber 1996) caused by sets of "particularly robust combinations of assumptions" (Boyer 2001b, 77). Here again Boyd and Richerson concur entirely. Like Boyer, they acknowledge that the outputs of cognitive processing vary significantly among individuals. Also like Boyer, they maintain that attractor positions arise from underlying continuities in cognitive processing. But Boyd and Richerson also suggest that the cumulative evolution of convergent practices or memes may partly be a matter of people unconsciously calculating the common denominators of numerous instances of the same behavior. For instance, they consider the possibility that variable instances of a given phoneme are processed by a child in such a way as to "compute the average of all the pronunciations that he hears. . . ."

> Here, mental rules are not transferred from one brain to another. The child may adopt a rule that is unlike any of the rules in the brains of its models. The rules in particular brains do not replicate, because no rule is copied faithfully. The phonological system can nevertheless evolve in a quite Darwinian way. (Boyd and Richerson 2000, 157–158)

The last sin on Boyer's list is to assume the presence of a general mechanism for culture learning. But Boyd and Richerson accept that highly structured cognitive architecture has an important causal role in patterns of cultural recurrence. Their point is that specialized cognitive capacities stored and transmitted genetically are, at best, insufficient to account for the bulk of transmitted culture. As they put it, "The single most important adaptive feature of culture is that it allows the gradual, cumulative assembly of adaptations over many generations—adaptations that no single individual could invent on their own. Cumulative adaptation cannot be based solely on innate, genetically coded information" (Boyd and Richerson 2000, 148).

Clearly, there is substantial common ground between the version of memetics espoused by Boyd and Richerson and the models presented by Boyer and, more generally, the cognitivist school. They agree that the transmission of culture is a matter of triggering similar outputs, not of simply downloading outputs from one mind to another. They agree that not all the mechanisms entailed in this triggering process are themselves culturally transmitted. They agree that cultural reproduction is not a matter of replication but of selection. And they agree that specialized cognitive architecture is implicated in at least some aspects of these selectional processes. So, where is the disagreement?

The disagreement hinges on the extent to which genetically prespecified mental capacities are implicated in patterns of cultural recurrence. In general, members of the cognitivist school are concerned with showing that innate and therefore universal features of cognitive organization are responsible for the attractor positions around which patterns of cultural innovation tend to congregate. By contrast, Boyd and Richerson argue that genetically transmitted capacities are only capable of explaining patterns of "learning enhancement"—that is, patterns of learning "from scratch." In order to explain the massive accumulation of cultural knowledge over generations, they would argue, we need to identify mechanisms of transmission that are extragenetic. At this point, Boyd and Richerson abandon the possibility of cognitive explanations for cultural recurrence and argue for a form of population thinking in which the causal factors they identify are units of culture themselves (memes, in other words).

Arguably, however, this whole debate is somewhat misdirected. The idea that cognitive explanations of culture must be reduced to genetically transmitted causes (and thus to patterns of learning enhancement rather than observational learning) would indeed be both mysterious and unnecessary. And, equally, the idea that cumulative cultural distributions can only be explained with reference to cultural properties themselves runs the risk of reifying culture and confusing the explanandum with the explanans (Sperber 1996). The reason for going beyond these alternatives boils down to this: the richly structured character of human cognition is not reducible to genetic causes but is an outcome of the same processes at work in observational learning and cumulative cultural adaptation.

Although cognitive developmentalists often display remarkable enthusiasm for nativist models of cognitive development, nature and nurture are really two sides of the same coin. All human cognitive capacities seem to be an expression of both biological (including genetic) and ecological factors. Indeed, debates about the relative importance of nature and nurture are somewhat tangential to the task of explaining culture. Whether or not one adopts a nativist or constructivist–empiricist epistemology, one clearly ends up with richly structured and universal features of mentation (Whitehouse 2001a). Nevertheless, a constructivist account of cognitive development tells us something very important—namely, that at least some aspects of human mental processing are not like conventional computer processing. Most computer programs operate on the principle of instruction, whereas organic learning systems mainly operate on principles of selection. Why is this important? Because selectional systems are constantly developing. When you input information into a computer, you need only do it once, and (unless you change or delete it) it remains there indefinitely. If you input the same information over and over, you merely create multiple tokens of the same information, and each token is the same. None of the preceding can be said of the way human memory works, for example.

A piece of encoded information may be available to recall for no more than a few seconds before all traces of it are lost forever. In another person, however, the same single input may leave traces for a lifetime. In yet another person, the same input may leave traces for a few days, but if repeated at regular intervals, produce permanent effects on the cognitive system. And these are only *some* common scenarios. So what determines the relationship between inputs and memory effects? The general answer would seem to be a combination of prior experiences and patterns (including intensities and modalities) of arousal. If we are to uncover the workings of the selectional mechanisms driving religion, then we must place these contextual factors at the heart of any model.

The Selection of Religious Phenomena Is Context Dependent

The development and maintenance of expert knowledge places heavy demands on memory. Since we cannot all be experts at everything, certain cultural concepts will be easier for some people to acquire than others. A competent pianist is likely to learn some aspects of guitar playing more rapidly than is somebody with no previous experience playing an instrument. A lawyer is likely to understand the minutiae of new legislation more easily than is a bricklayer. A medic will appreciate the potential applications of a new drug more immediately than will an artist. And so it is with religious experts. Of course, all religious people are experts of a kind, even if theologians, and religious professionals more generally tend to be more expert than others. Religious people are capable of acquiring certain kinds of new doctrinal or exegetical concepts within their own tradition more easily than are people who lack any substantial experience of that religious tradition. If we want to assess the chances of any particular religious concepts becoming widespread in a particular population, then we must begin by asking about the relevant conditions of prior learning and the ongoing conditions of transmission of expert knowledge.

Consider a simple illustration: Students in a theological college who have a solid grounding in Christian thought, are motivated to learn, and repeatedly reencounter the relevant doctrines, stand an extremely good chance of acquiring Holy Trinity concepts. By contrast, a class of disaffected juvenile delinquents who have a poor grasp of Christian thought, profoundly resent religious authorities and have only been told about the Holy Trinity on a single occasion, are extremely unlikely to recall the information and pass it on. The point may seem obvious, but it is of great theoretical importance, as we shall see.

Consider a very different case: Suppose that one of our more sheltered students at the theological college is taken to a thrash-metal concert for the first time. The experience may come as a considerable shock. For years to come, he may be able to recall a host of details about the experience as a vivid and richly encoded episode in his life experience. By contrast, certain other people at the concert, who go to similar gigs every week, might not recall anything distinctive about this particular occasion just a few months afterward. The theology student has a story to tell for the rest of his life (assuming you are patient enough to listen), whereas some other people who attended the same event will never be able to tell a soul about it.

The theory advanced in this book concedes that universal features of cognitive organization set limits on the memorability of would-be cultural phenomena. But the operations of memory are always context bound. The challenge is therefore to predict the likely recurrence of particular representational forms given specified patterns of prior learning, transmissive frequency, and arousal. Take, for instance, the cross-cultural recurrence of the concept "witch." Witch concepts are evidently more extensively transmitted in some populations than in others. Witch concepts appear to be easily acquired by anybody, based on forms of cognition and knowledge that are presumably universal. But that cannot explain why witches are a focus of great attention in one society and yet scarcely ever mentioned in another. Consider the case of the Azande of southern Sudan, among whom beliefs in witchcraft have been described as extremely virulent. In that particular society, witches are implicated in unfortunate happenings on an everyday basis (Evans-Pritchard 1937, 63–64). By contrast, the clergy of the Church of England are (on the whole) much less likely to attribute their daily misfortunes to witchcraft. Such a mode of explanation would seldom be entertained in the first place but, were it raised at all, would tend to be scorned by most vicars and bishops, if not by all members of their congregations. How are we to explain such differences between English and Zande populations? The key cannot be found in the cognitive apparatus taken out of its context of operation, because variables cannot be explained in terms of constants.

But a solution may emerge if we take into consideration variations in transmissive frequency.

Highly routinized religious regimes, including many varieties of Christianity, provide ideal conditions for the rehearsal and learning of complex theology with a heavy conceptual load. In such conditions, religious orthodoxies may develop somewhat snobbish views on "simple superstition," to the exclusion of at least some sorts of concepts (such as "witch") that require little repetition to acquire and spread.[2] By contrast, the conditions of transmissive frequency applying in witch-infested African societies may positively encourage a profusion of cognitively optimal concepts in the cultural repertoire on a more stable basis. This book is concerned above all with demonstrating the empirical productivity of a cognitive explanation of religion that takes the contexts of human thought and action into account.

Religious Transmission Is Partly Motivated by Explicit Religious Concepts

Until now, cognitive scientists have more or less entirely ignored the role of explicit religious ideas and sentiments in motivating religious behavior. The primary focus has been on how a generic, universal mind produces certain types of outputs regardless of differences in the contexts of operation. The properties of this generic mind are largely inaccessible to conscious inspection. According to Boyer (2002, 10), for instance, people experience a compulsion to participate in rituals because the rituals "activate . . . perfectly normal cognitive systems specialized in the detection of and protection against contaminants in the natural environment." And when things go bump in the night, people are inclined to attribute the causes of this to ghosts (or equivalent supernatural agents) for reasons we will examine at length in the next chapter. But people are not necessarily conscious of the operations of their contamination-avoidance mechanisms or the reasons why they sometimes attribute strange noises to ghosts rather than to natural causes.

Focusing on implicit motivations rather than on the reasons people are able to give for their behaviors may seem to have some tactical merits.[3] First, it could be argued that available data on explicit religious concepts are unreliable. Information gathered by ethnographic methods is reported in such a way that it is often difficult to distinguish people's actual explicit religious concepts from the ethnographer's (more or less distant) interpretation of those concepts. By contrast, the psychological evidence of implicit intuitive thinking, gathered mainly by experimental methods, is generally both precise and carefully controlled. Second, where implicit and explicit concepts conflict, the psychological evidence suggests that the implicit concepts are usually a better predictor of behavior. Third, a considerable literature in psychology shows that people can be easily manipulated to carry out actions in response to stimuli of which they are not consciously aware and will then fabricate explicit reasons for their behavior that have nothing to do with the real motivations driving it.[4] Much explicit knowledge would, on this view, seem to consist of post hoc rationalizations rather than providing a guide to what really motivates behavior.

The question is to what extent such arguments would justify a policy of routinely ignoring explicit knowledge and its potential motivating effects in the domain of religion. Some ethnographic evidence is overinterpreted, it is true. Moreover, it is often difficult to judge the extent to which anthropologists' generalizations about the beliefs of particular populations are based on careful scrutiny of counterevidence, potential biases, differences by age and gender, and so on. But even the methodological sloppiness of interpretivism and, more generally, of the postmodern autocritique have not managed to destroy the traditional empiricism of much ethnographic enquiry. To dismiss all the findings of anthropologists simply because of the vagueness or pretentious obfuscation of some scholars (some of the time) would be an overreaction. Likewise, while implicit and explicit concepts do sometimes conflict, this is not true all the time. Nor is it always the case that people's explicit notions merely provide post hoc rationalizations for unconsciously motivated behaviors. The balance of psychological evidence suggests that when we are mindful of our professed attitudes—and these are targeted at particular behaviors in specified contexts—explicit beliefs can provide a highly reliable guide to motivation (Fazio 1990). And this is precisely the situation that we often find in the domain of religious action, as well as in other domains of expert knowledge. In general, experts are people who have learned to override intuitive, implicit inferences and who have learned to apply explicitly formulated (often massively counterintuitive) principles in their stead.

When the ascetic refuses food despite the agonies of fasting, when a father brutalizes his beloved sons so that they may complete their initiations successfully, when an Anglican offers the other cheek in response to acts of aggression, the motivations for such behavior seem quite obviously to be shaped by explicit religious beliefs. Ascetics, initiators, and Anglicans share the same bedrock of intuitive knowledge about the world and the same emotional systems that would normally lead them to satisfy hunger, to protect their offspring, and to give vent to their anger when under attack. The only thing that makes these people different is that they defer to religious imperatives that explicitly exhort them to engage in behavior that runs against their ordinary thoughts and urges. How do people come to acquire such extraordinary motivations? To answer that, we have to understand how people acquire religious concepts in the first place.

A great deal of religious knowledge consists of cognitively costly concepts (Pyysiäinen 2001, 219). It requires considerable processing resources to learn

Buddhist teachings on the transcendence of suffering or the mysteries of the aboriginal dreamtime, for instance. Although these two sets of religious concepts are
acquired by very different methods, the processes of acquisition in both cases are
necessarily labor intensive. The transmission of a doctrinal orthodoxy necessitates
long-term study and continual consolidation. Learning the esoteric knowledge of
a mystery cult usually requires lifelong apprenticeship as well as deep philosophical rumination. The knowledge itself runs against the grain of natural intuitions,
which is why it is so hard to learn. So, why do it?

In the case of adherents to a doctrinal orthodoxy, religious enthusiasm is as-
sembled through techniques of verbal persuasion (described in chapter 5). In mystery cults, cosmological knowledge results from long-term reflection on the
meanings of veiled hints and clues supplied by the masters of the tradition (described in chapter 6). The apprehension of religious meanings in both cases is typically punctuated by moments of revelation. Suddenly, the relevance and value of
doctrine or ritual imagery become apparent—disparate elements fall into place,
and the world seems more coherent and meaningful. The challenge, as we shall see,
is to find ways of documenting and explaining these psychological phenomena in
adequate detail.

The same processes that enable religious concepts to be internalized and to
harden into fixed attitudes and identities also lie at the core of people's motivations to transmit their hard-won revelations. As much as religious experts value the
knowledge they have labored to acquire, so are they often passionately committed
to its preservation. People may bemoan the loss or obsolescence of technical
knowledge, of rules of etiquette and politeness, and so on, but the loss of religious beliefs and practices is usually a far more serious matter. By the end of this
book, we should be nearer to understanding why this is so often the case.

Culture in general—and religion in particular—are far from being infinitely plastic. There are material constraints on what people think and do, and some of the
most significant of these constraints derive from the regularities of human cognition. At the level of populations, patterns of thought and action become distributed through processes of selection, and considerable work has been done to lay
bare the nature of the cognitive mechanisms driving these selectional processes.
One school of thought, originally inspired by the work of Sperber, envisages cultural selection as an outcome of innate biases embedded in relatively fixed, generic
cognitive architecture. A second argument, from the new field of memetics, is that
distributions of cumulative cultural knowledge are caused by extragenetic biases,
located in the domain of culture itself. The truth, however, may lie somewhere in

between. Only some aspects of cultural learning can be understood in terms of cognitive "hardware." The spread of expert knowledge must also be explained with reference to context-dependent selectional mechanisms. Religions often incorporate forms of expert knowledge of this kind. To understand religious transmission in any depth, we must envisage the mind not as a fixed generic device, such as a computer, but as a constantly developing organic structure whose capacity for encoding, processing, and recall is defined by patterns of prior experience and learning. Having specified the nature of these patterns at the level of populations, we will be well placed to predict which types of concepts can become culturally widespread and with what consequences for social morphology. The theory advanced in this book makes a series of predictions of exactly that kind.

Notes

1. This is not always the case, of course. Some lay Christians, for instance, may have a richer grasp of the church's official theology than their minister or priest, but such cases are the exception rather than the rule.

2. The point is not that doctrinal orthodoxies attempt to exclude all such cognitively optimal concepts, but that they typically impose firm restrictions on which concepts of this sort are permitted or desirable and which are proscribed. This conceptual discrimination is justified on the grounds that the prohibited beliefs are readily activated in the absence of any thorough religious education (and hence associated with the "ignorant," the "unenlightened," the "childlike," the "savage," etc.).

3. I am grateful to Pascal Boyer for pointing these out to me.

4. For an illuminating discussion of the psychological literature on "hypocritical" behavior, see Myers 1998.

Cognitively Optimal Religion   2

HUMANS MORE READILY SOAK UP certain kinds of cultural knowledge than others. Consider the case of language: small children all over the world seem able, without deliberate instruction, to master rapidly vast quantities of lexical and syntactical information, as well as a range of other closely interconnected linguistic competencies (Chomsky 1986; Pinker 1994). Most (if not all) of these impressive abilities are species specific. Moreover, certain aspects of language acquisition follow the same pattern and sequence among children everywhere. Language would therefore seem to be a "natural" trait in humans. It need not follow, of course, that the human language faculty is the outcome of a specific, genetically transmitted device (e.g., an autonomous grammar module) or a suite of such devices.[1] Still, we do not need to resolve these issues in order to acknowledge the naturalness of language. To say that language is natural is, for present purposes, simply to assert that sufficient conditions for language acquisition are found in all human societies, without exception. Obviously, this would not be the case for all possible domains of culture. Sufficient conditions are not present in all societies for learning the rules of chess or the principles of calculus. But there are other patterns of knowledge that would seem to be just as natural as the acquisition of language.

For instance, people everywhere seem to acquire certain similar kinds of information about supernatural agents, rituals, and myths. Such concepts are clustered around a cognitive optimum position in the domain of religion. The cognitive optimum position constitutes a set of conditions favoring the selection of certain kinds of concepts found in all religious traditions, past and present. The cognitive optimum is essentially a universal attractor position, around which many cultural concepts, including religious ones, will be liable to congregate in the absence of countervailing tendencies. Much of this book will focus on particularly long-standing and widespread sets of countervailing tendencies. In this chapter, however, we will concentrate on various sorts of religious concepts that would seem to come naturally.

The Naturalness of Gods

One of the most substantial discoveries of the culture and cognition field is that concepts of supernatural agency (gods, ancestors, ghosts, witches, etc.) are naturally easy to generate, remember, and pass on. In the conditions provided by all human societies, such concepts breed like flies. Why?

A substantial body of work directed at answering that question has been led by anthropologist Pascal Boyer (e.g., 1990, 1992, 1993, 1994a, 1994b, 1996, 2001a, and 2001b). Boyer's starting point rests on the widely accepted finding in cognitive psychology[2] that people naturally organize their knowledge of the surrounding world in certain ways and come to do so in the course of childhood according to a somewhat fixed developmental schedule. Knowledge concerning inanimate objects, for instance, incorporates certain principles that are systematically different from those applying to animate beings. People everywhere assume that sticks and stones do not move unless an external force acts on them; by contrast, they assume that humans move around as a result of invisible properties buried inside them ("intentional states"). Thus, encounters with inanimate objects set off chains of inferences that belong to a mental domain (a chunk of largely tacit knowledge) that comprises a set of principles for intuitive physics. Consider the following examples of such principles: at about four months old, infants expect objects to move in continuous paths (rather than to materialize out of thin air); around six months, they develop some intuitions about the effects of gravity (and thus expect unsupported objects to fall to the ground); also during infancy, children come to appreciate that objects cannot be made to move at a distance. A rather different corpus of tacit principles similarly becomes established with regard to the interpretation of human behavior (a domain concerned with intuitive psychology). For instance, toddlers know that the behavior of other people is caused by properties that cannot be directly observed; slightly older children know that people can entertain false beliefs about the world.

These forms of "domain-specific" knowledge appear to be acquired by children quite naturally and are not subject to significant variation cross-culturally. Boyer's crucial discovery is that any concepts that minimally violate this sort of intuitive ontological knowledge are especially easy to notice and recall, as compared with straightforwardly intuitive concepts, as well as those that are merely "strange" (by the lights of a given culture).

Minimal violations of intuitive ontological knowledge come in two varieties. First, there are violations that consist of simply decommissioning a particular intuitive expectation. For example, ghosts are envisaged as being just like people, except that they do not conform to the principles of intuitive physics. They are assumed to think and emote like humans, but unlike corporeal beings and other physical entities, they can pass through solid objects. Boyer points out that such concepts entail breaches of intuitive knowledge. Second, there are violations that result from the borrowing of properties by one domain of intuitive ontological knowledge from another. These constitute cross-domain transfers of intuitive concepts. For instance, a statue of the Virgin Mary that is said to hear people's prayers is an inanimate object that has somehow acquired the psychological properties of a person. Ghosts and intelligent statues are counterintuitive concepts, but only minimally so. A statue that hears people's prayers, but only ten years before the prayers are uttered, is an even more profoundly counterintuitive concept. By contrast, a statue that is made of cheese has no counterintuitive properties and is merely a very odd kind of statue. In a series of brilliantly designed experiments, Boyer and his collaborators have shown that minimally counterintuitive (MCI) representations are easier to recall than intuitive, strange, or profoundly counterintuitive concepts (Boyer 2001a).

Experimental psychologist Justin Barrett (1998) first demonstrated that in laboratory conditions counterintuitive concepts in general are better recalled than intuitive items and that at least some counterintuitive concepts are better recalled than those that are merely odd.[3] Subsequent research by Pascal Boyer and Charles Ramble (2001) further supports that finding on the basis of cross-cultural studies and suggests also that simple violations (breach or transfer) are better recalled than more profoundly counterintuitive concepts in which more than two types of violation (breach *and* transfer) occur. Among the most important predictions of this work is that MCI concepts will, all else being equal, be easy to recall in all human societies, will therefore be easier to transmit, and will consequently be more widely distributed cross-culturally. On this view, we should expect concepts of ghosts and witches to be globally recurrent, whereas concepts of statues made of cheese or that can see into the future will be either localized or entirely absent from human cultures.

There is some evidence, however, that not all MCI concepts are equally contagious. Those that entail violations of intuitive knowledge concerning animate beings would seem to enjoy a particular selective advantage. Anthropologist Stewart Guthrie (1993) has argued that our species is strongly predisposed to seeing signs of human agency in almost any kind of situation. On the basis of the most unlikely inputs, we seem to have no difficulty discerning human faces or bodies in clouds, rocks, trees, and the dying embers of a campfire. We curse our computers when they crash, we scream in the dark when an object unexpectedly brushes against us, and we are easily seduced by advertisements—like the Michelin Man— that display a vast range of products behaving like people. This tendency to perceive humanlike presences everywhere may be glossed anthropomorphism.

More recently, Guthrie (2002) has observed that it is not merely a proclivity for the detection of humanlike features that is worthy of note, but a more general predisposition to attribute agency whenever perceptual inputs are sufficiently ambiguous. What arrests the attention when there is a rustling in the bushes is not necessarily the inference that a person is present but that an agent (an animal, a human, or perhaps a supernatural being) of some kind may lurk within. Barrett (2000) has pointed out that the presence of a hyperactive agent-detection device (HADD) in humans would have conferred considerable benefits in the conditions in which our ancestors evolved. Clearly, any failure to pay attention to signs that a predator is present would have been far more costly than the experience of innumerable false alarms. As an adaptation to the presence of predators, it is hardly surprising that activation of the HADD is often accompanied by a few goose bumps. Nevertheless, Steven Mithen (1996) has argued persuasively that the development of finely tuned cognitive machinery for dealing with agents also had evolutionary advantages for humans as hunters—not just as potential prey. Being able to track quarry required the ability to read the intentions of game animals, based on close study of their behavior. The ability to guess more or less accurately the intentions of other people would also have been valuable in the development of increasingly cooperative techniques of hunting.

If humans have a natural tendency to overdetect agents in their environments, then how does this bear on their equally natural tendency to acquire MCI concepts? A possible answer might be as follows: most instances of agent overdetection are easily discovered; thus it turns out to be the plumbing rather than a burglar. But signs of the presence of supernatural agents are not so easily explained away. It is true that the old cistern makes some strange noises, but who is to say that some of those unearthly sounds might not be caused by ghosts? That conclusion not only is hard to dismiss on the basis of counterevidence but also raises questions about the possible intentions of the ghosts in the cistern. In other words, supernatural-agent concepts provide a breeding ground for further chains of inferences. This is particularly obvious in the case of many kinds of gods who have access to strategic information (Boyer 2001a). The general rule of thumb is that if something is relevant to you, then you can be sure that the gods know about it. According to this view, god concepts drive a wealth of salient inferences, perhaps helping to account for the prevalence of such god concepts globally. But, whatever the details of the final explanation, it seems that MCI concepts, especially those concerning agents, are somewhat natural in humans. What other cultural traits might be said to congregate around the cognitive optimum position? Another candidate is ritual action.

The Naturalness of Ritual

If we think of rituals purely as actions, they undoubtedly have certain properties that are activated by default in all societies. These natural properties have to do with the procedural aspects of ritual. (The fact that rituals are also puzzling and potentially meaningful actions can be left aside for the moment.) Simple ritual procedures are easily and naturally acquired for two main reasons: The first is that they activate some rather powerful mechanisms dedicated to protection against contaminants. Second, whenever rituals are addressed to supernatural agents, they are capable of triggering tacit intuitive judgments about the appropriate forms that these rituals should take.

Important insights into the natural foundations of ritualization may be gleaned from the study of obsessive-compulsive disorder (OCD). Sufferers from that condition feel compelled to carry out certain actions in an obsessively repetitive fashion. These actions tend to be clustered around a particular constellation of themes, including attention to threshold or entrance; washing or grooming; touching, tapping, or rubbing; concern about symmetry or exactness; cleaning things; making nonsense sounds, words, or music; fear of harming others if insufficiently careful; and the list goes on (Fiske and Haslam 1997, 218). Although sometimes rooted in technically motivated procedures (such as hand washing), victims of OCD will repeat these procedures to a point that is vastly in excess of any practical requirements. Other routines, however, might have no obvious link to practical actions at all. Alan P. Fiske and Nick Haslam (1997, 219) compared a standard checklist of OCD symptoms (based on clinical observations) against ethnographic evidence on behavioral traits across fifty-two cultures, consisting of ritual contexts, work environment, and other activities. They concluded:

> Features resembling OCD symptoms are much more likely to occur in samples of rituals from the world's cultures than they are to occur in samples of work or other activities. In contrast, features resembling symptoms of other psychological disorders are rarer and do not discriminate as well between rituals and other activities. In the vast majority of cultures sampled, rituals contain more different OCD-like features than work or other activities.

Fiske and Haslam's interpretation of these findings focuses on the concern—expressed in OCD symptomology and in many rituals in their survey—with concepts and affective states relating to pollution and contamination and its effects.

It is easy to imagine how the evolution of contamination-avoidance mechanisms could result in a natural propensity for ritualization, albeit one that is carried to extremes by OCD sufferers (perhaps due to some malfunctioning of the neural circuitry in which these mechanisms are embedded). The risks of infection or contagion that arise from handling contaminants (ranging from feces to rotten meat) were real enough for our hominid ancestors. A system that is alert to the presence of such dangers, that carries emotional force (fear and revulsion), and that encourages the learning of contamination-avoidance procedures even when the nature of the threat is only vague or unspecified would certainly have been adaptive. From this, it is only a short step to the conclusion that people are naturally susceptible to learning and copying ritual procedures. As Boyer succinctly puts it, "Both rituals and obsessive pathologies seem to activate, albeit in a heightened and grotesque way, perfectly normal cognitive systems specialized in the detection of and protection against contaminants in the natural environment" (2002, 10).

Rituals might also be natural forms of human activity in a rather different respect. Rituals are, of course, actions, and humans are equipped with some highly specialized equipment for processing information of this sort. E. Thomas Lawson and Robert N. McCauley's (1990) theory of ritual competence shows that rituals in which MCI agents play a role have complex and ultimately bifurcating properties. The theory of ritual competence begins with the observation that all the crucial principles required for the invention and reproduction of rituals are supplied by ordinary cognitive mechanisms, particularly those associated with naïve psychology or "theory of mind." The technical term "theory of mind" (TOM) is used by developmental psychologists (e.g., S. A. Gelman et al. 1994 and Leslie 1994) to describe a domain of intuitive knowledge concerning the intentionality of animate beings. As previously noted, all normal adults assume that the behavior of other persons is caused by invisible properties (intentions) informed by beliefs that may or may not be correct. Among the crucial categories employed by the TOM are agent, action, patient, and instrument (see figure 2.1). Once these principles and categories have fully developed (approximately by school age), they remain roughly stable throughout life.

The principles and categories of TOM are utilized in the representation of ritual form in the same way as in the representation of all actions, except in one important respect. Lawson and McCauley maintain that religious rituals, unlike other kinds of actions, invest certain categories of participating persons or objects with special qualities. Thus, the agent, patient, or instrument used in a rite may be represented as having some special connection with the gods. From this apparently slight modification of schemes for the representation of ordinary actions, religious rituals acquire some rather complex structural properties.

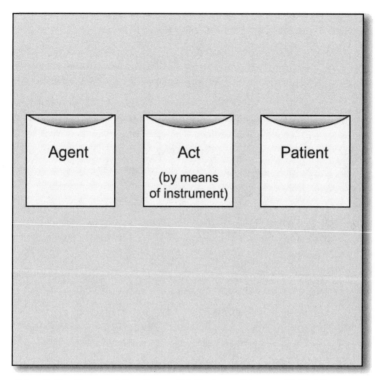

Figure 2.1.   Action Representation System (McCauley and Lawson 2002, 14)

Consider a simple nonritual action sequence in which a policeman bashes a bank robber with his truncheon. What Lawson and McCauley refer to as our "action representation system" specifies an agent (the policeman), an action (bashing), a patient or recipient of the action (the bank robber), and an instrument (the truncheon). Now consider a simple ritual action sequence in which a priest taps the shoulder of a candidate for ordination with a special staff. Here, the agent (priest) also acts (by tapping) on a patient (the candidate) using an instrument (the special staff). But in order for this rite of ordination to be effective, we have to assume that the priest is acting in place of a god (or similar superhuman agent). In other words, the agent in the action representation for such a ritual has some special qualities (in diagrammatic representations of such scenarios, Lawson and McCauley use an *S* to indicate the special qualities of the actor in the agent slot). The S-marker could occur elsewhere in a ritual. In sacrificial rites, for instance, the initial S-marker is associated with the patient slot. In Roman Catholic blessings, the initial S-marker is associated with the instrument slot. But now we must deal with a complication.

A priest who ordains another priest is not himself a culturally postulated superhuman agent (CPS agent). The ordaining priest is not a god. Rather, he is represented as having acquired the special ability to act on behalf of a god (or other CPS agent) by virtue of having previously undergone an enabling ritual, wherein he himself was a candidate for ordination. In Lawson and McCauley's model, the full structural description of any ritual would include not only the surface features of the ritual action in question but all the enabling rituals that its formal properties presuppose (although official and lay notions of how many enabling rituals are required in a given case may vary). The ways in which CPS agents enter into our representations of religious rituals therefore vary along two parameters: CPS agents may be most closely connected with the particular item or person that fills one of the various slots (i.e., roles such as agent, patient, or instrument) in the action representation system (referred to as the principle of superhuman agency, or PSA); at the same time, they may be more or less immediately involved, depending on how far back into the full structural description of the present ritual one would need to go into in order to derive the original intervention of a CPS agent (referred to as the principle of superhuman immediacy, or PSI) on which the efficacy of the present ritual depends. In a Roman Catholic blessing, for instance, the CPS agent is most closely associated with the instrument slot (being present in the water that is sprinkled on the patient); but this divine intervention requires the performance of a series of enabling rituals. In particular, the presence of a connection between the CPS agent and the holy water presupposes the execution of a prior ritual on the part of the priest (ritual preparation of the water), which in turn presupposes another prior ritual (ordination of the officiant), which in turn presupposes the ritual delegation of this authority to carry out ordinations (by Christ).

McCauley and Lawson propose that the structural depth of any given ritual, in terms of the PSI measure, might provide a fairly accurate measure of the "centrality" of that ritual in the religious tradition—that is, the ritual's relative dispensability. To put it slightly more succinctly, the fewer enabling rituals a given rite presupposes, the more fundamental and indispensable that rite will be considered to be within the wider religious system. In Roman Catholic thinking, for instance, the ritual of baptism should be more readily dispensable than the ritual of Holy Communion, since CPS agent involvement occurs at a higher level of structural depth in the latter than in the former (McCauley and Lawson 2002, 34). Intuitions concerning relative dispensability are, or course, postulated only at a tacit level (and need not accord with explicit exegetical and doctrinal knowledge). Accessing such intuitions would therefore require the deployment of quite sophisticated methods of psychological research, and some useful studies along these lines

Table 2.1.   Typology of Religious Ritual Forms

	Special Agent Rituals	*Special Patient/Instrument Rituals*
Level 1	Type 1	Type 2
Level 2	Type 3	Type 4
Level 3	Type 5	Type 6
Level 4	Type 7	Type 8
Etc.	Further Odd-Numbered Types	Further Even-Numbered Types

(McCauley and Lawson 2002, 28)

have already been carried out (Barrett and Lawson 2001; Malley and Barrett, forthcoming). McCauley and Lawson argue, however, that other ways of testing their claims about the centrality of rituals are available. For instance, one would expect to find historically that religious schisms and controversies tend to focus on proposed changes to relatively central rituals, whereas changes to less central rituals would more readily exhibit a pattern of accommodation by consensus (McCauley and Lawson 2002, 35).

In *Bringing Ritual to Mind* (2002), McCauley and Lawson develop the pivotal argument that all religious rituals can be divided into two types. The column on the right in table 2.1 consists of rituals in which the initial appearance of the CPS agent is associated with the instrument or patient slot. Since the types of rituals listed here are all accorded even numbers, McCauley and Lawson refer to them as even-numbered rituals (or more specifically as "special instrument" and "special patient" rituals). The column to left of that consists of rituals in which the CPS agent is most closely associated with the agent role, and these are referred to as odd-numbered rituals (or more descriptively as "special agent" rituals). On the basis of whether we are dealing with rituals of the odd- or even-numbered type, McCauley and Lawson claim to be able to predict (1) whether a ritual is reversible, (2) whether a ritual is repeatable, and (3) the relative degree of sensory pageantry and arousal associated with specifiable types of rituals.

Where the S-marker first appears in the agent slot, as in special agent rituals, the ritual should be reversible but nonrepeatable. The reason is simple: when gods act, their effects are decisive and permanent. An ordination or a wedding is effected by the god (via the priest or other officiant), and what god has done cannot be undone except by the god (or the god's representative). Hence, any reversal of the effects of such rituals could in principle be ritualized—accounting for the presence, for instance, of rites of defrocking or divorce. Unless such reversing rituals are performed, the rituals are nonrepeatable: neither can priests be reordained nor married couples remarried. Conversely, where the S-marker is in the patient slot (in "special patient rituals") or the instrument slot (in "special instrument rituals"), the rituals in question will be nonreversible but repeatable. In other words, there are no rituals for undoing the effects of, say, sacrifices and blessings. But, at the same time, there is no reason why such rituals should not be repeated over and over again.

Despite some problems with regard to McCauley and Lawson's more sweeping claims about the nature of ritual transmission (discussed in chapter 8), they present a groundbreaking theory of the role played by tacit intuitive knowledge in judgments of ritual efficacy. In particular, McCauley and Lawson make a persuasive case for the view that, at least at an implicit level, ritual actions are capable of generating powerful intuitions regarding repeatability, reversibility, relative centrality, and appropriate levels of sensory pageantry. Now, how do these intuitions fit with the previously discussed evidence concerning the similarities between OCD and institutionalized rituals?

If one considers the rituals of actual OCD sufferers, it is clear that notions of CPS agent involvement are inessential (and generally quite rare). The absence of such involvement means that these compulsive procedures fall outside the ambit of McCauley and Lawson's theory. But that is also true of many culturally stable and widely distributed magical rituals and taboos. What is often striking about such rituals is that they rather closely resemble technical procedures in certain respects. Consider the following instance of rainmaking magic among the Orokaiva (Williams 1928). The procedure begins by taking a certain kind of leaf, which is considered to look like a cloud, and crushing it in a pot. The rainmaker then procures an especially succulent stalk and squeezes it over the pot so that drops of liquid fall on the crushed leaf. Meanwhile, the words "rain come, rain come!" are muttered. Then the stalk is placed in the pot, and the whole concoction is carried indoors. To reverse the magic, the contents of the pot are taken out to dry and the rainmaker sweeps his or her hand across the sky, saying, "rain be finished!" No CPS agent involvement in this ritual is imagined to occur. But this is precisely one of the features that makes Orokaiva rain magic rather similar to the "rituals" of OCD sufferers. Both kinds of rituals incorporate obvious, univocal intentional meanings, and many (such as obsessive hand washing) are actually modeled directly on technical procedures. Above all, Orokaiva rain magic (along with a host of other ritual practices documented in that society) shows a great concern for the avoidance of contamination.[4]

In a nutshell, Orokaiva rain magic (in common with most rituals carried out by OCD sufferers) is very much like a technical procedure, specifically one that carries risks of pollution. We know that toothbrushing, for instance, has technical motivations concerned with dental hygiene and also that some care should be taken to avoid contaminants (e.g., wash hands beforehand; rinse brush after use; and store in specific holder or container). With regard to procedures of this sort, whether or not using standard physical causation concepts or notions of magical causation, actions matter more than intentions. When it comes to dental hygiene, it really doesn't matter what people brushing their teeth happen to think is the purpose of the procedure, as long as they perform it correctly. Likewise, there is good reason to suppose that the procedures performed among the Orokaiva to bring rain are assumed to be effective regardless of whether they are carried out with that aim in mind. If some ignorant person carried out the procedures without knowing what they meant, the rain should still come (as long as the procedures were carried out correctly). Introducing supernatural agents into our rituals changes the situation quite radically. And this is where the "ritual form hypothesis" may come into play.

In a series of recent experimental studies,[5] Barrett has shown that the presence of supernatural agents in the action representation system for ritual procedures biases people's intuitive judgments about the relative importance of agency versus action in a given performance. In one experiment, a sample of American Protestant participants was presented with the bare details of a fictitious ritual that had apparently produced a miraculous effect. Half the group was told that the procedure was connected with a supernatural agent, and the other half was simply told that this procedure and its effect occurred in some "other world," where normal physical causation might be expected to operate differently. One of the fictitious rituals was presented to the group as follows (Barrett and Lawson 2001, 194–195):

> Given that a special person cleans a trumpet with a special cloth and the village is protected from an epidemic, how likely is each of the following actions to protect the village from an epidemic? Please rate each action: 1 = extremely likely the action will work, 7 = extremely unlikely.
> a) A special person cleans a trumpet with a special plant.
> b) A special beetle cleans a trumpet with a special cloth.
> c) A special person cleans a trumpet with a special paper.
> d) A special dog cleans a trumpet with a special cloth.
> e) A special person covers a trumpet with a special cloth.
> f) A special person stuffs a trumpet with a special cloth.
> g) A special person cleans a trumpet with a special cloth.

The experiment therefore tested for the effects of various changes to ritual agents and ritual actions, respectively, on judgments of ritual efficacy. Participants in the "technical/magical" condition judged the presence of the right kind of agent to be significantly less important to the efficacy of the ritual than those who had been told that a supernatural agent was involved. Whereas, in many types of magical rites, performing the correct actions is all that matters, the insertion of supernatural agents naturally triggers social causal cognition, and having the correct intentions and ritual actors becomes more important than getting the actions right. Once this happens, other effects postulated by the ritual form hypothesis may be activated.

Recent empirical research (Malley and Barrett, forthcoming) designed to test some key features of McCauley and Lawson's theory suggests that considerations of ritual form do indeed influence implicit judgments regarding the repeatability, reversibility, and emotionality of rituals in which supernatural agents are presumed to play a role. Brian Malley and Justin Barrett's study concerned itself with selected rituals from three religious traditions: Hinduism, Judaism, and Islam. They began by contacting members of each of these traditions on an American university campus. They then sought to elicit, via interview, each person's opinions regarding the accuracy of McCauley and Lawson's predictions vis-à-vis a selection of familiar rituals:

> In interviews, we gave informants a simplified version of the Lawson-McCauley ritual definition and asked what actions in their religions might be rituals. For each ritual that informants identified, the interviewer asked for a description so as to determine how each informant understood each ritual's relation to a superhuman agent. We reserved the ultimate decision of whether a ritual was a special agent ritual for ourselves, however, because there was no practical way to explain the nuances of the Lawson-McCauley theory to informants. Follow-up questions ascertained whether informants regarded the ritual as reversible, repeatable, relatively emotional, and involving relatively high sensory pageantry for the patient. (Malley and Barrett, forthcoming)

In general, the intuitions of interviewees corresponded with those predicted by the ritual form hypothesis to a degree that was, albeit far from perfect, at least statistically significant. Some of Malley and Barrett's overall findings are presented in tables 2.2 and 2.3. The bold type indicates results that conflicted with McCauley and Lawson's predictions. It will be noted that the predictions regarding repeatability and reversibility fared better in relation to the Muslim rituals than did the Hindu and Jewish ones. The predictions of the ritual form hypothesis with regard to relative levels of sensory pageantry among rituals taken from the same tradition were only rather weakly supported. Nevertheless, when emotionality was substituted for sensory pageantry, the predictions were supported at a statistically significant level.[6]

If most of these data find adequate support from further studies, then the ritual form hypothesis would seem to be onto something important. The model seems to pick out some important natural biases in people's intuitions with regard to a number of aspects of rituals in which supernatural agents figure.

Before we move on, however, two brief caveats are required. First, in talking about the role of contamination-avoidance mechanisms and ritual form consider-

Table 2.2.   Overall Interview Results for Repeatability and Reversibility

Rituals	Special	Repeatable?	Reversible?
Hinduism			
Thread	Agent	No	**No**
Wedding	Agent	No	No
Abishekam	Patient	Yes	No
Aarthi	Patient	Yes	No
Raksha Bandhan	Instrument	Yes	No
Judaism			
Bris	Agent	No	No
Bar/Bat Mitzvah	Instrument	**No**	No
Wedding	Instrument	**No**	No
Conversion	Agent	No	*Mixed*
Mikvah	Instrument	Yes	No
Burning Chametz	Instrument	Yes	No
Lighting Shabbat Candles	Instrument	Yes	No
Havadalah	Instrument	Yes	No
Mezuzah	Instrument	**No**	**Yes**
Islam			
Marriage	Agent	No	Yes
Divorce	Agent	No	Yes
Hajj	Patient	Yes	No
Wudu	Instrument	Yes	No
Accuracy		**15 of 18**	**13 of 17**
		p=0.004	**p=0.025**

(Malley and Barrett, forthcoming)

ations, respectively, it may sound as if I am suggesting that there are two kinds of cognitively optimal rituals: the magical and technical, on the one hand, and the rituals that involve supernatural agents on the other. This is not the case. True, the rituals of OCD sufferers seem to be driven exclusively by an overactive contamination-avoidance mechanism. But that same mechanism, operating at more moderate levels, is probably capable of activation in a great many institutionalized rituals, including those that incorporate supernatural agents. Second, the predictions of the ritual form hypothesis can probably only come into play when the supernatural agents addressed in rituals have certain unusual mind-reading capacities. Barrett (2003) presents experimental data suggesting that having the right intentions when performing a ritual is only important if the supernatural agent is able to access those intentions. If not, actions are rated as more important than intentions in intuitive judgments of ritual efficacy (just as in the case of Orokaiva rain magic and similar rituals in which supernatural agents are not involved).

**Table 2.3.   Comparison of Emotionality and Sensory Pageantry
in Special Agent and Other Rituals**

	Special Agent	vs.	Special Instrument/Patient	Emotionality Prediction Fit?	Sensory Pageantry Prediction Fit?
Hindu	Thread	vs.	Abishekam	Yes	Yes
	Wedding	vs.	Aarthi	No	Yes
			Raksha Bandhan	Yes	Yes
			Abishekam	Yes	Yes
			Aarthi	—	Yes
			Raksha Bandhan	Yes	Yes
Jewish	Bris	vs.	Bar/Bat Mitzvah	No	No
	Conversion	vs.	Wedding	No	No
			Mikvah	Yes	Yes
			Burning Chametz	Yes	Yes
			Lighting Shabbat Candles	Yes	Yes
			Havadalah	Yes	Yes
			Mezuzah	Yes	Yes
			Bar/Bat Mitzvah	Yes	No
			Wedding	Yes	No
			Mikvah	Yes	Yes
			Burning Chametz	Yes	Yes
			Lighting Shabbat Candles	Yes	No
			Havadalah	Yes	No
			Mezuzah	Yes	Yes
Muslim	Marriage	vs.	Hajj	No	Yes
	Divorce	vs.	Wudu	Yes	Yes
			Hajj	No	No
			Wudu	Yes	No
		Accuracy		**18 of 23** **p=0.003**	**16 of 24** **p=0.076**

(Malley and Barrett, forthcoming)

Consequently, social causal cognition will not be activated, and the Lawson-McCauley hypotheses will not be applicable.

Whether or not rituals incorporate supernatural agents (of whatever kind), they are often associated with myths. The nature of that association is variable, as we shall see, but some social anthropologists have suggested that rituals and myths are really versions of one another: "The rite is a dramatization of the myth, the myth is the sanction or charter for the rite" (Leach 1954, 13). There are reasons to think that myths, like rituals, have some natural foundations.

The Naturalness of Myth

It is tempting to suppose that great works of literature, such as Homer's *Odyssey* or Shakespeare's *Othello*, are the products of distinctively literate minds. But, in fact, the wanderings of Odysseus or the tragic demise of Desdemona have much the same properties as any story, including those that we tell to defend our actions, to discredit our enemies, to entertain our children, or to explain a natural disaster. According to cognitive linguist Mark Turner, Western biases since antiquity have encouraged us to think that "the everyday mind is unliterary and the literary mind is optional" (1996, v–vi). But he argues, to the contrary, that

> The literary mind is not a separate kind of mind. It is our mind. The literary mind is the fundamental mind. . . . Most of our experience, our knowledge, and our thinking is organized as stories. The mental scope of story is magnified by projection— one story helps us to make sense of another. The projection of one story onto another is parable, a basic cognitive principle that shows up everywhere, from simple actions like telling the time to complex literary creations like Proust's *A la Recherche du Temps Perdu*. (M. Turner 1996, v)

The essence of a story, of any story, is that it represents a world that might have been (or might one day become) rather than a world that is. Stories are works of imagination. Until relatively recently, many psychologists assumed (more or less faithfully following Freud 1913 and Piaget 1962) that pretend play in young children reflected the early dominance of egoistic desire over logico-empirical learning. Child's play, according to this view, constituted a desperate (and constantly frustrated) effort to make the world as it should be, rather than as it is. This interpretation has been called into question by the findings of developmental psychologist Paul Harris. Harris shows that, from an early age, imaginative thinking involves forms of projection that are "well-attuned to social engagement," "not driven by frustrated desires," and capable of "amplifying" rather than merely ignoring, impeding, or violating "children's analysis of reality" (2000, 188). Nor is the natural tendency of children everywhere to construct fictional worlds a distinctively "childish" trait: "The capacity to imagine alternative possibilities and to work out their implications emerges early in the course of children's development *and lasts a lifetime*" (Harris 2000, xi, emphasis added).

Adults, like children, continually project possible scenarios onto the real world, without running the risk of conflating the actual and the fictional. What is more, they do this in ways that involve the "borrowing" of causal stories from one domain of knowledge in order to identify and evaluate possible outcomes of various scenarios in an entirely different domain. This is the essence of parable, as noted previously by Turner (1996). Exactly how these traits in human cognition evolved, and what selective advantages they conferred, if any, remains a matter of debate (for some well-substantiated hypotheses, see Mithen 1996). But few would argue with the fact that these traits universally emerge early in the phylogeny of cognitive development and remain stable and pervasive features of adult mentation. As Boyer puts it:

> We know that human minds are narrative or literary minds. That is, minds that strive to represent events in their environment, however trivial, in terms of causal *stories*, sequences where each event is the result of some other event and paves the way for what is to follow. People everywhere make up stories, avidly listen to them, are good judges of whether they make sense. But the narrative drive goes deeper. It is embedded in our mental representation of whatever happens around us. (2001a, 204; italics added)

Thus, people have a natural tendency to pay attention to causal stories that (1) relate to states of affairs that are not specified by observable, present realities and (2) are capable of driving inferences about other stories, on the principle of analogic reasoning. Does that mean that any story is as attention grabbing, readily recalled, and easily transmitted as any other? Certainly not. Consider how hard it would be to narrate a synopsis of Proust's novels or even to tell a funny but complicated joke without adequate rehearsal. Stories that cluster around the cognitive optimum position have at least two particularly obvious recurrent properties.

First, they are schematically organized into simpler units, each of which connects (often implicitly) a very few causes to a very few effects. As each effect may in turn be capable of triggering further effects, the process of narration is vulnerable to continual detours (although that is not the only common cause of digression, as we shall see). Narratives stabilize whenever particular chains of causes and effects are widely memorized and activated, in preference to other possible chains. But in the absence of special mnemonic support,[7] there are limits to the number and range of such chains that can be recalled on cue. An easy-to-transmit story must be a relatively *simple* story.

Second, cognitively optimal stories often take the form of "master narratives"— ones that supply a source narrative for a seemingly limitless range of target narratives on the principle of analogy or parable. Turner (1996) provides a particularly rich repository of illustrations of this point. Consider the simple case of proverbs:

> Proverbs frequently present a condensed, implicit story to be interpreted through projection. . . . "When the cat's away, the mice will play," said at the office, can be projected onto a story of a boss and workers. Said in the classroom, it can be projected onto a story of teacher and students. Said of sexual relationships, it can be projected onto a story of infidelity. With equal ease, we can project it onto stories of a con-

gressional oversight committee and the industries regulated by the committee, a police force and the local thieves, or a computer security device and the computer viruses
it was intended to control.

The presence of many possible source–target pairings, in any lengthy narrative, also raises problems of digression—in this case through the production
of stories within stories. Here, too, standardization is constrained by issues of
volume and complexity and the availability of mnemonic support.

Ethnographic research around the world has generated abundant examples of
myths and folktales that display much the same characteristics as proverbs, albeit
often in a less pithy and concise fashion.[8] Many such myths cluster rather obviously around the cognitive optimum position, insofar as they limit the range of
possible causal and analogical digressions, without any need for special mnemonic
support.

Do the theories summarized previously, which suggest that at least some of the
basic elements of religious traditions are naturally acquired, constitute an adequate
explanation of religion? Boyer and Guthrie argue that they are explaining the
propensity of humans to populate their worlds with gods and other supernatural
beings. Fiske and Haslam seem to have explained why ritual repetition is so compelling. Lawson and McCauley tell us how in turn the gods come to be implicated
in these rituals. Theories of cognitive linguists and developmental psychologists
meanwhile seem to explain the proliferation of myths-as-narratives, by which the
gods we have already invented and inserted into our rituals come to be known better as agents with various histories and agendas. Surely that is all we need, in order to have a religion?

There is nothing to prevent us from defining religion exclusively in terms of
traits that cluster around the cognitive optimum position. This will mean, of
course, that we would be obliged to classify certain patterns of thought and behavior (ranging from beliefs in fairies to the compulsive rituals of neurotics) as no
more or less religious than the receiving of the Eucharistic Host. Various interesting proposals from the "religion-is-natural" camp have been advanced that would
seem to avert such a conclusion (Boyer 2001a; Atran 2002; Barrett 2004). But
even if those proposals fail to convince, it would not be a crippling disadvantage
of the religion-is-natural argument that it casts its net rather widely. Although it
captures a number of concepts that people would be happy to call religious, it also
sucks in a great many other phenomena, seemingly remote from our folk notion
of the religious. What is wrong with that?

There is a more serious problem, however. Rituals, myths, and concepts of extranatural agency that cluster around the cognitive optimum position are, in a great many of the world's religions, differentiated from those that carry a heavier conceptual load (and thus require special mnemonic support in order to be transmitted). Nor is it simply a matter of difference. The heavier concepts are often the more highly valued ones. Herein lies a crucial gulf that divides the fairies from the gods. But it is not the only one.

In the following chapter, I will discuss the tendency for religious traditions to eschew certain cognitively optimal concepts and to peddle more complex bodies of knowledge in their stead. Religious people often maintain that the prohibited easy-to-transmit concepts are false, shallow, or misleading and that more compelling knowledge comes at a considerable cost. That cost may take different forms, ranging from traumatic initiations into cult mysteries through to protracted and demanding processes of religious education. In a sense, they are right: religion is seldom merely a cluster of naturally acquired concepts; it also often incorporates conceptually challenging bodies of knowledge. And therein lies the real plasticity of religion and its revelatory potential.

Notes

1. Debates continue to rage over the relative importance of genetic information in the development of specialized cognitive equipment for the acquisition of language. At one end of the spectrum of opinion, Turner (1996) argues that the notion of a genetically predetermined language acquisition device carries heavy theoretical costs in terms of inelegance and unnecessary complexity. It implies that we have evolved capacities for mastering a great range of possible grammars, and that whichever of these capacities turn out to be unnecessary for the particular language we happen to learn are somehow "switched off" in the course of development. At the other end of the spectrum, Fisher et al. (1998) have recently presented compelling evidence that at least some aspects of language impairment are genetically determined.

2. For instance, on the development of basic category distinctions, see R. Gelman 1990; Meltzoff and Moore 1994; Mandler and Bauer 1989. On the development of intuitive physics, see Spelke 1990. On the development of intuitive biology, see S. A. Gelman 1988. On the development of "theory of mind" (TOM), see Baron-Cohen 1995.

3. "Odd" concepts being merely violations of basic-level knowledge rather than of intuitive ontology.

4. For instance, after performing rain magic, the Orokaiva magician must observe certain OCD-like restrictions: "For some reason the rainmaker must skulk indoors, not venturing out nor ever looking at the sky" (Williams 1928, 177).

5. See Barrett 2001b, 2002a, 2002b, 2003; Barrett and Lawson 2001; Malley and Barrett, forthcoming.

6. No overall figures were collated on judgments of centrality, however, due to problems of availability and interpretation of data from both Hindu and Muslim traditions.

More recent studies (Barrett 2003) suggest a rather disappointing correlation between McCauley and Lawson's (2002) predictions and intuitive judgments of centrality, but we await publication of the full results.

7. Apart from regular rehearsal or the use of writing, or both mnemonic support may be provided by "mental maps" of various sorts—for example, where the verses of epic songs follow a geographical route in the local landscape (G. Lewis 1980).

8. Excellent examples include Richard Dorson 1972 and John LeRoy 1985.

Cognitively Costly Religion 3

SUPERNATURAL AGENT CONCEPTS, ritual procedures, and cognitively optimal narratives are distributed throughout human culture. They do not mark off a set of traits that are uniquely (or even distinctively) the province of the organized cult or church. Deities and ancestors have minimally counterintuitive properties, it is true, but so, too, do all kinds of culturally postulated agents ranging from cartoon characters (think of all the minimal violations of intuitive knowledge found in children's comics) through to a host of creatures that may even be subject to ritual treatments, such as fairies, ghosts, vampires, and even dear old Santa Claus. The rituals children perform on Christmas Eve or in preparation for visits from the tooth fairy, for instance, have all the properties one could want either from the contamination-avoidance theory or from the theory of ritual competence, described in the previous chapter. These procedures are even readily describable in terms of the ritual form hypothesis as special patient rituals with a very shallow structural depth (due to lack of prior enabling rituals).[1] And they come neatly packaged in a body of myths: readily assimilable narratives, for instance, about Santa's toy factory at the North Pole, his magical journey on a sled drawn by reindeer, and so on and so forth. All these ideas are beautifully structured around the cognitive optimum position. But is it religion?

Obviously, most adults who know anything about Santa Claus will say that we are not dealing here with a religious concept. This is not simply because they are in on the trick, but that is part of the reason. Santa Claus and the tooth fairy are excluded from the domain of religion in part because, like the characters in children's comics, they are regarded as fictional. But there is more to it than that. Many adults in Europe and North America sincerely proclaim a belief in ghosts. Few of them would consider ghosts to be a religious construct, however. On the face of it, this might seem to be explained by the fact that most Christian churches offi-cially regard ghoulish apparitions in much the same way as they regard wishing wells and horoscopes—as a lot of superstitious nonsense or a potentially danger-ous diversion from the "real" task of spiritual improvement or both. But that only begs the question: why would the members of Christian churches want to cast cer-tain kinds of supernatural constructs out into the cold? If the answer must be couched only in terms of factors internal to Christian belief systems, then it would hardly count as an explanation. We would still have to explain why Christ-ian belief systems take the forms that they do. What we require is a strategy that takes us out of the domain of any particular cultural framework and into the realm of general principles of human cognition. An initial question, then, is whether the Western tendency to differentiate between the fairies, the ghosts, and the gods (or their equivalents) is cross-culturally recurrent.

Cognitively Costly Gods

It is actually quite easy to find examples, throughout the ethnographic record, of traditional societies in which clusters of supernatural agents/rituals/narratives are classified into (1) those built around frankly fictional constructs, (2) those that posit "real" but relatively unelaborated constructs, and (3) those that demand very substantial cognitive investment in order to be adequately grasped and transmitted.

Let us begin with the fictions, taking (by way of illustration) two more or less random ethnographic cases: a traditional Amerindian population in lowland South America known as Wayú and some of the traditional cultures of South Africa. The Wayú tell many stories about godlike beings, heroic humans, ghosts, and unidentified (usually dangerous) spirits. Myths relating the deeds of godlike beings, in particular, have been interpreted by various scholars and missionaries as more or less coded illustrations of Wayú religious doctrine. Anthropologist Ben-son Saler (2002) has shown that this line of interpretation is almost certainly mis-taken. It is not merely the lack of evidence for a doctrinal system behind the stories that raises problems. Thanks to Saler's fine-grained ethnographic research, it is increasingly clear that Wayú storytellers do not regard the godlike beings in their narratives as real. This was not immediately obvious. Saler (2002) had been tape-recording a corpus of myths about Wayú godlike beings when the narrator suddenly asked him if he believed the stories:

> I sensed one of those glorious moments in ethnographic fieldwork when a win-dow unexpectedly opens on a topic of considerable importance, and I thought deeply about how I should reply. Apparently, I thought deeply for too long a time, for the myth-teller punctuated my silence by declaring, "We don't believe that these things happened." In a follow-up discussion the myth-teller stated flatly that

Maleiwa, Juya, and other godlike beings in the traditional narratives don't actually exist. It is entertaining and instructive to tell stories about them. Further, the multiple meanings of some of the terms used to name them lend themselves to rhetorical artifice. But the godlike beings of myth are what we would call fictional characters. . . . Other informants with whom I subsequently discussed this matter for the most part supported the myth-teller. Without further laboring the point, let me give it as my opinion that the godlike beings of Wayú myth are not themselves religious objects. They do serve, however, as discursive devices for talking not only about Wayú religion but about many aspects of Wayú life, and particularly the cognized and experienced tensions and contrasts of that life.

Stories collected in South Africa have often been more immediately recognizable to Europeans as fictional narratives. In part this is because many European tales, such as the Uncle Remus stories and *Aesop's Fables*, probably have African origins (Werner 1968). In Bantu stories, Brer Rabbit takes the form of a hare, and Brer Wolf or Fox is usually a hyena. Meanwhile, as Alice Werner (1968, 26) observes:

> The Zulu stories [that] have been collected . . . are more or less like our own fairy-tales: about chiefs' sons and beautiful maidens, lost children, ogres, witches, enchanters, and so forth; but they also have their hare stories. . . . Much the same may be said of the Basutu, only they give some of the hare's most famous adventures to the jackal. . . . And some of the same incidents are told by the Zulus of a queer little being called Hlakanyana, a sort of Tom Thumb, apparently human, but by some people identified not with the hare, but with a kind of weasel.

The point about all these stories, whether or not spread about in Africa, South America, or Europe, is that they are populated with characters who are regarded by normal adults as imaginary and nothing more. As parables, they are often highly instructive, providing wise and timely advice as well as comfort and entertainment. But the minimally counterintuitive concepts involved are considered neither real nor as appropriate objects of worship or propitiation.

Thus, a distinction seems to be made by people all over the world between cultural representations relating to a fictional world and those that relate to "real" supernatural agents, the rituals they require, and the stories that are associated with them. But the "real" ones are *also* often sharply differentiated into two main types: There are those, like European ghost concepts, that enjoin minimally counterintuitive concepts, simple rituals, and ripping yarns—all of which are easy to acquire and pass on. By contrast, most societies also postulate very much more complex otherworldly forces (ranging from gods and ancestors to more amorphous entities) that are hard to understand and demand enormous cognitive resources to manage and transmit.

Consider the case of the Mali Baining peoples of Papua New Guinea, among whom I conducted fieldwork from 1987 to 1989 (Whitehouse 1995, 1996c). The Mali Baining traditionally regarded their surrounding forest as populated with spirits (*sega*).[2] Although normally invisible to humans, except in dreams and as rare apparitions, the *sega* appeared to one another as perfectly normal men and women, whose lives were more or less identical to those of real people. The trees in which they lived appeared to them as houses (complete with doors and windows), and the forest undergrowth furnished the materials for their beautifully kept gardens. Humans, of course, could see only jungle, and so they sometimes blundered into a *sega*'s garden or destroyed their houses when clearing new land for cultivation. At such times, the *sega* became a problem, visiting all kinds of misfortunes on the human interloper. At other times, the *sega* might be petitioned for assistance, in luring game animals or retrieving a lost hunting dog. For these purposes, simple rituals were performed using spells passed on among kinsmen or acquired by purchase or barter from more distant sources. Beyond that, people knew very little about *sega*. Stories floated around, from time to time, about encounters with these forest spirits. But little effort was made to develop an elaborate (let alone a consistent) corpus of knowledge about the *sega*. They were "just *sega*," and that was that. Concepts of *sega* are clearly clustered around the cognitive optimum position.

In stark contrast, the Mali Baining also postulated concepts of the supernatural that were the focus of a great deal of rumination, and that presupposed highly elaborated bodies of cultural knowledge. Such concepts also required performances of complicated rituals that were extremely costly in terms of labor, materials, and cognitive resources. Prior to missionization of the Mali Baining (which began in earnest during the last century), these activities were focused around complex cycles of dances, thought necessary to ensure the fertility and growth of humans, game, and crops. Following the spread of Christianity, other kinds of complex cosmology and ritual emerged in the form of a new religious movement, known as the Pomio Kivung. Let us begin, though, with the precontact tradition.

Mali Baining religion traditionally took the form of a secret male cult, into which boys were initiated approximately every six to eight years. As in many other parts of Papua New Guinea, initiations involved a period of isolation of the novices at a remote location in the forest, the endurance of painful ordeals, and the imposition of secrecy (enforceable on pain of death). During Mali Baining initiations, a series of strange objects (mostly masks and instruments) were revealed to novices. They were taught to make such artifacts themselves and were required to paint some of them using blood agonizingly extracted from their tongues. The culminating rites involved an elaborate series of dances in which novices wore the masks they had constructed. The heavy frames of their costumes were supported by a pin (made of sharpened cassowary bone) that was forced through the skin at the base of each dancer's spine. Throughout the process of initiation, novices were given to believe that every detail of the masks, instruments, rituals, tortures, and dances had deep inner meanings that only the elders were capable of grasping fully. The unraveling of these meanings was largely a matter of personal revelation rather than direct instruction, and this was expected to take place very gradually (over the lifespan).

During my field research, I spent many hours tape-recording interviews with ritual experts—heavily punctuated by conspiratorial smiles and knowing glances on the part of my interlocutors—in an attempt to form a picture of their exegetical knowledge. Much of what I was told, however, was so cryptic as to be virtually unintelligible. In the face of my frustration, the elders constantly emphasized that there was a system of knowledge behind the rites of initiation, evidently relating to the "hidden" causes of human and animal fertility and reproduction. Even though I never grasped that system, few (if any) of its elements could be described as cognitively optimal. For instance, ritual experts talked of "power" (or "heaviness") rather than about supernatural agents; fragments of myths were offered to me as clues rather than narrated as complete, readily assimilable stories; vast amounts of detailed information about the properties of the natural world and of the secret ritual artifacts pertaining to them seemed to be intricately connected in the minds of elders in ways that I simply could not begin to grasp. Whereas my questions about *sega* were answered with easily intelligible stories, spells, and rituals, all my attempts to inquire into the meanings of male cult activities were met with seemingly endless strings of complex and puzzling statements, replete with technical details that seemed capable of integration only by minds very much more highly trained in these matters than my own. My own data on these topics leave a lot to be desired. But systematic, longer-term studies of Melanesian initiation rites are currently underway, and these are yielding increasingly solid and extensive evidence that initiators really do preside over bodies of exegetical knowledge that are remote from the cognitively optimal position.[3]

A fuller story has been published with regard to the Pomio Kivung religious tradition among the Mali Baining (Whitehouse 1995). Most of my informants were members of this Christian-syncretic organization that enjoined a complex set of beliefs about God and the ancestors—beings that collectively formed a so-called Village Government. The Village Government kept the living under constant surveillance and was greatly pleased by pious thoughts and deeds. When satisfied that the morals of Pomio Kivung members had been perfected, the ancestors would return, bringing cargo and, eventually, establishing heaven on earth.

Pomio Kivung ancestors, along with the Christian God, could quite reasonably be classed as simple supernatural agent concepts. They possessed the minimally counterintuitive properties of omniscience and incorporeality—both of which, of course, are consistent with the cognitive optimum position. On closer inspection, however, the Pomio Kivung tradition also sustained a body of ideas about the Village Government that was vastly more complex and difficult to transmit than Mali Baining concepts about *sega*. By far the most salient feature of the Pomio Kivung ancestors was that they exemplified certain moral properties. What made the ancestors different from ordinary people, quite apart from the counterintuitive attributes, was that they were morally perfected beings and therefore incapable of committing sinful acts. The intentional and behavioral traits attributed to ancestors were, in these respects, nonstandard rather than counterintuitive. But they were also intrinsically difficult to conceptualize.

Concepts of sin in the Pomio Kivung may be loosely defined as violations of the Old Testament Decalogue. Although borrowing from the biblical Ten Commandments, however, Pomio Kivung authorities taught a very much more intricate and encompassing version of them. For instance, the commandment "thou shalt not kill" was taken to mean all forms of injury against oneself or others, including verbal injury (what we might call "character assassination"). And the commandment forbidding deceit was interpreted to cover the communication of false information of all kinds, whether intended or not. So broad, in fact, was the remit of the *tenpela lo* ("ten laws") of the Pomio Kivung that it was literally impossible for ordinary mortals to avoid committing sins, and much of their ritual lives were taken up with the performance of absolution rituals to reverse the effects of daily sinfulness. A vast amount of energy in the public oratory and general discourse of the Pomio Kivung was devoted to creating representations of ancestral beings capable of being "without sin" and to tackling the problems faced by ordinary people in emulating them.

Each local community in the Pomio Kivung held lengthy meetings at least twice every week, which all followers of the movement were normally required to attend. At these meetings, designated orators would present sermons, highlighting evidence of sinfulness in the congregation and castigating transgressors. Sufficient time was also set aside at these meetings for detailed monologues on each of the ten laws (one law being covered at each meeting and, thus, all ten in any given five-week period). Through these methods of routinized transmission, a large corpus of knowledge relating to Pomio Kivung cosmology, morality, eschatology, and history or mythology was sustained in a remarkably standardized form with little opportunity for unintended variation across both time and space. As I have argued at length elsewhere (Whitehouse 1995, 2000a), the moral characteristics of the Village Government, on which people were urged to model their own lives, were simply too complex and multifaceted to be learned and reproduced intact without continual reminding and consolidation. Unlike the more cognitively optimal ideas of the Mali Baining concerning *sega*, the concepts of the Pomio Kivung cannot be easily or "naturally" acquired and transmitted. They require special mnemonic support in the form of routinized narrative rehearsal.

There are, then, a number of ways in which concepts of a supernatural realm can become culturally widespread. We have seen that they can coalesce as a set of make-believe ideas, practices, and stories. They could also form a domain concerned with "real" supernatural agents—like the *sega*—who are genuinely regarded as malevolent, but who are also sometimes sought out for assistance. Either way, we are dealing with concepts clustered around the cognitive optimum position. In stark contrast, we have seen that people can have much more complex ideas about supernatural agents, which are neither easy to remember nor intrinsically very plausible. The latter concepts require costly support in terms of both memory and motivation. Much the same pattern can be noted in the way different kinds of rituals are transmitted.

Cognitively Costly Rituals

In many respects, Mali Baining rituals concerned with interactions with *sega* resembled the rain magic of the Orokaiva, discussed in the previous chapter. Consider the following rather typical example of such a ritual that was performed to retrieve a lost hunting dog, called Kaukau:

> [The magician] obtained some lime powder and went to a secluded place at the edge of the village. There he clasped the lime powder in his hand, close to his mouth, and murmured [a formula]. . . . Then he opened his hand and blew off the lime powder. If it had stuck to his hand, the lime powder would have been "cold," indicating that Kaukau was dead. In this case, however, the powder dispersed on the wind. He then held up his hand. If the wrist bone made a cracking sound, then Kaukau would be very distant; if his elbow cracked, then Kaukau would be quite near; if his shoulder cracked, Kaukau would be very close at hand. His elbow cracked. (Whitehouse 1996c, 176–177)

Just like Orokaiva rain magic, this ritual addressed to the *sega* entailed actions with readily transparent meanings. Inert powder would have corresponded to a motionless body, whereas animated powder, carried by the wind, indicated a living, moving body. The relative distance of points along the magician's arm corresponded to the relative distance of the lost animal. Such simple iconic principles as those in the rituals of Orokaiva magicians leave little scope for alternative, symbolically motivated interpretations. It so happens that Mali Baining magic appeals to supernatural beings (the *sega*), but the beings are attributed no special cognitive powers. Spells have to specify out loud what is required of the *sega*; otherwise they cannot be expected to know. Hence, actions are assumed to be more consequential than intentions for the purposes of an efficacious performance. In all these respects, rituals addressed to the *sega* are, without exception, clustered tightly around the cognitive optimum position.

Once again, we find a very different pattern of ritualization in the precontact fertility cult of the Mali Baining and in the Pomio Kivung. Just as concepts of supernatural agency migrate dramatically away from the realms of natural cognition, so the same may be said of the way ritual meanings are constructed. In the secret male cult, for instance, every detail of the rituals is assumed to be pregnant with hidden meanings. There is nothing obvious about the intentions underpinning the tongue bleedings or the piercing of the dancers' skin at the bases of their spines. As traumatic episodes, the first experiences of painful operations of this sort trigger long-lasting memory effects, encoding all kinds of disconnected fragments of the ritual process. Through subsequent involvement in these rituals and through encounters with other primes and triggers, cult members grope their way slowly toward ever-deeper understandings of the anological codes that structure and motivate rituals of this kind. The resulting bodies of esoteric knowledge contain concepts and systems of interlocking connections that are just about as far from natural cognition as possible.

In the Pomio Kivung, ritual exegesis also drifts away from the cognitive optimum position but for different reasons. In one rather obvious sense, Pomio Kivung rituals *could* be easily and naturally understood, in terms of intuitive judgments of well-formedness. The ancestors are mind-reading beings whose presence is capable of activating social causal cognition and all that follows from that. For instance, absolution rites in the Pomio Kivung, by the lights of the ritual form hypothesis, are special patient rituals, and for all the reasons Robert N. McCauley and E. Thomas Lawson provide, as noted in the last chapter, these absolution rites are capable of triggering tacit intuitions about repeatability, nonreversibility, and levels of emotionality. Saying they are capable of that, however, is not to say that this implicit knowledge is indeed activated. People mostly do not interpret routinized ritual procedures in that way. For instance, it is quite common for Pomio Kivung followers, when carrying babes in arms, to manipulate the bodies of infants through the absolution rites. If one assumes that ancestors have mind-reading capacities and that the efficacy of the rituals depends therefore on observing the correct intentional states, such behavior would make no sense. What I think is really happening, however, is that the absolution rituals are being processed *implicitly* as automated procedures in which actions are all that matters, and intentional states are quite irrelevant. This, indeed, is probably a typical feature of all circumstances of ritual routinization.[4] By contrast, *exegetical* knowledge for these kinds of rituals is organized and transmitted in a more or less exclusively *explicit* way, through the endless reiteration of the meanings and significance of absolution rites, temple rituals, and the whole system of Pomio Kivung practices. This explicit level of understanding is profoundly disconnected from the level of procedural competence: people's knowledge of why they perform their rituals is cognized very differently from their knowledge of how to perform them. And that explicit knowledge has little about it that is natural or cognitively optimal. On the contrary, it requires constant review and reiteration to acquire and maintain.

Cognitively Costly Narratives

Just as CPS agent concepts and rituals come in both cognitively optimal and cognitively costly guises, so it is with stories and myths. We have seen how naturally people acquire and pass on simple folktales and proverbs, but transmission of sacred cycles of mythology typically involves a great deal more effort. To understand why, it is first necessary to appreciate a fundamental difference in the ways in which people represent the functions of sacred myths and everyday stories and folktales, respectively. Folktales are everywhere construed as freestanding narratives in the sense that they can be used with impunity for almost any analogical purpose or even just simply to entertain. This is not to say that they are of questionable status as accounts of factual events. The situations or episodes they describe may be passionately held to be true or regarded as partly or wholly fictional; but the point is that nobody assumes that these stories were devised exclusively as a means of illustrating some set of absolute higher truths. Any general lessons contained in folktales are what they purport to be, and nothing more. They are not automatically referred to an entirely separate body of knowledge for which they merely serve as a timely reminder or illustration. In religious systems, however, cycles of mythology may assume precisely that form. They are often seen as mnemonic aids for the transmission of revelatory knowledge that is intrinsically hard to represent (as will be shown in detail in chapter 5).

In some religious traditions, the explicitly acknowledged function of myth (whether or not the myths are considered to be historically accurate) is to dramatize doctrinal teachings that have supposedly been fixed for all time. Consequently, the causal chains of religious narratives are often far less "natural" than those of everyday folklore. The stories do not have to cohere as stories but only as illustrations of coherent doctrine. In some other religious traditions, meanwhile, myths become even more fractured. They are typically delivered piecemeal as highly esoteric clues that can only be reassembled through years of careful contemplation. In mystery cults, myths provide scattered and fragmented triggers for processes of "spontaneous exegetical reflection" (discussed at length in chapter 6), memorable in themselves but meaningful only through the long-term investment of massive cognitive resources.

It seems possible, then, to distinguish two very different dimensions to religion, involving contrasting ways of generating and transmitting ideas about supernatural agents, rituals, and myths:

1. On the one hand, we have aspects of religious thinking in which people's ideas about the spirit world tend to be simple, vague, and frequently contradictory. The rituals associated with these supernatural agents are easy to learn and closely analogous to technical procedures insofar as their meanings will be readily decipherable. If the supernatural agents in question are accorded special mind-reading capacities, then exegetical knowledge will be built around social causal cognition and implicit evaluations of well-formedness that stem from those intuitions. Stories about spirits in this domain will circulate quite freely as minor variations on simple themes, and no attempt will be made to standardize the corpus. In short, there will be just as little investment of cognitive resources in the transmission of this kind of cultural knowledge as is devoted to the make-believe constructs.

2. On the other hand, we often find a more "weighty" dimension to religious experience, in which notions of extranatural agency are massively more complicated, in which rituals have elaborate meanings (whether or not officially codified or constructed around multiple layers of spontaneously generated exegesis), and in which stories (if they survive at all) become only a means to an end (e.g., a framework on which to hang abstract doctrinal knowledge or a veiled clue to the nature of esoteric mysteries) and no longer an end in themselves.

The sorts of cultural traits referred to under point one, clustered around the cognitive optimum position, are as natural as language itself. The traits listed under point two are found in the vast majority of human populations and appear to have been around for a very long time (how long, as we shall see, is a matter of contention). It follows that explaining the transmission of the cognitively costly aspects of religion is a different kind of enterprise from explaining the transmission of language or minimally counterintuitive concepts. A comprehensive theory of the way standard cognitive architecture operates in all known human environments would be sufficient to explain why humans learn to speak or entertain concepts of ghosts. But that is not sufficient to explain religion. Transmitting a religion also requires the development of forms of mnemonic support that are costly to maintain in terms of the most basic human resources: labor, time, and energy. A set of viable supports, once established, can bring about appropriate conditions for its propagation. The next chapter explains at the most general level possible why this is so, before we proceed to a more detailed examination of the mechanisms involved.

Notes

1. McCauley and Lawson attempt to rule out such a conclusion (2002, 14–16), and some of the problems with this strategy will be discussed in chapter 7.

2. For a fuller account of *sega*–human relations, see Whitehouse 1996c.

3. We await, in particular, the publication of exceptionally long-term and fine-grained research conducted by Pascale Bonnemère and Pierre Lemonnier on initiations among the Ankave of Papua New Guinea. Some preliminary findings are presented in Bonnemere (1996).

4. Evidence from Malley and Barrett (forthcoming) that Muslims, Jews, and Hindus do not necessarily have any strong intuitions about where to insert the S-markers in their rituals further supports that conclusion.

THE THEORY OF MODES
OF RELIGIOSITY

II

The Theory of Modes of Religiosity 4

I T HAS LONG BEEN RECOGNIZED that religion encompasses two very different sets of dynamics: Max Weber (1930, 1947) distinguished routinized and charismatic religious forms; Ruth Benedict (1935) contrasted Apollonian and Dionysian practices; Ernest Gellner (1969) explored the opposition between literate forms of Islam in urban centers and the image-based, cohesive practices of rural tribesmen; Jack Goody (1968, 1986) developed a more general dichotomy between literate and nonliterate religions; Victor Turner (1974) distinguished fertility rituals and political rituals as part of an exposition of the contrasting features of what he called "communitas" and "structure"; Ioan M. Lewis (1971) juxtaposed central cults and peripheral cults; Richard Werbner (1977) contrasted regional cults and "cults of the little community"; Fredrik Barth (1990) distinguished "guru" regimes spread by religious leaders and "conjurer" regimes in which religious revelations inhere in collective ritual experiences. These are just a few of the many attempts to characterize a fundamental divergence in modalities of religious experience and practice (Whitehouse 1995, chapter 8; Peel 2004; Laidlaw 2004). At the root of all such dichotomous models is a recognition that some religious practices are very intense emotionally: they may be rarely performed and highly stimulating (e.g., involving altered states of consciousness or terrible ordeals and tortures); they tend to trigger a lasting sense of revelation and to produce powerful bonds between small groups of ritual participants. By contrast, certain other forms of religious activity tend to be much less stimulating: they may be highly repetitive or "routinized," conducted in a relatively calm and sober atmosphere; such practices are often accompanied by the transmission of complex theology and doctrine and also tend to mark out large religious communities composed of people who cannot possibly all know each other (certainly not in any intimate way). But all the great scholarship so far devoted to understanding these contrasting sets of dynamics suffers from two major shortcomings: The first is that none of the theories advanced in the past was sufficiently comprehensive; each theory focused on just a few aspects of the two modes of religious experience and action. The second major shortcoming is that none of the existing theories explained adequately why we get two contrasting forms of religious experience in the first place.

This chapter introduces the theory of divergent modes of religiosity, which I term "doctrinal" and "imagistic" (Whitehouse 1995, 2000a). The aim of the modes of religiosity theory is to tie together all the features of the two modalities of religious experience that other scholars have already identified and to explain why these contrasting modalities come about in the first place. This theory advances a set of hypotheses amenable to empirical investigation, concerning the causal interconnections between a set of cognitive and sociopolitical features.

Modes of Religiosity and Memory

In order for particular religions and rituals to take the form that they do, at least two things must take place: First, these religious beliefs and rituals must take a form that people can *remember*. Second, people must be *motivated* to pass on these beliefs and rituals. If people cannot remember what to believe or how to do a ritual, these beliefs and rituals cannot be passed down from one generation to the next, and so the religious tradition would not be able to establish itself. Equally, if people do not think that particular beliefs and rituals are important enough to pass on, the beliefs will mutate or become extinct. That being said, memory and motivation have the potential to present far bigger problems than one might suppose. Some religious activities are performed very rarely. Unless some very special conditions apply, there is a real risk that people will forget the details of what these activities mean and even forget how to perform them correctly. A potential solution to this problem is to have a very repetitive regime of religious transmission. One advantage of such a strategy is that a substantial corpus of complex cosmology can be reproduced in this fashion. People can learn difficult concepts, dogmas, and stories—and will remember these in the long run—if they repeat them frequently. But this can produce problems of motivation. Continually listening to sermons and performing the same rituals over and over might become extremely boring. And if people are bored, there is a danger they won't continue to follow, or pass on, the religion. There are solutions to all these potential problems, and these solutions have profound consequences for the forms that religion can take. But before we can go into that, we need to grasp the general nature of memory functions (see figure 4.1).

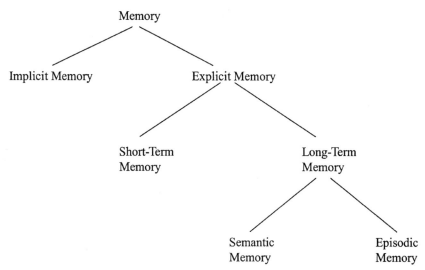

Figure 4.1.   Types of Memory

There are basically two kinds of memory—implicit and explicit (Graf and Schachter 1985). Implicit memory deals with things we know without being aware of knowing (such as the varied forms of procedural competence required in successfully riding a bicycle).[1] Explicit memory deals with things we know at a conscious level and can be further subdivided into two types—short-term and long-term.[2] Short-term memory enables us to hold onto concepts for a matter of seconds (e.g., a new phone number, which we might remember just long enough to write down before forgetting). Long-term memory enables us to hold onto concepts for hours—and in some cases for a whole lifetime. Long-term memory can also be subdivided into two types—semantic and episodic.[3] Semantic memory consists of general knowledge about the world (e.g., how to behave in restaurants or what is the capital city of France). We can seldom recall how or when we acquired this sort of knowledge. By contrast, episodic memory consists of specific events in our life experience (e.g., our first kiss, the death of a beloved relative, and the day war broke out). These types of memory are activated somewhat differently in doctrinal and imagistic modes of religiosity.[4] And these differences go a long way to explaining the divergent sociopolitical features of the two modes.

The Doctrinal Mode of Religiosity

In the case of the doctrinal mode of religiosity, ritual action tends to be highly routinized, facilitating the storage of elaborate and conceptually complex religious teachings in semantic memory, but also activating implicit memory in the performance of

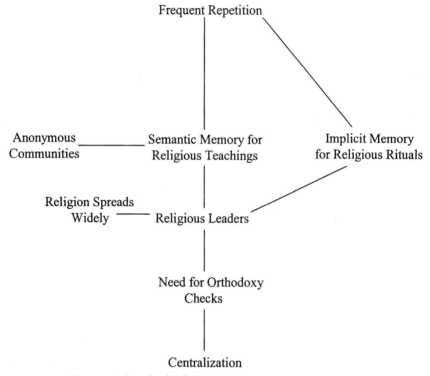

Figure 4.2.   The Doctrinal Mode of Religiosity

most ritual procedures. These cognitive features are linked to particular social morphology, including hierarchical, centralized institutional arrangements, expansionary potential, and dynamic leadership. The specific hypotheses enumerated in the following are summarized in figure 4.2:

I. Frequent repetition activates semantic memory for religious teachings.

    One of the most conspicuous features of the doctrinal mode is that the transmission of religious teachings is highly routinized (i.e., frequently repeated). A great advantage of frequent repetition is that it allows the establishment of a great deal of explicit verbal knowledge in semantic memory. Doctrines and narratives that would be impossible to learn and remember if they were rarely transmitted can be effectively sustained through repetitive sermonizing. Repetition, however, can lead to reduced levels of motivation. In detailed empirical studies of this phenomenon, I have labeled this the "tedium effect."[5] But many routinized religions are successful at holding onto their followers through a variety of mechanisms, including supernatural sanctions (such as eternal damnation) and, more positively, incentives (such as eternal life and salvation). Of course, the power of these mechanisms depends on people believing the religious teachings. In order for people to believe in a set of doctrines, the doctrines have to be cast in a highly persuasive fashion. This is commonly achieved, at least in part, by special techniques of oratory established over time through processes of selection. Routinized religions tend to be associated with highly developed forms of rhetoric and logically integrated theology, founded on absolute presuppositions that cannot be falsified.[6] All of this is commonly illustrated by poignant narratives that can easily be related to personal experience.[7] In addition, the heavy repetition of explicit beliefs increases their accessibility and relevance in everyday settings.[8]

2. Semantic memory for religious teachings and the presence of religious leaders are mutually reinforcing features.

   Where religious ideas are expressed in words (e.g., transmitted through oratory), it is likely that the orators themselves will rise above the common herd. Most religious traditions of this sort have celebrated leaders who may take the form of gurus, messiahs, prophets, divine kings, high priests, mediums, visionaries, disciples, or simply great evangelists or missionaries. The very fact that there are so many different types of, and terms for, religious leadership is an index of how widespread and important the phenomenon is. Partly through their skills as orators, these leaders become marked out as special. But at the same time, their pronouncements (real or attributed) provide the central tenets of a belief system, and their deeds become the basis for widely recounted religious narratives, transmitted orally. Both forms of knowledge are stored primarily in semantic memory.

3. The presence of religious leaders implies a need for orthodoxy checks.

   Where religious leaders are upheld as the source of authoritative religious knowledge, their teachings must be seen to be preserved intact. At the very least, the credibility of any such tradition depends on its adherents *agreeing* what the teachings are, even if other traditions hold to alternative (and perhaps conflicting) versions. We might call this the principle of agreement. Agreement depends partly on effective detection of unauthorized innovation, and then on its effective obstruction and suppression. Religious routinization contributes to both detection and suppression by conferring a selective advantage on standardized or orthodox forms over nonorthodox ones. The link between routinization and detection is especially straightforward. Frequent repetition of a body of religious teachings has the effect of fixing it firmly in people's minds. In literate traditions, the teachings might also be written down in sacred texts, and thereby fixed on paper (at least to some extent). But the crucial thing is that standardized versions of the religious teachings become widely shared and accepted through regular public rehearsal and reiteration.[9] Once this has happened, the risks of innovation going undetected become remote. Rather more complex is the role of routinization in the obstruction of unauthorized innovation, to which we now turn in points 4 and 5.

4. Frequent repetition leads to implicit memory for religious rituals.

So far, we have considered only the effects of frequent repetition of religious teachings; but what about the effects of routinized ritual performances? Rituals that are performed daily or weekly rapidly come to be processed, to a considerable extent, in procedural or implicit memory.[10] There can be little doubt that at least some Christians, for instance, spend significant portions of church services simply going through the motions. This is not a slur on people's religious commitments. It is simply a psychological reality that repetitive actions lead to implicit behavioral habits that occur independently of conscious thought or control. Although potentially accessible to conscious representation (e.g., for the purposes of teaching a child or newcomer how to behave in church), liturgical rituals may not, in the normal pattern of life, trigger very much explicit knowledge at all.

5. Implicit memory for religious rituals enhances the survival potential of authoritative teachings stored in semantic memory.

To the extent that people do participate in routinized rituals "on autopilot," this reduces the chances that they will reflect on the meaning of what they are doing. In other words, frequent repetition diminishes the extent to which people come up with personal theories of their rituals.[11] And they are more likely to accept at face value any official versions of the religious significance of their rituals. The processing of routinized rituals as implicit procedural schemas really opens the way for religious authorities to tell worshippers what to believe, especially when it comes to the meanings of their rituals. At the same time, the provision of a standardized orthodoxy tends to limit individual speculation. The causal role of routinization in the suppression of unauthorized innovation is, here again, governed by principles of selection. It is not that frequent enactment of rituals *prohibits* exegetical innovation, but it tends to reduce the volume and elaborateness of exegetical reflection, leading to relatively low rates of unauthorized innovation across populations of religious adherents. The question "relative to what?" will be answered later in this chapter through an examination of processes of exegetical reflection and independent innovation in the imagistic mode.

6. The need for orthodoxy checks encourages religious centralization.

Not all innovation is a bad thing. The principle of agreement simply requires that innovation is seen to originate from authoritative sources and is accepted or observed by all loyal followers. Routinization may have the effect of insulating orthodoxies to some extent from unintended innovation, but it does little to obstruct the determined heretic. The problem here is clearly one of policing. As soon as a routinized religion becomes well established, we tend to see the emergence of a central authority and some sort of ranked, professional priesthood.[12] It becomes the task of delegated officials to police the orthodoxy across the tradition as a whole, and there will often be a proliferation of sanctions for unauthorized innovation and heresy (ranging from excommunication and ostracism to torture and execution).

7. Semantic memory for religious teachings leads to anonymous religious communities.

Where religious beliefs and practices are frequently repeated, we have seen that at least part of this religious knowledge is organized in semantic memory. This means that the knowledge itself becomes separate from particular episodes in which it is acquired. For instance, a Christian may believe certain things (e.g., about the significance of the crucifixion) and may do certain things (such as participating in weekly church services), but that is not the same as remembering how and when all this knowledge was acquired. In other words, many of the beliefs and acts that define a person's identity as a Christian are not remembered as special episodes.[13] In consequence, many aspects of what makes somebody a Christian are really abstracted properties that, in principle, could be ascribed to anybody. And, in fact, they do get ascribed to anonymous others. To understand why, it is useful to think about the issues in a concrete way. If you ask a regular church-going Christian to tell you what happened at a service or mass three years ago, he or she wouldn't be able to remember the actual event. That person could tell you, though, what happened, because it would have been the same thing that always happens. In other words, what makes a particular episode distinctive gets forgotten. This of course includes the makeup of the congregation: people in the congregation come and go, people die, people move in and out of the area, and visitors may come and go. If it is a big congregation, there may be many people there who do not know each other personally. Thus, one's memories for Christian rituals are not memories for a particular group of people. What it means to be a regular churchgoer is not to be part of a particular group but to participate in a ritual scheme and belief structure that anonymous others also share.[14] Of course, the anonymity principle only comes into operation if the religious community is large enough to ensure that no individual follower could possibly know all the other followers. And it turns out that there are factors at play in routinized religions that encourage rapid spread and, therefore, large-scale religious communities. One of the most important of these is the emphasis on oratory and religious leadership.

8. The presence of religious leaders is conducive to the religion spreading widely.

The fact that the religious teachings are expressed in oratory, on the part of great leaders (or their deputized representatives), means that these teachings are readily transportable. Only one or a few proselytizing leaders or good evangelists are required to spread the Word to very large populations.[15]

In sum, the doctrinal mode of religiosity consists of a suite of mutually reinforcing features. When these features coalesce, they tend to be very robust historically and may last for centuries and even for millennia. At the root of all this is a set of cognitive causes deriving from the ways in which frequently repeated activities and beliefs are handled in human memory.

The Imagistic Mode of Religiosity

The sorts of practices that lead to the coalescence of imagistic features are invariably low frequency (rarely enacted). They are also, without exception, highly arousing. Examples might include traumatic and violent initiation rituals, ecstatic practices of various cults, experiences of collective possession and altered states of consciousness, and extreme rituals involving homicide or cannibalism. These sorts of religious practices, although taking very diverse forms, are extremely widespread.[16] Archaeological and historical evidence suggests they are also the most ancient forms of religious activity.[17] As with the doctrinal mode, the coalescence of features of the imagistic mode derives its robustness from the fact that these features are causally interconnected or mutually reinforcing. Once again, this claim rests on a series of testable hypotheses, depicted in figure 4.3 and enumerated in the proceeding:

1. Infrequent repetition and high arousal activate episodic memory.

Rarely performed and highly arousing rituals invariably trigger vivid and enduring episodic memories among the people who participate in them. It appears to be a combination of episodic distinctiveness, emotionality, and consequentiality that together result in lasting autobiographical memories.[18]

These memories can be so vivid and detailed that they can take the form of (what some psychologists call) flashbulb memories.[19] It is almost as if a camera has gone off in one's head, illuminating the scene, and preserving it forever in memory. The effects of infrequent performance and high levels of arousal should be thought of in terms of processes of selection. Religious practices that are rarely performed, but which elicit low levels of arousal, are unlikely to be passed on: people will rapidly forget the procedures, and especially their meanings, during the long gaps between performances;[20] even if they could remember some aspects of the rituals, their lack of thought about these practices for long periods would not be conducive to high motivation. In short, rarely performed religious practices that survive tend to involve high levels of arousal, and this is due to the triangular nexus of causes indicated in figure 4.3.

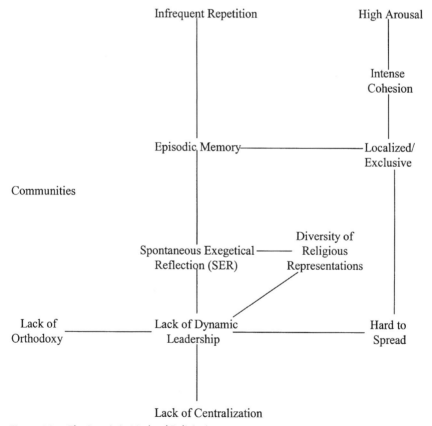

Figure 4.3.   The Imagistic Mode of Religiosity

2. Activation of episodic memory triggers spontaneous exegetical reflection, leading to expert exegetical frameworks stored in semantic memory.

The combination of infrequent repetition and high arousal may provide excellent conditions for remembering the details of religious procedures, such as ritual actions. But it does not seem to help people to remember verbally transmitted information, such as doctrines and narratives.[21] It turns out that this needn't matter. In fact, the meaning and salience of rare, climactic rituals usually lies in their capacity to trigger spontaneous exegetical reflection (SER)—often experienced as personal inspiration or revelation. The key to understanding this lies in the fact that episodic memory is a type of explicit memory. This means that rare, climactic rituals are processed at a conscious level. Not surprisingly, people tend to reflect extensively on these experiences, and speculate about their significance and meaning.[22] This eventually results in elaborate, if idiosyncratic, exegetical knowledge stored in semantic memory. An important factor here is that elevated arousal is occasioned typically by sensory stimulation (often using a variety of channels—auditory, visual, kinesthetic, olfactory, etc.). This in turn encourages people to draw associations between different images evoked in religious ceremonies, which are rooted in the way perception is organized (McCauley 2001). Two points need to be borne in mind here. The first is that rare and climactic rituals evoke abundant inferences, producing a sense of multivalence and multivocality of religious imagery, experienced as personal and unmediated inspiration. The second requires a separate hypothesis, illustrated in point three.

3. SER leads to a diversity of religious representations.

The personal experiences and revelations triggered by rare, climactic rituals tend to be quite unique. They may converge on certain themes and central ideas, but there is nothing resembling the kind of uniformity of belief that characterizes doctrinal orthodoxies. The principle of agreement, if it is invoked at all, applies only to the ritual procedures themselves and not to their meanings.[23] If exegesis is verbally transmitted, it is restricted to "experts" whose adherence to the principle of agreement may well be asserted but seldom demonstrated.[24]

4. SER and representational diversity inhibit dynamic leadership.

If a fertile and compelling array of religious beliefs and interpretations is generated independently through personal reflection, dynamic leadership is almost impossible to establish. If a leader tried to come forward at rare, climactic rituals to advance an intricate and coherent body of doctrine, people might listen. But they would very rapidly garble or forget what they had been told and, at least in the long run, their own inspirational ideas are likely to be more compelling than the content of a single oration. In such circumstances, admittedly, the possibility remains open for an individual, group, or class to be elevated socially, and for this to be expressed in the structure and choreography of rituals and the accordance of ritual precedence to persons of high standing. But leadership of this sort is primarily symbolic rather than dynamic.[25]

5. Lack of dynamic leadership, lack of centralization, and lack of orthodoxy are mutually reinforcing.

The fact that each person experiences inspiration as coming directly from the gods or ancestors, rather than being mediated by leaders or priests, means that there is no place here for centralized authority. And there is no orthodoxy over which such an authority might preside.

6. High arousal fosters intense cohesion.

The high arousal involved in the imagistic mode tends to produce emotional bonds between participants. In other words, there is intense social cohesion.[26] People who are bound together in this way tend to form rather small and localized communities.

7. Intense cohesion and episodic memory foster localized, exclusive communities.

Where rituals are remembered episodically, each participant remembers who else went through the rituals with them. Ritual groups are based on memories for shared episodes, in which particular coparticipants feature. Consequently, religious communities tend to be exclusive: you cannot be a member unless people remember you as part of a previous cycle of religious activities; by the same token, you cannot very easily be excluded once you are in (i.e., your participation cannot be easily forgotten). This tends to give rise to fixed and exclusive ritual groups in which there is no easy way of adding to, or subtracting from, the established membership.

8. Localized and exclusive communities and lack of dynamic leadership inhibit spread or dissemination.

Unlike the beliefs and practices of the doctrinal mode, traditions operating in the imagistic mode do not spread widely.[27] Since religious understandings are inspired by collective ritual performances, the unit of transmission is the entire ritual group (not a small number of talented orators). It follows that the spread of such traditions would be inefficient and costly: either the local group must perform its rituals with neighboring groups, or the local group must be mobile (i.e., migratory or nomadic). But either way, the practices are likely to mutate as soon as they get passed on.[28] In part, this is because of the lack of leaders and religious hierarchies capable of policing an orthodoxy, and in part it is because each ritual community is likely to be fiercely exclusivist (and therefore will tend to emphasize local distinctiveness over regional unity).

Modes of Religiosity Contrasted

The key features of doctrinal and imagistic modes of religiosity stand in stark contrast to one another, as represented in table 4.1. It will be observed that these contrasting features are of two types: First, there are cognitive features, concerned with differences in the way religious activities are handled psychologically. Second, there are sociopolitical features, concerned with contrasts in social organization and politics at the level of groups and populations. This clustering of sociopolitical features has been widely recognized for quite a long time, but what is new about the theory of modes of religiosity is the way it places these features together in a single model and then explains the clustering of features in terms of a set of cognitive or psychological causes.

The theory advanced here operates on principles of selection. Modes of religiosity constitute attractor positions around which ritual actions and associated religious concepts cumulatively tend to cluster. Innovations remote from these attractor positions cannot survive.[29] For instance, a new prophet might discourse on his elaborate personal revelations, and audiences might be eager to listen. But if that discourse is to crystallize into a stable body of teachings, it must be subjected to regular reiteration and safeguarded by a system of effective policing. If not, it

Table 4.1.   Contrasting Modes of Religiosity

Variable	Doctrinal	Imagistic
Psychological Features		
1. Transmissive frequency	High	Low
2. Level of arousal	Low	High
3. Principal memory system	Semantic schemas and implicit scripts	Episodic/flashbulb memory
4. Ritual meaning	Learned/acquired	Internally generated
5. Techniques of revelation	Rhetoric, logical integration, narrative	Iconicity, multivocality, and multivalence
Sociopolitical Features		
6. Social cohesion	Diffuse	Intense
7. Leadership	Dynamic	Passive/absent
8. Inclusivity/exclusivity	Inclusive	Exclusive
9. Spread	Rapid, efficient	Slow, inefficient
10. Scale	Large scale	Small scale
11. Degree of uniformity	High	Low
12. Structure	Centralized	Noncentralized

will be garbled or simply forgotten. Likewise, a new ritual might be invented to mark the effects of a rare event, such as a solar eclipse. But if that ritual is to establish the basis for a new religious tradition, it must be sufficiently arousing, shocking, and personally consequential to drive subsequent revelations based on SER. If not, it too will fail to stabilize as a tradition. History is obviously littered with such failures.

Religious practices commonly satisfy at least one or other of the two sets of psychological conditions specified in table 4.1. The activation of these conditions provides the underlying causes of the distributed (population-level) effects depicted as the "sociopolitical features" of religion. But it would not make sense to try to single out any one of the psychological causes as somehow prior to any of the others. There is no independent variable driving the rest, only a set of conditions that some patterns of human activity manage to satisfy, thus accounting for their cultural success.

Modes of Religiosity in the Real World

Anybody who has studied a particular religious tradition in any detail will know that religions are neither doctrinal nor imagistic in terms of the features identified in my model. In some cases, a religious tradition that incorporates all the elements of the doctrinal mode also exhibits some of the features of the imagistic mode. At the same time, this religion may embrace a large population of lay adherents who have little or no access to the tradition's complex body of revelatory knowledge, and so could hardly be said to be motivated by it. Some rituals might be low in frequency and elicit low levels of arousal. Other rituals might be neither frequent nor particularly rare and instead are scattered across an intermediate range of performance frequencies. Some frequent rituals may be completely lacking in known exegesis, and some rarely performed rituals might be associated with quite an elaborate and standardized exegetical corpus. These kinds of scenarios might seem to disprove the claims of the theory of modes of religiosity. And if they do not, then what counts as falsification?

In the first place, as noted in the previous section, modes of religiosity are attractor positions. They do not specify a set of law-like rules for building individual behavior. The claim is not that all instances of ritual action conform to one or another mode of religiosity. Indeed, that would be impossible by definition, since roughly half the variables with which the theory is concerned itself (the sociopolitical features of table 4.1) relate to distributed population-level attributes rather than particular instances of thought or behavior (even though it is the latter that cumulatively cause the former). So we cannot say that a particular ritual, for instance, is doctrinal or imagistic. We can only say that its long-term reproduction through the innumerable thoughts and actions of many people results in the coalescence of features specified by the modal theory. These features, in other words, are discernible only as marked tendencies within a religious tradition, taken in the round.

What the theory of modes of religiosity sets out to explain, then, is the *tendency* for religious systems to gravitate toward divergent attractor positions. It is only through these processes that intrinsically hard-to-acquire revelatory knowledge can be generated and culturally transmitted. This kind of knowledge, stored in semantic memory, might be quite unevenly distributed within a tradition. In the case of the imagistic mode, such bodies of expert knowledge take many years to develop and mature. Consequently, the less experienced members of the tradition do not yet have access to the full motivating force of its revelatory knowledge (and their participation often has to be coercively enforced by the elders or experts). In the doctrinal mode, it is possible in principle for everybody to have access to revelatory knowledge; that has clearly been the aim (if not the outcome), for instance, in many post–Reformation Christian traditions. But it is also possible for the doctrinal corpus to be largely confined to elites. In many parts of the world, the "little traditions" (Redfield 1955) of rural tribespeople and peasantries are founded on versions of elite religious practices that (for the laity) lack a systematic justification in doctrine and narrative. In the absence of pedagogic support and effective policing, we often find that lay versions of world religions migrate away from both of our modal attractor positions and settle around more easily acquired, intuitive concepts and practices (the cognitive optimum position) that consequently require neither routinization nor high arousal to maintain. Yet another possibility, and a particularly common one in some parts of the world, is for modes of religiosity to interact in complex ways.

Religious traditions founded on interacting modes of religiosity encompass large populations, but at the same time, they are composed of many locally distinctive ritual communities. The cohesion of the latter may readily be projected onto the wider religious community, and such processes appear to have been crucial in many large-scale and bloody religiously motivated wars (see chapter 7). In other cases, however, the effect of the imagistic mode is not necessarily to intensify commitment to a set of principles codified in language but, rather, to provide a substitute for such principles as the main source of religious motivation. It is precisely within those populations that lack access to the authoritative corpus of religious teachings—and so cannot be adequately motivated by these teachings— that we find the greatest profusion of imagistic practices. Elitist discourses would have us believe that the prominence of the imagistic mode among the uneducated and dispossessed is symptomatic of ignorance. Expressed more precisely, and less snobbishly, routinized religious rituals that lack a persuasive justification in dogma (i.e., learned via instruction) will die out unless they are either naturalized (through the proliferation of cognitively optimal versions) or motivated by forms of religious experience and understanding that are at least to some significant extent internally generated. A model for this sort of motivational base is provided the world over by the ancient imagistic mode of religiosity.

Since the possibilities afforded by modal dynamics are quite numerous and complex, it might seem as though the theory forbids nothing and is therefore unfalsifiable. That is not the case, however. Chapter 9 attempts to set out predictions of the theory of modes of religiosity in a way that could be systematically falsified by empirical data from psychology, archaeology, historiography, and ethnography.

The Origins of Modes of Religiosity

The presence of the imagistic mode almost certainly predates the emergence of the doctrinal mode by a very substantial margin. The former appears in the archaeological record at least as far back as the Upper Paleolithic period, whereas the latter appears probably no less recently than the emergence of Bronze Age civilizations (Whitehouse 2000a, chap. 8). Obviously, the first fully modern humans had very much the same cognitive equipment as modern peoples, so why did it take so long for both modes of religiosity to emerge, and why are not both modes universal?

The answer almost certainly lies in the fact that processes of experimentation with patterns of ritual behavior and revelatory thinking are not random. The features that comprise our divergent modes of religiosity probably do not coalesce in the absence of some kinds of triggers located outside the mode dynamics themselves. It is hard to imagine, for instance, why a band of peaceful hunter-gatherers with abundant resources would have occasion to experiment with the extremely costly patterns of behavior needed to get the development of modes of religiosity underway. Indeed, many modern-day hunter-gatherers with sufficient territory at their disposal do not experiment in that way, even when surrounded by groups with elaborate religious models of this kind. Instead, egalitarian foraging bands (Woodburn 1982) seem to make do with relatively simple rituals and concepts of the supernatural clustered around the cognitive optimum position. In order for our distant ancestors in the Upper Paleolithic period to have adopted forms of religion operating in the imagistic mode, there would have needed to be significant external pressures.

A particularly obvious pressure for at least some ancestral populations would have been the advancing ice sheets. For instance, we know that the increasingly harsh conditions of the last ice age triggered new and often more dangerous strategies of cooperative hunting. It is possible that, initially, low-frequency, high-arousal group activities of this kind became linked with attempts to manipulate the environment through the performance of rituals. Cohesive units formed through the communal performance of low-frequency, high-arousal rituals would have been capable of wiping out, displacing, or absorbing less cohesive bands of hunter-gatherers competing for the same resources (under conditions, of course, of growing scarcity). This helps to explain the creative explosion of artistic imagery apparently associated with terrifying initiation rites in the Upper Paleolithic period (Pfeiffer 1982; Whitehouse 2000a, chap. 8). It suggests the development—perhaps for the first time—of complex bodies of revelatory religious knowledge based on processes of SER. Such traditions, once established, would have been very robust. Ritual experts may have tried to communicate their elaborate revelations by word of mouth, but unless their attempts to transmit information in that way could become routinized and centrally policed, it is hard to see how the doctrinal mode could become established. One reason why doctrinal religions seem to have been slow to get off the ground is that there were no external pressures to carry ritual innovations in that direction until the emergence of large-scale agricultural societies (Whitehouse 2000a, 169–172). Only then did the seasonal labor cycles and the increasingly complex nature of social cooperation foster the routinization of ritual and the centralization of religious authority, allowing other core elements of the doctrinal mode to coalesce (Whitehouse 2000a, chap. 8).

An alternative cognitive account of the emergence of doctrinal orthodoxies is presented by Pascal Boyer's theory of the emergence of professionalized religious guilds (Boyer 2001a). Like me, Boyer dates the emergence of doctrinal orthodoxies no earlier than the rise of complex societies, approximately six thousand years ago. His story begins, however, before the first centralized states began to take shape. To the list of cultural traits that cluster around the cognitive optimum position Boyer adds another set of concepts pertaining to the classification of humans into different natural kinds.[30] People all around the world tacitly presume that the other humans they encounter can be classified according to innate properties. Explicit versions of this kind of thinking—taking, for instance, the form of racist discourses—may be highly variable in content. But what matters for Boyer's theory is that almost any kind of trait that can be associated with some people and not others is liable to trigger intuitions about inherent categorical differences (regardless of how absurd these categories may seem by the lights of scientific biological knowledge). There are those who speak this language rather than that, who have these kinds of bones rather than those kinds (e.g., based on principles of descent), and—most importantly from the point of view of religious thinking—there are those who have particular qualities that make them better equipped than others to deal with supernatural agents. These qualities may be construed in local cultural registers as invisible marks or perhaps even as physical appendages to internal organs. But something makes these people different, and whatever it is finds abundant support in tacit essentialist reasoning. Long ago, when all societies were very small scale, religious specialists served only a group of locals. But when larger populations came together with the emergence of city-states, religious specialists, by virtue of their essentialized differences from ordinary folks, were naturally compelled to form guilds.

As such guilds became professionalized, they came under pressure to protect their share of the market. The solution, according to Boyer, was to establish a distinctive, standardized, easily recognizable, and securely patented brand. But that required the assistance of literacy. Texts would become the guarantee of both exclusive truth and inclusive orthodoxy. Once this happened, the heyday of the lone specialist dealing in local concepts and rituals had passed. The literate guilds instead supplied *general truths* for all and, wherever possible, sought the backing of powerful economic and political interests at the heart of the state machine. Religious systems were now established around "coherent . . . generally *integrated* . . . apparently *deductive* . . . and *stable*" religious doctrines (2001a, 278, emphases in original).

With the rise of more complex and regionally standardized doctrinal systems came a tendency to "downplay intuition" (Boyer 2001a, 278) and thus to exclude the beliefs and practices associated with the cognitive optimum position. Thus, as religious supermarket chains started to squeeze the corner-shop specialists, the wares that were on offer came to be more explicitly and coherently organized. According to Boyer, preliterate religious traditions had "no systematic doctrine of supernatural agents . . . [and] no theory of what these agents are like, what they do, where they reside, etc." (2001a, 266).[31] The wares of the local religious specialist did not amount to "such a thing as 'religion' as a special domain of concepts and activities" (Boyer 2001a, 267). Thus, according to Boyer, the emergence of professionalized religious guilds produced for the first time an explicit notion of religion as a demarcated domain of thought and action.

Boyer's theory brilliantly welds Gellner's Weberian sociology and Goody's theory of literacy to the main findings of social and evolutionary psychology in a fashion that is both highly original and rhetorically compelling. But there are also problems with Boyer's account. To begin, Boyer advances a series of correlations that run rather strikingly against the grain of available empirical evidence. For instance, are the concepts of preliterate, localized traditions necessarily clustered more substantially around the cognitive optimum position than, say, the belief systems sanctioned by literate elites? Detailed ethnographic evidence on a great range of small-scale nonliterate cultures strongly suggests otherwise. Australian Aboriginal ideas about the "dreamtime" (or "dreaming") provide a good case in point. Extensive direct study of these traditions has revealed the presence of dauntingly elaborate bodies of philosophical and cosmological knowledge that require many years of intensive contemplation to develop and mature. In attempting to convey a sense of the scope and complexity of Aboriginal religious thought, one anthropologist sums up the evidence as follows:

> Australian Aborigines have incredibly subtle, philosophically challenging mystical cosmologies that posit a spiritual plane of existence that was prior to the world of sensory experience (in the "dreamtime") but now lies behind or parallel to it. Mervyn Meggitt . . . describes how the old Walbiri man who was his spiritual guide eventually told him gently that he, Meggitt, had reached his philosophical depth and could follow no longer into the mysteries of the cosmos. Probably no Westerner has ever fully penetrated these Aboriginal philosophical realms. (Keesing 1981, 333–334)

Similar comments have been made with regard to the cosmologies of small-scale, nonliterate societies in Amazonia (Reichel-Dolmatoff 1971), Africa (Griaule 1975), and Melanesia (Juillerat 1992). The overall impression from ethnographic research is that nonliterate societies, in general, do not deal in religious concepts that are closer to the cognitive optimum than those of literate societies. The cognitive optimum is a natural attractor position (present in all societies), but countervailing tendencies are by no means limited to complex societies with literate, professionalized religious guilds.

The role accorded to literacy in Boyer's model also raises important issues. Boyer rightly points to a close correlation between the presence of literacy and the homogenization of regional traditions policed by professional guilds. A crucial question, to which archaeology may hold the key, is whether the emergence of literacy helps to create doctrinal orthodoxy, or as I would suggest, the emergence of doctrinal orthodoxy creates some of the pressure to develop systems of writing. It would help, of course, to know whether early signs of literate innovation occur alongside the emergence of religious standardization or whether one tends to precede the other. Recent studies of the origins of professional religious guilds promoting standardized concepts of a doctrinally complex nature suggest that these features predate the advent of literacy in a number of key locations (Mithen 2004; Johnson 2004). It would therefore appear that the presence of doctrinal orthodoxies favors the subsequent development of writing systems, rather than being caused by them. But even if Boyer's account turns out to provide a better fit with available data, we still have to explain how the complex systems of concepts associated with doctrinal orthodoxies come to be successfully disseminated in a population. The theory of modes of religiosity might help to solve at least some of these problems.

For a start, the modes theory does not attempt to correlate particularism and orality with the cognitive optimum position, on the one hand, and universalism and literacy with cosmological complexity on the other. Consequently, it is not threatened by ethnographic data demonstrating the tendency of many small-scale, nonliterate traditions to drift away from the cognitive optimum position. On the contrary, the modes theory was built with data of that sort in mind. The challenge all along has been to show precisely *how* the localized religions of Papua New Guinea managed to generate profoundly complex revelations associated with mystery cults in the absence of either routinized forms of education or external mnemonics (e.g., systems of writing). The solution, I have suggested, is one that was discovered way back in human prehistory and has remained part of the cultural repertoire of many populations ever since—from the "simple" societies of such regions as Melanesia to the complex polities of Europe and elsewhere. It takes the form of what I have called the imagistic mode of religiosity.[32]

Through elevated arousal, cognitive shocks, and the creation of consequential events, the rituals of the imagistic mode set off trains of exegetical thinking that are enduring and (over time) capable of generating highly elaborate semantic knowledge. The motor driving this process is a stock of episodic memories for traumatic ritual ordeals. These are the general conditions, I would suggest, in which the great philosophers of Aboriginal Australia, Amazonia, Africa, and Melanesia (as well as of other small-scale, nonliterate societies) come into existence. But philosophers are found in complex societies as well. Some of these are very much like the ritual experts of precontact New Guinea—the spiritual fathers of Hellenistic Mithraic cults, for instance, or the high priests of many contemporary pagan cults in Europe and North America. But another kind of philosopher was also born with the advent of the doctrinal mode of religiosity. What made this new breed of religious experts different was that their knowledge could be transmitted *verbally*, via highly repetitive regimes of teaching and reminding. And these methods of transmission opened the floodgates to processes of standardization and the policing of emergent orthodoxies.

The independent development of the doctrinal mode requires that a number of elements initially fall into place. For a start, of course, there must be inspired individuals with a complex and compelling message to communicate. According to Boyer's model, such persons only came into existence along with the establishment of religious guilds. According to the modes theory, by contrast, such figures have been around for very much longer than that. What they lacked throughout most of human prehistory was a means of transmitting their knowledge by word of mouth. They required a forum for teaching complex knowledge to attentive and credulous audiences—a setting, in short, that allowed forms of routinized oratory and instruction.

Many factors could have been implicated in the establishment of such forums in different places at different times. An acceleration in the pace of ritual life, caused by periods of drought, famine, or disease, might be a contender. The development of more routinized forms of organized labor might be another. But whatever the triggers,[33] transmission of complex religious knowledge by means of language required methods of sustained reiteration.

Still, this would not have been enough on its own. Even if we concede that routinization could (help to) explain the susceptibility of audiences to particular teachings (as will be argued at greater length in the next chapter), we still have to explain what motivated their interest. Complex teachings would have to be *persuasive*, and persuasiveness depends on the use of all those devices that Boyer associates with literate guilds: coherence, integration, rhetoric, and plausibility. Literacy might assist in the perfection of some of these features of the doctrinal mode, thus helping to explain the concomitant emergence and spread of writing systems, but it does not explain why doctrinal orthodoxies come into existence in the first place.

This chapter has attempted merely to summarize the theory of modes of religiosity at a very general level. As an introductory overview, it may have raised more questions than it has answered. A much fuller account of my central claims now follows. Focused heavily on the psychological variables driving the model, particularly the complex relationships between memory, codification, frequency, transmission, and arousal (chapters 5 and 6), this account is intended to fill in many of the gaps in my earlier volumes and in the preceding précis.

Notes

1. The dividing lines between explicit and implicit memory are difficult to draw (for a fine overview, see Schachter 1987), but evidence from studies of normal cognition (e.g., Roediger 1990) and amnesic patients (e.g., Graf, Squire, and Mandler 1984) show that such a distinction (or a series of more fine-grained distinctions) is difficult to avoid (although see Baddeley 1997, chap. 20). Many of these issues are discussed more fully in chapters 4 and 5.

2. This particular distinction has a long history and certainly predates cognitive science. It is apparent, for instance, in William James's (1890) discussion of primary and secondary memory, and the first experimental studies of short-term memory date back to the same period (Jacobs 1887).

3. The distinction between semantic and episodic memory was first fully developed by Tulving (1972) and is now used by psychologists studying a wide range of phenomena, including amnesia, aphasia and agnosia, story grammars, schemas and scripts, and framing and modeling. For a thorough overview, see Baddeley 1997.

4. See Whitehouse 1992, 1994, 1995, 1996a, 1996b, 1996c, 1998, 2000a, 2000b, 2001a, 2001b.

5. See, for instance, Whitehouse 2000a, 44–46, 115, 142–143, 148, 155.

6. For the most part, dogma is interwoven by strings of logical implications. Since the range of possible strings is far greater than those that happen to be exploited by religious teachers, standardization necessitates frequent rehearsal (i.e., a routinized regime of doctrinal transmission).

7. See, for instance, Whitehouse 1995, chap. 7, and 2000a, 60–63.

8. Powell and Fazio (1984), for instance, have shown that the motivational force of explicit beliefs is at least partly a function of frequent rehearsal.

9. For a fuller discussion of this point, see Whitehouse 2000a, 151–153, 172–180. Some criticisms of this aspect of my argument notwithstanding (e.g., Boyer 2002), I accept that literacy is a precipitating condition (perhaps even a necessary condition) for the independent invention of doctrinal mode phenomena (Whitehouse 2000a, 179–180), but it is not essential for their reproduction (Whitehouse 1992).

10. See in particular chapter 5.

11. Some (admittedly preliminary) experimental support for this claim comes from a study by Barrett and Whitehouse of spontaneous exegetical reflection (SER) generated by repeated performances of an artificial ritual modeled on the Catholic practice of self-crossing. This study suggested that levels and volume of SER correlate inversely with degree of repetition and habituation.

12. This argument is elaborated in Whitehouse 2000a, chapter 8. For a similar (and fuller) overview of these processes, see Diamond 1998.

13. The reality is a bit more complicated than that. Consider, for instance, conversion experiences in some Christian traditions, which appear to be constructed around episodic memories. From the viewpoint of my argument, three points are crucial to make about these sorts of phenomena. First, where episodic memory plays a significant role in the doctrinal mode, it is typically in relation to highly personalized rather than collectively experienced episodes (episodes of the latter sort tend to produce something altogether different—an imagistic domain of operation, discussed in the proceeding). Second, these highly personalized episodes tend to be subjected to such frequent verbal reiteration that they eventually give rise to quite rigidly schematized, even stereotyped, narratives (thus dissolving into the standardized schemas of semantic memory). Third, religious experiences encoded in episodic memory are invariably superfluous to the doctrinal mode in the sense that the reproduction of the doctrinal tradition in a recognizable form does not depend on their preservation. In short, being a member of a doctrinal tradition (e.g., a Christian) minimally presumes some level of commitment to schemas encoded in semantic memory—no more and no less.

14. See Whitehouse 1992 and 2000a, 9–12, 40–41, 50–52, 113–117.

15. See Whitehouse 1992, 1994, and 2000a, 72–80.

16. For ethnographic examples, see Lowie 1924, Turnbull 1962, Meggitt 1962, Allen 1967, Strehlow 1965, Barth 1975, 1987, Tuzin 1980, Herdt 1981, 1982.

17. See Lewis-Williams 1997 and Pfieffer 1982.

18. The evidence here is somewhat complex, but useful overviews are presented by Conway 1995 and Christianson 1992.

19. This term was first coined by Brown and Kulik 1977, and has since been examined in a variety of major studies (discussed at greater length in chapter 6). The role of flash-bulb memory in recall for ritual episodes has been most extensively discussed in White-house 1996a, 2000a; McCauley 2001; McCauley and Lawson 2002; and Atran 2002.

20. The only cases of low-frequency, low-arousal rituals known to me are ones that use external mnemonics or a compositional hierarchy of ritual elements (i.e., rarely performed rituals composed of an assortment of more frequently performed rites) or both. For examples, see McCauley 2001 and Atran 2002. But such exceptions seem to prove the rule—not only because they are hard to find but because they always constitute practices that are inessential to the reproduction, in a recognizable form, of the doctrinal traditions in which they occur.

21. A recent pilot study by Barrett and Whitehouse suggests that recall for rarely transmitted verbal exegesis is extremely poor, and even more so for rarely transmitted behavioral procedures. In this study, a class of one hundred first-year anthropology students participated in an artificial ritual requiring them to carry out a series of unusual actions. They were told that the purpose of this was to learn about the pressures of ethnographic field-work, especially the effects on stress levels among researchers of having to participate in strange activities. Participants were instructed not to write down what they had heard. The theological statement was delivered loudly and slowly, to maximize the chances of successful encoding. Participants then completed a short questionnaire asking them to rate their emotional states during the performance. Seven weeks later, participants completed a questionnaire asking them to record the action sequence they had performed, the stated reasons for the experiment, and the fictitious theology they had heard. The elements and sequence of the ritual actions were recalled more or less perfectly by the entire class. By contrast, recall for the fictitious theology and even for the stated reasons for the experiment was virtually nil. This particular experiment was unsuccessful, insofar as it was intended to establish correlations between emotional self-ratings and recall for various aspects of the artificial ritual. The lack of significant variation in recall performance made this impossible. Nevertheless, our findings do suggest that the cultural reproduction of ritual actions does not require very great frequency (even quite rarely performed actions sequences will be well-remembered). By contrast, even the simplest exegetical and theological concepts cannot survive relatively long transmissive cycles. In order to be learned in the first place, and sustained in semantic memory in the long run, they must be repeated and rehearsed.

22. All rituals have the potential to trigger SER by virtue of being irreducible to any set of technical motivations (see the introduction). Nevertheless, frequent repetition can reduce the likelihood of an internal search for symbolic motivations being initiated by causing habituation and reliance on implicit procedural knowledge. This is not the case with respect to low-frequency, high-arousal rituals activating episodic memory. Whenever recall for the rituals is triggered, this will involve recall of an explicit kind that is, in turn, eminently capable of setting off a search for symbolic motivations.

23. See Barth 1975 and Whitehouse 2000a.

24. See especially Whitehouse 2000a, chapter 4.

25. In other words, the position of leader (if it exists) does not afford opportunities to transmit, shape, or direct any systematic program of belief and action.

26. See, for instance, Aronson and Mills 1959 and Mills and Mintz 1972.

27. Ethnographic evidence for this is presented in Whitehouse 2000a; historiographical evidence is presented in Whitehouse and Martin 2004.

28. Classic ethnographic studies include Williams 1928, Schwartz 1962, and Barth 1987 (for an extended discussion, see Whitehouse 2000a).

29. There are exceptions, however. If transformed into more intuitive variants or provided with exceptional forms of mnemonic support, certain concepts and practices remote from our modal attractor positions can indeed survive. But, either way, they cease to contribute to the transmission of *revelatory* knowledge or to the distinctive social morphology of religious traditions. These issues are discussed in detail in later chapters.

30. For a slightly different view of how this works, see Hirschfeld 1996.

31. Boyer is here describing the case of a contemporary nonliterate religious tradition, that of the Buid of the Philippines (Gibson 1986). But he uses this case to illustrate the *general* situation that he suggests obtained prior to the rise of the first civilizations.

32. Possible factors triggering the emergence of the imagistic mode are discussed in Whitehouse 2000a, chapter 8.

33. A detailed investigation of these issues was begun at a conference on the historiographical and archaeological evidence for modes of religiosity, held at the University of Vermont in August 2002, funded by the British Academy and the Templeton Foundation, and published in the present series (Whitehouse and Martin 2004).

Ritual and Meaning in the Doctrinal Mode   5

IN THE LAST CHAPTER, we noted that the doctrinal mode of religiosity entails (among other things) highly repetitive patterns of ritual performance and verbal transmission. I suggested that routinization was linked to the activation of implicit memory for ritual procedures and to semantic memory for verbally codified teachings, including ritual exegesis. This chapter examines the psychological implications of religious routinization in much greater detail, postulating at least five levels of cognitive processing entailed by high-frequency ritual transmission and focusing on the disconnectedness of "how-type" (procedural) knowledge of these kinds of ritual actions from "why-type" (exegetical) knowledge. The latter places great demands on memory. In this respect, novices would seem to require heavier repetition of cardinal principles of exegesis than more experienced members of the tradition, and consequently a delicate balance between the demands of acquisition and learning and long-term maintenance and consolidation must be achieved if the concepts are to survive. In particular, reproduction of religious knowledge with a heavy conceptual load presents challenges to the motivational systems of religious adherents. Insufficient repetition can lead to poor acquisition as well as to patterns of decay and distortion of the orthodoxy, while excessive repetition can produce tedium and reduced commitment. Routinized religious oratory, as we shall see, must weave a narrow path between relevance and redundancy. These arguments are built around psychological theories relating to processes of learning, analogical thinking, and memory.

The Distinction between Implicit and Explicit Memory

Within cognitive psychology, studies of learning attach considerable importance to the difference between knowing *how* to do something and knowing *that* something is the case. Neil Cohen and Larry Squire (1980) originally proposed the labels "procedural" and "declarative" memory to designate these two kinds of knowledge. In the case of procedural memory, recollection is unconscious—that is, we may know how to do a particular thing, such as ride a bicycle, without being aware of what it is we are remembering. By contrast, declarative memory entails conscious acts of recollection. The distinctiveness of these memory systems is supported by evidence from amnesic patients, many of whom display massive deficits with regard to declarative memory but whose procedural memory systems may be unimpaired. Peter Graf and Daniel L. Schachter (1985) and Daniel Schachter (1987) subsequently proposed a theory of implicit and explicit memory along lines closely resembling the procedural or declarative distinction. A problem with Cohen and Squire's earlier model was that it merely described, but did not explain, certain patterns of cognitive impairment associated with amnesia. One possibility is that amnesiacs suffer from encoding or "activation" problems. Activation theory (e.g., Graf, Squire, and Mandler 1984) suggests that implicit memory (but not explicit or declarative memory) is handled by dedicated neural structures that operate automatically and are relatively independent of other brain functions. Processing theory (e.g., Roediger and Blaxton 1987), meanwhile, suggests that implicit and explicit memory systems, whether or not they also correspond to discrete neural architecture, have different proprietary inputs. In this view, implicit or procedural memory processes data presented by perceptual systems, whereas explicit or declarative memory is geared up to process the outputs of internal cognitive mechanisms (see figure 5.1).

The general relationship between implicit and explicit memory presented by the processing theory seems intuitively plausible, up to a point, but, clearly, the construction of implicit knowledge is not always driven by our experiences. Some forms of implicit knowledge seem to result from the repeated application of explicit rules. For instance, learning to drive a car may begin by encoding a set of verbal instructions, such as "press down on the clutch pedal before engaging the gear stick; then apply pressure to the accelerator while slowly releasing the clutch." John Anderson (1983) develops a detailed model, known as ACT* (pronounced "act-star"), to account for the processes by which declarative knowledge is trans-

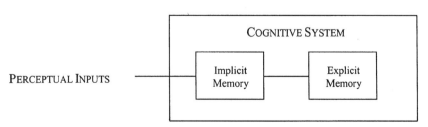

Figure 5.1.   The Relationship between Implicit and Explicit Memory in Processing Theory

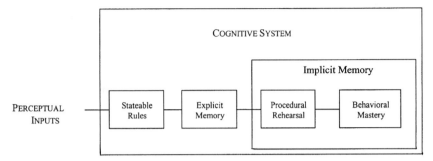

Figure 5.2.   The Relationship between Implicit and Explicit Memory in the ACT* Model

formed through repeated rehearsal (i.e., by practicing) into automatic, habitual, and thus implicit skills. In its general outline, the ACT* model (see figure 5.2) contrasts starkly with the picture presented by processing theory. Nevertheless, this contrast does not necessarily amount to a contradiction. The relationship between implicit and explicit memory is most profitably envisaged as a two-way street. Annette Karmiloff-Smith's recent theory of "representational redescription" (RR) may help to explain why.

The Theory of Representational Redescription

According to Karmiloff-Smith (1992), learning is a recursive process in which perception dynamically interacts with internal cognitive processes, producing progressively more explicit and consciously accessible understandings. Karmiloff-Smith envisages learning as a four-phase process. In the first phase, procedural competence may develop through empirically driven experimentation or through the application of explicit instructions. Once a set of embodied skills and habits has been established, it takes the form of unconscious or implicit knowledge. As such, it is informationally encapsulated—it cannot be modified by information from other parts of the cognitive apparatus. A nice illustration of this feature of implicit knowledge is provided by Roy D'Andrade (1995, 144–145), who points out that Americans driving in England may be able to combine implicit driving skills with explicit knowledge of the "drive on the left" rule, but when suddenly presented with a risk of head-on collision will feel compelled to swerve to the right (with potentially disastrous consequences). Implicit knowledge is "informationally encapsulated" in the sense that it cannot take into account explicit knowledge, even when this is a matter of life and death.

Thus, Karmiloff-Smith argues that implicit knowledge is bracketed off from knowledge in other domains, even (as in the driving example) within the domain to which it becomes attached. Encodings at this level are "procedure-like" and "sequentially specified" (1992, 20), giving rise to increasingly fluent behavioral repertoires and correspondingly rapid and automatic perceptual and sensorimotor adjustments. Phase one in Karmiloff-Smith's model thus culminates in "behavioral mastery," which she refers to as "level I" (i.e., Implicit).

The next phase consists of the formation of more explicit representations—the progressive reformulation of implicit knowledge as a set of inductively derived principles (level EI). This is a process by which the internal processing apparatus reformulates information encoded in the input systems as a set of essential elements or metonymical features. Nevertheless, this sort of internally processed inductive knowledge is initially inaccessible to consciousness. As such, it cannot be brought into accordance with implicit representations contained in the input systems. Internally generated explicit knowledge, however, exercises greater control over inferential processes than the implicit representations from which it was constructed. Expressed somewhat differently, theoretical considerations override purely empirical ones. In some domains, this can result in a marked, albeit temporary, deterioration of behavioral mastery.

This claim is supported by evidence relating to a wide range of domains that at least some (but not all) forms of learning follow a U-shaped curve and are not simply a matter of steadily improving proficiency. A striking example is the apparent deterioration of object-manipulation skills between ages four and six. Four-year-olds confronted with the task of balancing a set of bricks approach the problem like little empiricists. Regardless of whether the bricks are asymmetrical or have visibly or invisibly unequal weight distribution, four-year-olds use them to construct viable towers. This task is performed using implicit procedural knowledge, encoded in the child's input systems, that considers not whether the observable properties of a given block should make it balance in a particular position, but only whether it does balance. With practice, the sensorimotor and perceptual skills of four-year-olds become sufficiently refined that they may be described as having achieved "behavioral mastery" of the task of constructing towers out of building blocks.

At around age six, however, theoretical principles of weight distribution override empirical considerations (Karmiloff-Smith 1992, 82–87). Symmetrical blocks that have been invisibly and unevenly weighted so as to violate the six-year-olds' geometric-center theory are simply rejected by these children as "unbalanceable," even though four-year-olds (unconstrained by the geometric-center theory) can incorporate the blocks successfully. There is, in other words, a deterioration of behavioral mastery, attributable to the executive control of quasi-theoretical assumptions about weight distribution and gravity. At around age eight the task of balancing blocks, including those with invisible, uneven weight distribution, becomes possible again, even though the geometric-center theory can still be shown to be operative.

Theory and empirical evidence are reconciled in the block-building performances of these older children. Karmiloff-Smith provides similarly persuasive evidence for the RR model in relation to the construction of knowledge in several other domains (including language, number, theory of mind, and notation). Of course, learning in a given domain does not have to proceed unilineally. As predicted by Anderson's ACT* model, explicit and declarative knowledge may provide a starting point for procedural learning in a particular domain or subdomain, giving rise to (rather than resulting from) the development of procedural skills.

Thus, Karmiloff-Smith's model involves a sort of reconciliation of knowledge encoded in the input systems, on the one hand, and generated by internal, interdomain computations on the other. This is a process in which our representations become available to consciousness but, initially, cannot be verbalized (level E2). Further processing of such intuitive knowledge across domains can lead to its recodification as a "cross-system code" (Karmiloff-Smith 1992, 23) capable of being verbally described (level E3).

Karmiloff-Smith provides a concise illustration of her general argument by describing how people learn to play the piano. A novice pianist has to laboriously practice sequences of individual notes before being able to remember them as discrete strings capable of being reproduced automatically and fluently. Such fluency amounts to behavioral mastery and, as such, constitutes learning only at an implicit level, engaging online cognitive functions. Processing of such knowledge is fast, mandatory, informationally encapsulated, and so on. Anyone, like myself, who has failed to advance much beyond this level in learning to play an instrument, will recognize the difficulty of remembering a piece that one has not played for a long time. Strings of notes and chords, internally fluent, are often hard to combine into an integrated piece. The cues that allow sudden recollection of the links between one musical string and another, or the reactivation of whole strings that were temporarily forgotten, elicit irreducible and automatic units of knowledge. Starting again within a string is extremely difficult, and changing the sequential, procedural features of a string in accordance with a conscious plan proves virtually impossible during the experience of playing. More advanced musicianship requires RR, such that

> the knowledge of the different notes and chords (rather than simply their run-off sequence) becomes available as manipulable data. . . . The end result is representational flexibility and control, which allows for creativity. Also important is the fact that the earlier proceduralized capacity is not lost: for certain goals, the pianist can call on the automated skill; for others, he or she calls on the more explicit representations that allow for flexibility and creativity. (Karmiloff-Smith 1992, 16)

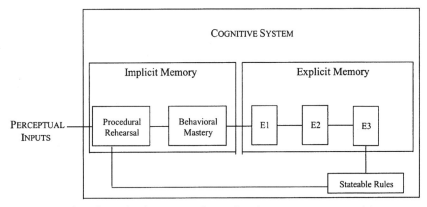

Figure 5.3.   The Relationship between Implicit and Explicit Memory in RR Model

The development of explicit theoretical musical knowledge, unlike the achievement of behavioral mastery at the piano, allows the transfer of knowledge within the domain of music (encompassing many instruments) but also between domains (such as mathematics and musical notation). At the most explicit level (E3), such knowledge can be verbalized as advanced musical theory, capable of informing and being informed by similarly explicit knowledge in any domain. It follows, of course, that learning in a given domain does not have to proceed unilineally. The development of new forms of behavioral mastery is driven by explicit knowledge. But the reverse is also true: new skills are capable of driving new forms of explicit knowledge. Nevertheless, intradomain learning cannot proceed downward (i.e., E3-E2-E1, etc.). As with any two-way street, traffic on each side must proceed in one direction only (see figure 5.3).

Representational Redescription in Routinized Ritual

Karmiloff-Smith's (1992) account of implicit knowledge (encoded in procedural form and specifying behavioral sequences that are bracketed off from other representations) reads almost like an attempt at defining routinized ritual. Her notion of "bracketing" is especially interesting: she is referring to the informational encapsulation of implicit knowledge, disallowing both intra- and interdomain representational links. Consider the procedural knowledge entailed in weekly Christian church services. These may involve various alterations of posture, coordinated among worshippers in the congregation, as sequences of standing, sitting, and kneeling. Although engaging the same sensorimotor and perceptual apparatus as more or less identical alterations of posture in secular contexts, the ritual setting provides invariable linkages between varied postures and particular context-dependent activities that are specified in advance. Thus, standing in the middle of a service may be invariably linked with the activity of singing, kneeling with praying, and sitting with listening, even though there is no obvious instrumental connection between these specific activities and the bodily postures they require. There is no technical reason why people should not be able to sing, pray, and listen in any of the three stipulated postures. Infants and toddlers brought to church every week therefore have to learn the stipulated character of ritual bodily practices as something fundamentally different from instrumental uses of the body in everyday life (where bodily postures may be an instrument of communication or of modifying the material environment or the conditions of bodily experience itself). In this sense, any given unit of ritual behavior is bracketed off both from non-ritual behavior and from other units of ritual behavior; it is informationally encapsulated insofar as behavioral mastery operates independently of other more explicit considerations; it is automatic and mandatory, in that one stands, sits, and kneels without any need for conscious reflection and in swift (automatic) response to cues from the environment.

Although people who attend church regularly do not need to have quasi-theoretical knowledge of the links between standing and singing, kneeling and praying, and sitting and listening, such knowledge is bound to emerge over time. A developmental story might run like this. Preschoolers regularly attending church may rapidly learn to sit, stand, and kneel in response to some of the same cues that trigger automaticity in the behavioral repertoires of church-going adults (e.g., movement in the rest of the congregation). Around age six, this behavior may have undergone RR, such that the child's behavior reflects quasi-theoretical links between particular activities and ritual bodily postures (e.g., standing up requires singing and vice versa, whereas sitting down requires shutting up!). This might lead to a deterioration of behavioral mastery, as in experiments designed to test object-manipulation skills (discussed earlier). It would be particularly interesting to test this intuition, for instance, by putting regular church-going children of various ages through an unorthodox service wherein some singing occurs in a kneeling posture. Would six-year-old children describe the singing as "praying," and would four- and eight-year-olds simply describe it as "singing?" By age eight, one might anticipate reconciliation of empirically driven and quasi-theoretical knowledge of Christian services, such that singing-while-kneeling was simply an unorthodox way of singing.

The RR model suggests that routinized forms of ritual transmission establishing behavioral mastery at the performative and procedural level will gradually generate quasi-theoretical procedural knowledge. All this may well constitute learning only at an implicit level, however. It is possible in principle, and probably quite common in practice, for Christians to participate in liturgical rites on autopilot (so to speak), without actually reflecting on how they know what to do at any given stage. Nevertheless, quasi-theoretical principles (such as the rule: "genuflect while praying") are always potentially accessible to verbal report. It is the same with geometric-center theory, which adults normally apply when balancing blocks without necessarily being conscious of doing so. But when asked why they do not try to balance a block on its edge, few people would have difficulty explaining that most of the weight of the higher block must be distributed across the surface of the lower one.

Routinized Ritual and Exegesis

Procedural knowledge of ritual, whether or not empirically based or governed by quasi-theoretical principles, is only concerned with how to perform a ritual; it is not concerned with why it is performed. The why-type question has to be answered at an explicit level—it is a request for declarative knowledge or exegesis. Repetitive rituals are commonly accorded extensive exegesis. In attempting to explain this in cognitive terms, it is tempting to hypothesize that explicit, why-type knowledge of rituals is reflexively derived from implicit how-type knowledge—as through an advanced process of RR, for instance. This is extremely unlikely, however.

In the case of routinized rituals, spontaneous exegetical reflection (SER) is not automatic. Experienced worshippers often cannot say why they perform a particular habituated ritual action, even though (or perhaps partly because) they may suspect that it has some authoritative theological justification. When worshippers are pressured to reflect on questions of symbolic motivation in the absence of externally derived exegesis, they seem to do so not with reference to implicit procedural knowledge, but with reference to thematically connected schemas entertained at an explicit level. For instance, a Catholic asked to explain why she crosses herself with holy water on entering the church for Mass may have no idea at all why she does this. But, when pressed, she may associate it with the practice of removing one's shoes on entering a mosque, on the grounds that both represent an act of respect or a process of cleansing.

This sort of backward justification can be examined most easily in relation to highly repetitive rituals for which official exegesis is systematically unavailable. Although comparatively rare, such cases do exist—indeed, they are particularly prominent in logocentric traditions that entertain ambivalent attitudes toward ritualism on doctrinal grounds. Such attitudes are readily apparent in early Protestantism, particularly in its more Calvinistic manifestations (Collinson 1997). Similarly, the Judaic notion of a "natural law" has led some Jewish theologians to doubt the explicability, if not the efficacy, of sacrifice (see Herrenschmidt 1982, 33). In some cases, such ambivalence gives rise to ritual forms that lack a strong official justification and exegesis. A particularly clear example of this is the *puja* ritual, as described among Jains of Jaipur (Humphrey and Laidlaw 1994). Caroline Humphrey and James Laidlaw explain that ritualism in general, and the *puja* in particular, occupy a dubious position in Jainism. Although a highly repetitive (often daily) ritual for practicing Jains, the *puja* is not accorded official exegesis. Indeed, it is widely regarded as an empty ritual of which it is the responsibility of individual worshippers to endow with meaning through highly personalized and largely private processes of SER.

The *puja* ritual is performed in temples elaborately decorated with representations of ascetic renouncers, saints, and protector deities. The most important of these are marble, stone, or metal statues of ascetic renouncers, invariably assuming postures of meditation. The *puja* consists of a wide range of acts in which these idols are bathed, presented with offerings, anointed, and addressed in song, prayer, chants, and acts of meditation. At a procedural level, the *puja* consists of numerous units of action, conceptualized sequentially and taxonomically. For instance, the *pushpa puja* is a unit of action in which flowers are placed on an idol; it is construed in sequential terms as the third stage in the performance of a complete *puja* ritual, but it is also envisaged taxonomically as a special type of *anga* (limbs) *puja* that, in turn, is a special type of *dravya* (material) *puja*. Humphrey and Laidlaw show that procedural knowledge of the *puja* consists of both implicit, experientially driven performative competence and quasi-theoretical principles relating to ritual sequence and taxonomy. Considerably less convergence is apparent, however, in relation to people's reflexive representations of why the ritual actions entailed in the *puja* take the form that they do.

For instance, interviews with worshippers produced a wide variety of spontaneous reflexive commentaries on the *pushpa* (flower) *puja*. To one Jain, this action meant that her knowledge should blossom like a flower; to another, it meant that his feelings should be soft and gentle like a flower; to another, it meant that the scent of flowers should increase the pleasure of worship; to another, flowers encapsulated a notion of purity, and so on. Moreover, some interviewees claimed to have no reflexive knowledge in relation to the *pushpa puja* and appeared to be operating only at the procedural or implicit level. As one informant observes: "I do not know the reason why I put flowers, I just do it" (Humphrey and Laidlaw 1994, 35).

In their discussion of reflexive commentaries on the Jain *puja*, Humphrey and Laidlaw observe, "the problem appears to be a superabundance of meanings—meaning untamed" (1994, 36). Their solution to this problem hinged on a notion of ritual as a special type of action that lacks intrinsic intentional meaning. Nonritual actions, such as placing a lid on a pot of water suspended over a fire, have an intrinsic intentional meaning. As long as we can reasonably attribute to the cook certain basic understandings about the physics of heating liquids, he or she is clearly intending to trap heat in the pot and hasten the process of boiling or to prevent unwanted materials from falling into the pot or both. In contrast, we cannot make such inferences about the intentions of ritual actors because their actions are stipulated in advance and lack intuitive relations between means and ends. Since intentional meaning is not contained in ritual actions themselves, the attribution of a much less constrained range of meanings seems to be possible. In other words, ritual meaning appears to be up for grabs, and so in cases like the Jain *puja* where tight control over the range of exegesis is not exercised by religious authorities, we find an apparently limitless range of meanings being bandied about.

Humphrey and Laidlaw's data are highly instructive, and their theoretical arguments fundamentally persuasive 1994). Nevertheless, if we are slightly more precise about the cognitive principles undergirding the *puja*, the forms of knowledge it sustains seem to be less mutable than Humphrey and Laidlaw suggest. Procedural knowledge with regard to the *puja* is quite tightly constrained in that the varieties of habituated ritual action that count as *pujas*, as well as the rules governing their sequential recurrence, are quite widely shared and finite. For most people, that is probably all you need to know in order to participate fully and competently in the *puja*. The interview data just summarized suggest that Jains probably do not speculate to any great extent on why they perform the *puja*, or why it takes the various specific forms that it does. But insofar as people do engage in this sort of reflexivity—for instance, as a result of direct questioning by ethnographers—they come up with conceptually simple exegetical commentaries. Those who say that flowers are placed on the idol because they have a pleasant aroma appear to be offering a technical motivation for this type of *puja*. Exegesis of this sort is often derived from closely related cultural schemas and idioms, which might, for instance, conceive of inner states (such as serenity) as capable of blossoming. In principle, the potential repertoire of such interpretations is quite wide, but from the viewpoint of the individual worshipper, this repertoire is constrained by the limitations of semantic memory and the cognitive resources invested in exegetical speculation. Presumably, most Jains do not try to memorize lists of possible meanings of the *puja* (even if some do) and, in practice, are only able to remember a few exegetical possibilities at any given time, if they are entertained at all. The only conceptually complex exegetical commentaries cited by Humphrey and Laidlaw appeared to derive from written sources or the verbally transmitted teachings of ascetics. But in order for such representations to have a significant impact on lay religious sensibilities, they would need to be both widely and frequently transmitted. Since neither is the case, the exegetical meanings of the *puja* for most Jains are, far from being fecund and untamed, somewhat *limited*.

The *puja* ritual, although not unique, is something of an odd case. Its theoretical importance, as far as the present argument is concerned, is that it illustrates the unconnectedness of procedural and exegetical knowledge in relation to highly repetitive rituals. This is most clearly seen where official exegetical discourses are not effectively imposed, and so even in principle could not be causally connected to the reproduction of implicit ritual knowledge. But routinized religion is seldom this short of official exegesis with respect to its rituals. In most cases, children are told from an early age various explicit meanings of the liturgical rituals in which they participate. By the time they reach adulthood, most devout Roman Catholics would probably have little difficulty providing quite elaborate and convergent commentaries on the significance of Holy Communion. Now, this kind of official exegetical knowledge tends to be conceptually much more complex and difficult to remember than the sorts of reflexive, internally generated interpretations proffered by Jains in relation to the *puja*. Exegetical commentaries on Holy Communion would involve hard-to-grasp notions of omniscient agency, transubstantiation, redemption, and so on. Such concepts are clearly not spontaneously generated by each religious adherent. Rather, they are *learned* via processes of intensive reiteration and consolidation.

Routinization, Doctrine, and the Tedium Effect

Although the routinization of ritual somewhat discourages SER, it provides excellent conditions for the transmission of complex exegesis and doctrine. People who congregate regularly (every day or every week) to perform public rituals constitute potential audiences. All large-scale religions incorporate routinized ritual forums for the transmission of verbally codified religious knowledge. In some cases, the role of orator or teacher is accorded exclusively to experts (e.g., a professionalized priesthood); in others it is possible for all (or nearly all) participants to be experts to some extent and to alternate between the role of speaker and audience, teacher and pupil. In some traditions, the forum for doctrinal transmission is restricted to particular audiences, such as the members of a monastic order or some other kind of religious elite. But regardless of how the knowledge is distributed and the labors of transmission divided, those who possess this knowledge must have undergone an intensive education in order to acquire it.

It may seem rather obvious that conceptually complex knowledge needs to be rehearsed and reviewed in order to be learned. Nevertheless, no systematic attempt has been made to demonstrate the levels of repetition needed to transmit religious knowledge of varying degrees of conceptual complexity. Nor do we know what rates of reiteration are required to maintain intact complex strings of propositional or doctrinal knowledge once these have been thoroughly learned. A recent pilot study[1] suggests, however, that repetition is important not only for learning religious doctrines, but also for ensuring that they are remembered in the long run. In this study, a class of religion students heard twice-weekly repetitions of the four noble truths of Buddhism over four weeks. Recall for these doctrines was tested after the second repetition (time one), after the eighth repetition (time two), and after a six-week interval, during which period no further repetition took place (time three). Students were awarded two points for complete recollection of a noble truth, one point for partial recollection, and zero points if nothing was recalled. Thus overall scores could range from zero (no recall of any noble truths) to eight (complete recall of all four noble truths). On this scale of 0 to 8, the time one mean score was .91 (11.4 percent), the time two mean score was 3.2 (40 percent), and time three went down to 1.18 (14.7 percent). These findings seem to suggest that eight repetitions, each spaced by a few days, are not necessarily sufficient to transmit even quite limited doctrinal information (the time two score is not impressive, although motivational factors in genuine cases of religious transmission may produce better results). Rather more interestingly, we observed a very rapid decay in recall for the information that *had* been successfully learned.

In the absence of more substantial research in this area, we can at least say that the transmission of doctrinal knowledge probably requires more frequent repetition than the maintenance of that knowledge once it has been learned (although some ongoing rehearsal or consolidation would seem to be required). If that hypothesis is roughly correct, then it follows that the degree of routinization of religious transmission in traditions that emphasize, for instance, daily or weekly sermonizing and recitation would seem to be unduly excessive. Although this may be useful for those who are still learning the intricacies of a doctrinal orthodoxy, more experienced adherents (presumably the majority at most such gatherings) are forced to endure a considerable amount of redundant repetition. One effect of hearing the same parables and teachings over and over again can undoubtedly be varying degrees of boredom. In some cases, it can lead to what I have described as the tedium effect (Whitehouse 2002a; see also chap. 4)—a state of low morale arising from overfamiliarity with religious formulae and routine.

It might be objected that many religious adherents attest to a somewhat pleasurable, or at least comforting, experience of routinization. Far from finding repetition dull or tedious, many worshippers would say that ritual habituation provides reassurance and perhaps even a mildly hypnotic euphoria in the face of an uncertain, stressful, and fast-moving world. While in no way wishing to deny the reality of that experience, various independent indices of the tedium effect are widely apparent in such traditions, suggesting that people's conscious appraisals of their experience are not the whole story. For instance, all routinized religions forbid specific stereotyped expressions of boredom during their most high-frequency ritual performances, and many impose specific sanctions or "penances" for such faults. In spite of these measures, lengthy religious orations on familiar topics *everywhere* elicit overt signs of boredom among audiences, ranging from fidgeting and glazing of the eyes through to daydreaming and even slumber. When people say that their experiences in these circumstances are comforting, this may well be due to what psychologists call "cognitive dissonance" (Festinger 1957). In many carefully replicated studies, it has been shown that people will generally rate mundane tasks as more interesting when the payoffs are minimal. If the payoffs are substantial, those performing the tasks will freely admit that they found the activities boring, because they can justify their participation in terms of its rewards. That is not to say that the poorly rewarded participants are lying. Since they are unaware of their implicit motives for participation, they seek an alternative (post hoc) rationalization that seems to them perfectly true.

Another objection, of course, might be that at least some very repetitive rituals appear to be highly arousing. The affective quality of routinized doctrinal transmission undoubtedly can be enhanced by techniques of impassioned oratory (including the timely deployment of aggressivity, humor, dramatic emphasis, narrative etc.), as well as various forms of sensory stimulation (e.g., gospel singing, incense, visual effects, wailing, and hugging). The use of drama can also raise the emotional tonus of the occasion (e.g., as members of the audience deliver shocking confessions or experience miraculous healings). Although all these elements can play a role in staving off tedium, we need to be cautious when making inferences about elevated emotional states. My own hunch is that arousal varies inversely with frequency of ritual repetition. If one participates for the first time in a routinized possession cult or charismatic church, one might achieve states of very high excitement; but is it really possible for the "old hands" in such traditions to maintain these arousal levels when they have seen it all many hundreds of times? This seems unlikely, but it is, in the end, an empirical question. Indicators of physiological arousal can now be measured precisely by noninvasive techniques, and so relative levels of arousal among groups of participants with varying degrees of experience is, in principle, open to investigation.

Routinization, Relevance, and Revelation

We are still left with the challenge of explaining what motivates the truly enthusiastic supporters of routinized religions. This is no minor matter. It is generally the enthusiasts who create or shape the traditions others then follow. They are usually the ones who carry the great burdens of preserving and policing the orthodoxy. And they are the ones who often catch and hold the attention of audiences, infecting them with a sense of enduring revelation. Obvious examples of infectious oratory are provided by a range of contemporary Christian evangelical traditions.

According to anthropologist Brian Malley, American Protestant churches, on the whole, have displayed a remarkable resilience to the tedium effect, apparently by using patterns of religious repetition as a means of establishing the relevance of doctrinal orthodoxy to everyday life experience:

> Most sermons seek to connect doctrinal ideas with people's life situations, thus illuminating the relevance of Christian teaching for people's lives. It is this relevance [that] seems to me to counteract the tedium effect and is the reason that imaginative preachers are much in demand. It may be worth considering that the survival of highly doctrinal Christianity is not due to the political exclusion of alternatives but to preachers' creative ways of linking doctrine to daily life. The repetition may be driven less by the danger of inadvertent heresy than by the need to keep the ideas cognitively primed. Such an account of repetition is perfectly compatible with the overall dynamic proposed by Whitehouse. (Malley 2004)

Consistent with Malley's assertion, I have suggested elsewhere (Whitehouse 2000a, 93–94) that the effectiveness of the doctrinal mode depends in large part on the establishment of a dialogical relationship to complex religious teachings. One might argue that doctrinal reiteration couched in a "conversational" idiom (cf. Harding 1987) provides an exceptionally fertile array of schemas capable of activation in a vast range of common settings. This is what I think Malley means when he suggests that the "cognitive priming" of religious discourse ensures its everyday relevance. Moreover, additional mechanisms of cognitive priming are suggested by recent developments in the psychological study of analogical reasoning.

Keith Holyoak, Dedre Gentner, and Boicho Kokinov describe analogical reasoning as the "ability to think about relational patterns" (2001, 2). Construed in these general terms, analogy is a pervasive feature of most (if not all) cognitive activity. As such, the study of analogical thinking promises to generate increasingly integrated theories of mind. While psychologists have tended to specialize in the study of particular aspects of memory, learning, perception, emotion, and so on, research on analogical thinking must take into consideration all these processes insofar as they constrain or shape and, in turn, are constrained or shaped by each other. We know, for instance, that the capacity to draw analogies between related concepts depends on one's "memory state" at the time of testing (Kokinov 1990, 1994), that visual illustrations of problems can trigger different analogical solutions than verbal illustrations of identical problems (Kokinov and Yoveva 1996), and that verbal analogy is commonly used in emotional manipulation as a means of persuasion or to elicit empathy (Thagard and Shelley 2001). Partly because analogical thinking is intricately connected with processes of remembering, perceiving, emoting, and so on, we find that analogies are constructed rather differently in the real world as compared with the psychologist's laboratory. Kevin Dunbar calls this the "analogical paradox":

> On the one hand, the results of the past twenty years of research on analogical reasoning have found that unless subjects are given extensive training, examples, or hints, they will be much more likely to choose superficial features than deep structural features when using analogies. . . . On the other hand, such results are at odds with the data that we have collected from naturalistic settings. In both science and politics, we have found that structural analogies are not a rare event. People very frequently access structural and relational features when using analogy. The differences between the ways that analogy is used in naturalistic versus laboratory settings provide important insights for all models of analogical reasoning and shed new light on the nature of complex thinking. (2001, 313–314)

In laboratory conditions, studies of analogical reasoning generally present participants with two related problems. In a classic study, Mary Gick and Keith Holyoak (1980) presented participants with a story about a doctor who seeks to destroy a tumor using rays. The doctor's problem is that the high-intensity rays needed to destroy the cancer would pass through healthy tissue, thereby destroying it in the process of destroying the cancer. The "convergence solution" is to direct a number of low-intensity rays at the tumor from different angles, converging to produce a single high-intensity ray at only the required location within the patient's body. Gick and Holyoak found that approximately 10 percent of people presented with this story will arrive at the convergence solution without assistance of any kind. If, however, those hearing the first story are later presented with a second analogous story and its solution, they perform better when trying to solve the radiation problem. Consider the following analogue story. An army general wants his men to attack a fortress, but the roads leading to it are mined to explode if large numbers of troops march along them. He solves the problem by dividing his men into smaller groups that converge on the fortress simultaneously. Armed with this problem and its solution, 80 percent of people tested could then solve the radiation problem. But Gick and Holyoak's most striking finding was not that many people used one story to solve another, but that they only seemed to do this when explicitly encouraged to draw an analogy in order to solve the problem. Dunbar's point is that people are much more likely to use distant analogies to solve problems in naturalistic settings than in the laboratory. The question, of course, is *why*?

Dunbar's explanation has to do, in part, with patterns of encoding in the two kinds of settings. In laboratory experiments such as the ones originally carried out by Gick and Holyoak, participants are not usually expecting to have to use "source" stories to construct analogous stories of their own. Consequently, they do not actively contemplate the structural features of the source story to any great extent. Encoding focuses more on superficial features (e.g., extraneous details rather than underlying themes). In the real world, by contrast, people often attend to the structural properties of particular problems and their solutions on the assumption that this information may prove to be useful in solving subsequent problems of a thematically similar kind. Dunbar suggests that this is particularly the case in domains, such as science and politics, where processes of creative problem solving figure prominently. It is also particularly the case in the domain of religion. But the principles of analogical thinking used by scientists and politicians are deployed slightly differently by adherents of a doctrinal orthodoxy.

In highly routinized religions, people regard the corpus of orthodox religious teachings as a special set of source problems and their solutions that are intended to be applicable to indefinitely many target problems or solutions in the real world. What makes them special is that although they are acquired in specifiable ways (e.g., from the speeches of particular holy men and pages of text), they are not felt to originate in these sources. The explicit claim made, ad nauseam, by religious enthusiasts is that the original source is some higher power. They have been explicitly taught that this is so, and can probably say quite a lot on the subject, but their sense of it being true also has to do with the fact that the origins of religious teachings are intrinsically obscure. This obscurity is a direct result of heavy repetition. If a group of religious adherents is told a particular sacred narrative many times, there comes a point at which the narrator knows that the audience knows the story and the audience knows that the narrator knows that they know the story. Telling this particular story is not equivalent to an everyday act of communication. In particular, it is not reducible to the general technical motivation that normally underpins speech—namely, to impart information. Moreover, just as the purpose of the narration is unlike that of ordinary speech, so the intentions of the speaker cannot be inferred in a normal way. Are the intentional states of this particular speaker revealed in this retelling, or are we glimpsing the intentional states of countless previous narrators? The agency responsible for this kind of ritualized speech is indeterminate and opaque (Bloch 2004). We are left, then, with a void, a gap in our understanding, which is resolved by some official explanation—the intentions behind the narrative come from God (or from whatever or whomever). But official explanations only partially resolve the matter. Such explanations still don't explain why narratives of this kind seem to provide such salient or relevant food for analogical thought.

A possible explanation for the salience effect is that when people apply religious teachings to everyday situations, they implicitly realize that the source–target pairing they have produced is of a rather special kind. In ordinary analogical thinking, source concepts derive from semantic knowledge that is only provisionally true (it might have to be updated). By contrast, in the kind of analogical thinking used by devotees of a doctrinal orthodoxy, the source concepts are absolutely true, and are not transmitted in a way that reveals the intentions that gave rise to them. The invulnerability of such concepts to processes of questioning or updating makes their applicability to everyday situations seem to be rather impressive—and to use Malley's term (Sperber and Wilson 1986), *relevant*. But since the knowledge in question does not come from you or me, neither does its relevance in the world. This, as the guardians of the orthodoxy reassure us, must come from Elsewhere.

The cognitive operations associated with religious routinization are varied and complex. With regard to ritual actions, at least five main kinds of knowledge would seem to be activated. First, ritual procedures are managed by implicit memory systems, are driven by empirically based learning, and are giving rise to what Karmiloff-Smith calls "behavioral mastery." Such knowledge allows worshippers, at least in principle, to perform repetitive rituals without conscious reflection, in automatic response to environmental cues. Second, routinization triggers intuitive, quasi-theoretical knowledge concerning ritual procedures. Although mostly implicit, such knowledge may also be available to verbal report, *if*, for instance, people are encouraged to reflect on the matter. Third, frequently repeated rituals are processed as verbally transmitted procedural rules—for example, "kneel when praying" or "stand when singing"—that are encoded in semantic memory. Such knowledge is most likely to be stated when instructing children or novices how to conduct worship; it may itself have been acquired verbally or be internally derived from implicit rules. In the ACT* model, such knowledge drives learning of type 1, but (since it may also derive from type-2 knowledge) it is not essential to the development of knowledge of types 1 or 2. Fourth, routinization can produce internally generated, speculative exegesis concerning why rituals take the specific form that they do and why they must be performed. This type of knowledge is explicit, but it is not automatically generated and is not caused by knowledge of types 1, 2, and 3. If official exegesis is also available, people may refrain from producing speculative interpretations of their own or at least be fearful or embarrassed about communicating them. Of course, people simply may not be bothered to reflect on their rituals in this way, unless encouraged to do so. At any rate, such reflexivity is likely to generate relatively simple exegetical observations. Fifth, routinized rituals are commonly associated with externally derived exegesis, often regarded as authoritative, which is obviously also explicit and offline. Knowledge of type 5 tends to be highly elaborate and hard to learn, requiring frequent and extensive transmission in order to be sustained in a stable form. Doctrinal transmission can be highly motivating but routinization also runs the risk of inspiring tedium and demoralization.

Routinized transmission produces both opportunities for, and constraints on, the construction of religious thinking. Substantial repetition is necessary for the learning of complex doctrinal knowledge. Some degree of ongoing rehearsal seems to be necessary to maintain that knowledge. Routinization of rituals may reduce the risks of unintended innovation by suppressing the volume and elaborateness of independent reflection on the meanings of rituals. Cognitive dissonance effects may also contribute to subjective positive evaluations of participation, as a source of comfort or reassurance, for instance. At the same time, verbal reiteration is capable of raising levels of commitment to a religious orthodoxy by increasing the motivational force of attitudinal stances. Such effects probably are enhanced by encoding conditions that foster analogical creativity (especially by directing people's attention to structural properties of potential source–target pairings). But this kind of creativity is special insofar as the origins of the doctrinal knowledge used to interpret experience are unknowable. When such knowledge turns out to be applicable in everyday settings, this seems intrinsically mysterious. When religious authorities tell us that this is the work of God, our intuitions are unable to deliver a rival explanation.

When all these features operate in concert, the doctrinal mode would seem to be quite robust. Its revelatory knowledge can be remembered by a large number of followers, and they will be motivated to keep the tradition alive and to pass it on to future generations. But there is a downside. Gaining access to complex doctrinal knowledge is time consuming and labor intensive. The process of learning must be accompanied by incentives and sanctions. Ongoing commitment must be earned by techniques of oratory and persuasion that are themselves hard to develop and master. Any serious deterioration in the frequency of transmission, the quality of orations, or the policing of the orthodoxy could contribute to a decline in levels of commitment as well as patterns of unintended deviation from authoritative scripts. But, then again, overpolicing and excessive routinization can inspire tedium and lowered motivation, even if cognitive dissonance combined, perhaps, with sanctions (or limited opportunities) for defection might help to prevent the flock from dwindling. But at the core of every religion is a set of salient and valued revelations. To keep these alive in circumstances of routinized transmission is no simple matter. In the next chapter, we will see that low-frequency, high-arousal rituals face few of these problems.

Note

1. This study was devised in collaboration with Justin Barrett and carried out at the University of Vermont by Luther H. Martin.

Ritual and Meaning in the Imagistic Mode   6

R ITUALS THAT ARE ONLY RARELY PERFORMED are also typically felt to be personally consequential, extraordinary, and emotionally arousing occasions. These features result in long-lasting episodic memories. But the memories are problematic. They specify at least some of the details of what happened in a particular ritual performance, but they do not specify the *meanings* of those happenings. Rituals are capable of being accorded a wide range of symbolic motivations, but people do not reflect extensively on matters of symbolism in the absence of very special inducements. Theologians and art critics (for example) engage in that kind of activity, but only because they have undergone an extensive, routinized education into that peculiar mode of intellectual activity, backed up by complex systems of rewards and incentives. Where no such educational framework exists to support exegetical reflection, why should it happen at all? The answer presented in this chapter is that especially vivid episodic memories trigger a search for meaning, and this search becomes all the more complex and elaborate in cases where the episode itself is open to a rich variety of possible interpretations—as in the case of rituals. The search is protracted, in fact potentially unending, because the memories that drive it endure throughout the lifecycle. But even if the mysteries of such rituals pursue us to the grave, they undergo important transformations as our exegetical knowledge matures. In this regard we will see, once again, that the theory of representational redescription (RR) is potentially instructive.

Emotion and Episodic Memory

Neuroscientists have long recognized that negative affect in animals is linked to indelible memory for one-off events (LeDoux 1992). A considerable volume of research has been devoted to understanding the biological mechanisms linking arousal and memory effects, much of it centered around studies of the effects of localized neurological damage on various types of amnesia in both humans and animals (Mishkin and Appenzeller 1987). It is now widely accepted that the "limbic system" plays a crucial role in memory. The limbic system comprises a number of complex, distinguishable brain structures, including the amygdala and hippocampus. A broad range of evidence suggests that the hippocampus contributes to processes of memory formation (Squire 1992). Nevertheless, different sorts of memory (e.g., procedural, semantic, and episodic) may well recruit rather different subcortical circuits, in which the role of the hippocampus varies significantly. Joseph LeDoux (1992) has suggested that the amygdala is implicated, perhaps uniquely, in the processing of especially emotional events. Another possibility, explored by P. E. Gold (1992), is that negative arousal or "stress" enhances episodic recall for detailed inputs primarily through the activation of high brain glucose levels. According to this proposal, it is not (necessarily) that different systems of memory recruit systematically contrasting structures and circuits, but rather that one general memory mechanism might produce different effects as a result of different amounts and types of biochemical reinforcement. Elsewhere I have presented a general sketch of how such processes might occur, based on a modified version of Gerald Edelman's (1992) theory of neuronal group selection (Whitehouse 1996a, 2001a). Martin Conway (1995) meanwhile provides a highly instructive and concise overview of the arguments for both dual-route and general mechanisms for memory formation. Either way, there is significant evidence for a distinctive profile of neurological processing associated with the encoding of emotionally arousing memories.

This hypothesis is also prompted by psychological research on memory in real-world conditions. One of the main areas in which work of this sort has recently proliferated is in the study of "flashbulb memory" (FM)—a term originally coined by Roger Brown and James Kulik (1977) to describe a type of episodic memory in which images of photograph-like vividness are "printed" in memory, apparently due (at least in part) to the unique and emotional character of the event. Brown and Kulik hypothesized that exceptionally surprising, arousing, and personally consequential events trigger a "now print" mechanism, producing exceptionally vivid, detailed, and enduring episodic recall. Among the key features of FM are (1) an ability to retrieve extraordinarily fine-grained background information about the reception event, such as visual or tactile impressions not directly relevant to the action sequence and (2) a set of "canonical" categories of recall, specifying the location of the event, the action sequence, who was involved (e.g., as news bearer), the type and intensity of arousal (in self and others), and the aftermath.

In their pioneering study of recall for ten exceptional events, Brown and Kulik (1977) found that both consequentiality ratings and self-reported levels of arousal and shock correlated strongly with the incidence of FM. In light of these findings, they postulated that FM resulted from processes of encoding at or around the re-ception event. Levels of surprise and arousal, they suggested, had to be high at en-coding but not so high that input and processing systems were impaired. In addition, the event would have to score highly in terms of personal consequential-ity. According to Brown and Kulik, these conditions would be sufficient to initiate FM effects, comprising fine-grained contextual detail and at least some canonical categories of recall, as I indicated previously. Drawing on the neuroanatomic mod-els of R. B. Livingston (1967), they suggest that FM resulted from quite specific properties of neural functioning involving limbic and reticular systems and exten-sive, diffuse emissions across the cortex. And Brown and Kulik argue that such properties, allowing effective transmission of information about exceptional and consequential situations (in the absence of elaborate external mnemonics), would have conferred palpable benefits in the circumstances of hominid evolution.

Brown and Kulik recognize that factors other than encoding contributed to long-term recall for traumatic episodes. According to the original FM hypothesis, episodes that produce FM are (by definition) deemed personally consequential at the time of encoding. But such episodes do not always prove to be actually con-sequential. If the consequences of such episodes prove to be profound and nu-merous, there may be many opportunities for subsequent narrative rehearsal. Retelling the story of "what happened" may produce long-term memory for the story itself, perhaps enriching and extending the information available as genuine FM. Nevertheless, since much of the latter information would be encoded non-verbally, Brown and Kulik proposed that narrative-based memory would not in-terfere with recall for the reception event itself.

The FM hypothesis has attracted both considerable interest and criticism among psychologists working on memory. Ulric Neisser and his colleagues have generated a particularly extensive body of critical commentary and subsequent re-search. In his early writings on FM, Neisser (1982) argues that encoding condi-tions may be quite irrelevant to the production of FM effects. Subsequent narrative rehearsal alone, he suggests, might be sufficient to account for the canon-ical structure of vivid episodic memories. Nevertheless, a year after Neisser's hy-pothesis was first advanced in print, Eugene Winograd and William Killinger (1983) published a study showing dramatic differences in richness of episodic re-call for the Kennedy assassination among children between the ages of one and seven years at the time of the shooting. In particular, those aged seven years in 1963 remembered considerably more details than those who were aged six, and more still than those who were aged five. As Gillian Cohen (1989, 130) puts it:

> The results did not support Neisser's view that the vividness of flashbulb mem-ories is produced by frequent rehearsal because self-reported amount of discus-sion was only weakly related to the amount of detail recalled. Moreover, if recall

depends on reconstruction subsequent to the event, it is difficult to see why the age at encoding has such a strong effect on retention. Winograd and Killinger concluded that, because older children were capable of a deeper level of understanding, their encoding of the event was more elaborate and they formed a richer memory representation.

In a recent systematic survey of the arguments and evidence raised against the FM hypothesis, including the studies by Ulric Neisser, Eugene Winograd, and M. S, Weldon (1991), Martin Conway (1995) concludes that Brown and Kulik's argument emerges remarkably unscathed. Much of the criticism it has attracted, while attempting to challenge the preeminence of encoding processes in FM effects, has more or less ignored Brown and Kulik's original claims about the nature of these processes and has consequently failed to test them. According to the FM hypothesis, high ratings for personal consequentiality at encoding are a *necessary* condition for the activation of FM. And yet all but one of the many subsequent studies ostensibly presenting evidence against (at least some aspects of) the FM hypothesis have failed to build in measures of personal consequentiality at encoding (Conway 1995, 41). According to Conway, this failure may be decisive in explaining the absence of genuine FM effects among participants in at least some investigations. By contrast, studies engaging the FM hypothesis directly have been rather more successful in generating supporting evidence for Brown and Kulik's original formulation, and in replicating the data on which it was founded.

Conway focuses in particular on three studies that have generated unequivocal evidence for FM. The first, conducted by David Pillemer (1984), examined recall among American subjects for the attempted assassination of Ronald Reagan in 1981. The second, conducted by Neisser, Winograd, and Weldon (1991), studied recall for the 1989 earthquake in Loma Prieta, California. In particular they compared recall between two categories of subjects: (1) those in the earthquake zone and (2) residents of Atlanta, far away from the affected area. The third, conducted by Conway himself (and his coworkers) studied recall for the resignation of Margaret Thatcher in 1991 (Conway et al. 1994). Here, a crucial comparison was made between the memories of UK citizens and those of other countries. In the case of the study by Pillemer, elevated arousal at encoding but not personal consequentiality seemed to be important in activating FM. Conversely, in the study by Neisser, Winograd, and Weldon, FM effects were prevalent among those directly experiencing the earthquake, suggesting the importance of personal consequentiality, whereas elevated arousal did not appear to be a factor. The study by Conway et al. investigated a more complex array of variables, including several potentially discrete aspects of personal consequentiality (e.g., prior knowledge, importance, and subsequent patterns of retrieval), and found that *both* increased affect and consequentiality correlated with the incidence of FM. Conway (1995) concludes that while the studies by Pillemer and Neisser, Winograd, and Weldon provide some tentative evidence that either elevated affect or high ratings for personal consequentiality (but not necessarily both) are sufficient to activate FM, all three studies suggested that encoding rather than subsequent rehearsal was the key factor in producing these effects.

Major news events, such as resignations, assassinations, and earthquakes, readily lend themselves to studies of FM because of the relative ease of locating subjects with recall associated with the same event. Nevertheless, as Conway points out (1995, chap. 4), the most arousing and personally consequential events in people's lives are typically ones that affect not large populations, but individuals or small groups. Certainly, news items concerning politicians one has never met are unlikely to induce the degree of intense emotion and even trauma capable of being activated by events of direct, personal experience. And, interestingly, it is recall for episodes of the latter sort that provides the most powerful evidence for FM. This, as we shall see, may be of particular importance for understanding the mnemonic effects of direct participation in rare and traumatic religious rituals.

Some highly arousing and intensely personal experiences can, of course, be widespread. For instance, the onset of the menarche is a predictable aspect of puberty in girls, but it can be a surprising, distressing, and decidedly private experience associated with low rates of subsequent narrative rehearsal. In a study involving ninety-nine women, Pillemer et al. (1987) found that vividness and detail of recall for first menstruation correlated strongly with lack of prior education and support. Women who had received thorough medical and practical advice and knew what to expect were very unlikely to recall their first menstruation at all. By contrast, women who were ill-prepared and thus were, in varying degrees, shocked and frightened by their first menstrual episode, commonly experienced FM effects in relation to their experiences.

Other studies of recall for unique, traumatic episodes among both children and adults tell a similar story. For instance, John C. Yuille and Judith L. Cutshall (1986) showed that subsequent recall for a robbery and fatal shooting was more detailed and accurate on the part of witnesses reporting the highest levels of stress at encoding than among the comparatively low-arousal group of witnesses. Lenore C. Terr (1979, 1983) has shown that the young victims (aged five to fourteen years) of a single kidnapping episode produced highly detailed and vivid FM in subsequent tests of recall. A wide range of studies of survivors of traumatic episodes, especially Vietnam War veterans, shows a clear connection between extreme negative arousal and enduring episodic memories.[1]

Of course, it is one thing to discover that detailed and vivid episodic recall can often be gathered from trauma victims by means of cues provided by professional investigators, and quite another to understand processes of retrieval in natural settings. Much has been learned about this from studies of psychogenic illness and posttraumatic stress disorder (PTSD). Following are some standard criteria for diagnosis of PTSD:

1. Recurrent and intrusive recollections of the event
2. Recurrent distressing dreams of the event
3. Sudden acting or feeling as if the traumatic event were recurring (includes a sense of reliving the experience, illusions, hallucinations, and dissociative [flashback] episodes)
4. Intense psychological distress at exposure to events that symbolize or resemble an aspect of the traumatic event[2]

   The last of these criteria presents important clues to processes of *retrieval* of FM for traumatic episodes. Resemblance between the encoded memory and subsequent inputs might take a wide range of forms. Sven-Ake Christianson and Lars-Goran Nilsson (1989) report the experience of a rape victim on seeing the same distinctive pattern of brickwork that had been visible at the time of the attack. This woman experienced sudden and vivid recall of the rape, exhibiting the "live quality" originally discussed by Brown and Kulik. In many cases, reactivation of sensory information, encoded at the time of the trauma, is sufficient to trigger processes of substantial episodic retrieval. In other cases, more conceptually driven analogues may elicit recall. Retrieval may be highly distressing, and sufferers from PTSD often avoid the primes and triggers for FM. Such avoidance is not necessarily a conscious process, and so-called repression of traumatic memory may also be a factor.[3] If successful long-term avoidance of retrieval occurs at all, then this would not seem to be a typical result of *singular* traumatic experiences (except where states of dissociation, induced for instance by drugs or hypnosis, interfere with encoding).[4] Terr (1991) discusses at some length the effects of type 1 trauma (a single negative episode) as distinct from type 2 trauma (repeated negative episodes) on subsequent patterns of recall. Type 1 trauma produces what he calls "etched-in" memories (1991, 14)—essentially, FM effects associated with massively detailed and vivid recall.

   Thus, there is a substantial body of evidence from psychology (both experimental and clinical) that elevated arousal and personal consequentiality are intimately connected to the formation of enduring and vivid episodic memory. It seems that FM in particular results from conditions *at encoding*, rather than from patterns of subsequent narrative rehearsal. Some of the best evidence for these conclusions comes from studies of recall for highly traumatic life experiences. Following an extensive review of this literature, Conway (1995, 93) observes:

Perhaps the most striking finding . . . is the incidence of flashbulb memories following highly stressful and traumatic experiences. Memories resulting from unique, one-off, traumatic experiences are highly detailed, can be intrusive, the patient avoids cues that might lead to recollection, and the healing process involves the patient coming to terms with his or her autobiographical memory more generally. The events that lead to this pathological recall of flashbulb memories are clearly among the most personally consequential and significant of all life events and are typically associated with intense emotional experiences.

Episodic Memory and Ritual

Some rituals clearly exhibit all the features associated with FM effects. Rites of initiation, for instance, are obviously personally consequential for those who take part. But in many cases they are also extremely shocking and traumatic—involving such practices such as head-biting, showering with red-hot coals, and evulsion of the fingernails in Australian Aboriginal initiation rites (Strehlow 1965); whipping, burning, mutilation, and extreme physical deprivation in Melanesian fertility cults (Barth 1975); and agonizing circumcisions in many African societies (Turnbull 1962). Such practices, documented all around the world and over many millennia, have been variously described as ecstatic (I. M. Lewis 1971), Dionysian (Benedict 1935), autoerotic (G. Lewis 1980), and simply sadistic (Bateson 1936). A major category of these forms of ritual action, particularly associated with cults of initiation and circumcision, might be dubbed "rites of terror" (Whitehouse 1996a), since they entail not only extreme physical agony but also deliberate psychological tortures, aimed primarily at arousing fear among novices or candidates.

We might reasonably expect the victims of ritualized violence to recall many aspects of their experiences for long periods, perhaps even for the rest of their lives. Unfortunately, no systematic studies have yet been conducted of people's memories for such rituals, but it would be very surprising if episodes of ritualized violence were more poorly recalled than other terrifying episodes. It is tempting to suppose that low-frequency rituals are composed of procedures that could only be transmitted successfully as a result of being stored in episodic memory. If arousal levels became too low, episodic memory would not be activated, and the details of the ritual procedures would be forgotten. On a selectionist account, the low-frequency rituals that survive would always be the highly arousing ones. In some of my earlier work on this topic (Whitehouse 1992), I advanced an argument very much on these lines. In the case of initiatory ordeals, however, there are reasons to doubt that the situation is that simple. Novices may be so terrified during their initiations that subsequent recall, though vivid and haunting, may only specify rather disjointed elements of the ritual process. If so, episodic recall of this sort would not provide a sufficient body of knowledge to enable initiated persons, at a later date, to organize the same rituals for a younger generation of novices. How, then, are the gaps to be filled? Fredrik Barth (2002, 15–16) points to a plausible answer, at least in respect to Baktaman initiation rites in inner New Guinea:

> I have noted in my ethnographic account, but not made any point of, the Bakta-man rule that the next senior cohort/set, those who have preceded the new set of novices, are supposed to have a special responsibility during the latter's initiation: that of "showing" their juniors the initiation (Barth 1975, 49f). This has seemed to me unimportant, since the management of the initiation was invariably in the hands of the cult master as chief initiator. [Nonetheless], the next senior cohort was present during most of the episodes of the ritual, and sometimes assisted in minor ways in its staging. Whitehouse now makes me wonder if this is perhaps essential to the reproduction of the substantive body of the tradition: that it is in their role of "showing" their juniors, and not as terrified novices, that a cohort properly assimilates the substance, the corpus of knowledge and ritual acts, that composes an initiation. The two modes of memory may be functioning for com-plementary purposes within the tradition: salience and value are generated through the flashbulb mechanisms associated with the terror-induced heightened experi-ence, while mastery of substance is only achieved [the] second time round, and with further repetitions, when schematic memory becomes established.

Moreover, Michael Houseman (2002, 20) independently reaches a very similar conclusion with regard to initiation rites cross-culturally:

> Contrary to what . . . [Whitehouse's] account may appear to suggest, initiation is not a once in a lifetime experience. Indeed, the most frequent experience men have of initiation is not as novices, but as members of the initiating community in the course of other initiations subsequent to their own. While one's experience as a novice probably does result in a number of haunting memories, it is surely as per-sons who direct the novices' (and the uninitiated women's) behaviour, who prepare and inflict hardships upon them, who comfort them afterwards, who reveal secrets to them, and so forth, that participants acquire (under the direction of ritual lead-ers) that which may truly be said to be transmitted through such rituals, namely, the organization of the ritual action itself.

Barth's and Houseman's criticisms, on this score, are well taken. Both suggest that it is subsequent and repeated involvement in the coordination of initiation rites for fresh cohorts of novices that provides the richly schematized knowledge of the ritual process needed for confident orchestration of initiations as experi-enced elders. On current evidence, this seems a valuable corrective to the arguments presented in some of my earlier publications. But if the one-off ordeals of novices in initiations are not sufficient to allow subsequent transmission, why should they be necessary at all? Given my hypothesis that massively elevated negative arousal in one-off ritual ordeals is a reliably recurrent feature of the imagistic mode *in general* (see chapter 4), there had better be a good answer to this question.

Episodic Memory and Spontaneous Exegetical Reflection

The fact that a ritual is rarely performed does not mean that the procedures comprising it will necessarily be hard to recall, even in the absence of elevated arousal and cognitive shocks. Moreover, as Barth and Houseman suggest, what is especially rare is the highly emotive experience of being the subject of such rituals, for there may be ample opportunities to witness the ritual procedures again and again from the rather different perspective of organizer, helper, or observer. The importance of elevated arousal in low-frequency rituals is not that it contributes to recall for ritual *actions* (although it may be a factor here) but that it sets in motion a search for ritual *meanings*.

As indicated at the very beginning of this book, rituals are special kinds of actions. Part of what makes them special is that they are irreducible to technical motivations and therefore open in principle to a wide range of symbolic motivations. In chapter 5, it was suggested that highly repetitive rituals become so habituated that the knowledge of how to carry them out may (at least some of the time) be activated at an implicit level. This would almost certainly serve to reduce the rate and volume of conscious reflection on the *meanings* of such rituals, at least across the religious membership as a whole. But low-frequency ritual procedures cannot be cognitively processed in that way. The question is whether such rituals lead to especially intense processes of spontaneous exegetical reflection (SER).

SER is essentially a process of analogical reasoning. If we see a group of people with bodies painted red jumping up and down, we may well ask why they have painted themselves in that fashion, why they are leaping about, and what possessed all of them to come to a particular spot at this particular time in order to behave in that way. Let us assume that we lack any suitable scripts for the interpretation of this behavior in terms of technical motivations. We know, for instance, that the jumping is not an exercise to keep them fit, that the body paint does not identify them as members of a sports team, and that they did not come together to participate in a training session. In fact, let us say that we know this is a ritual precisely because nobody (who knows about these things) would dream of suggesting that the behavior in question is reducible to a set of technical motivations. Our attempts to interpret the behavior must, in these circumstances, turn on analogical principles. Perhaps the red paint tells us that these people are like newborn infants, or that they have been "ignited" by the "fire" of the spirits, or that they are warriors who have "washed" in the symbolic blood of their enemies? The range of possible symbolic motivations will always be vast (although, of course, the conceptual content on which the human imagination does its work will obviously differ in interesting ways from one cultural setting to the next). The mechanism for making connections between all the concepts that might potentially be activated is analogy.

What limits the actual connections that will be made between ritual actions and possible layers of interpretation is the relative creativity and longevity of analogical associations. Creativity is a measure of the extent to which ritual actions serve as a prime to other potential associations. Longevity is a measure of how long the associations endure in memory, thereby in turn potentially serving as primes for further acts of creative analogical thinking. There is good reason to suppose that the activation of FM for ritual procedures helps to amplify the creativity and longevity of analogical associations. It produces especially rich and fertile processes of SER that gradually come to cohere as substantial bodies of expert knowledge stored in semantic memory. Let us begin with the issue of creativity.

In the process of recalling life-changing events, people often show a marked tendency to identify symbolic (especially portentous) properties in those episodes (Pillemer, Rinehart, and White 1986). Indeed, according to Daniel Wright and George D. Gaskell (1992), the search for meaning in extraordinary episodes lies at the core of the cognitive processes that produce FM effects in the first place. The surprising nature of the episode triggers a frustrated search for relevant meanings, and when no suitable schema can be found, a new one is established. The new schema specifies a host of unconnected details, due to the absence of any organizing theme. The challenge of making sense of episodic memories of this kind is greatly exacerbated by ritualization.

Not only do low-frequency, high-arousal rituals fail to trigger suitable schemas in the minds of those undergoing them for the first time, but they clearly constitute episodes for which symbolic motivations would be expected to exist (as I noted previously). In other words, rituals are by their very nature puzzling activities that invite *interpretation*. The mechanisms of FM meanwhile encourage extremely close attention to potential structural features of specified episodes that might serve in the future as a foundation for analogical interpretation. This combination of ritualization and FM effects would create a powerful trigger for intensified analogical thinking.

The ethnographic record shows that low-frequency, high-arousal rituals tend to generate rich exegetical knowledge based on loose and fluid thematic associations, where concrete properties of ritual choreography and paraphernalia are felt

to stand for more abstract processes such as plant growth, spiritual transformation, mammalian gestation, and so on. Nevertheless, it is sometimes only possible to infer these iconic processes on the basis of indirect evidence, since they
may not be explicitly stated by participants. One such body of evidence might
relate to the clustering of particular images in a ritual sequence—for instance,
images of substances that naturally increase in volume and thus appear to symbolize or instantiate mystical processes of natural fertility and growth (especially
where people say that the ritual is "good for the crops," even if they do not tell
you how or why). Another body of evidence might focus on the sequential occurrence of imagery as, for instance, ritual choreography evoking images of physical death or decay followed by images of gestation and birth may appear to
express a notion of spiritual rebirth and regeneration. Sometimes, such interpretations are supported by esoteric mythology (Juillerat 1992; Poole 1982). In
other societies, no such corpus of secret but explicit verbal information appears
to be available (Gell 1975; Barth 1975). Either way, the majority of ritual participants (e.g., novices, observers, and junior initiators) seem to struggle if asked
to supply verbal explications of the meanings of ritual imagery. That kind of
elaborate semantic knowledge seems to be available only to senior ritual experts.
The theory of RR may help to explain why this is by revealing certain key aspects of the longevity of analogical thinking associated with low-frequency,
high-arousal rituals.

Representational Redescription and the Imagistic Mode

Karmiloff-Smith's model of RR (1992), as summarized in the previous chapter,
focuses exclusively on forms of learning that result from behavioral rehearsal or
repetition. Not only is rehearsal or repetition the means to behavioral mastery, but
further repetition is what drives the redescription of this knowledge at progressively more explicit levels. Whereas behavioral mastery is the incorporation of au-
tomatized habits, its more explicit redescription appears to consist of the
development of schemas or scripts, culminating in "semantic memory"—a body
of encyclopedic knowledge about the world, manipulable via higher-level, explicit,
interdomain principles of logical motivation, thematic association, and so on. But
where, in all of this, do we locate enduring memory for distinctive, rare (or
unique) events?

The first point to make is that procedural knowledge concerning rare and
climactic rituals is consciously entertained. Episodic memory is a form of explicit memory. When people recall episodes of initiatory tortures, for instance,
their memories are potentially stateable. Chains of events, specifying the procedural sequences of such rituals, are not habituated or automatic and can only

be entertained as explicit knowledge. Although the rituals may incorporate units of habituated action, many of the more extraordinary features will be recalled episodically and, therefore, available to self-report. From the viewpoint of a recently initiated young man, his ritual ordeals take the form, in memory, of a series of exceptional (and no doubt disturbing) episodes. For years to come, he will be able to remember some of what happened, who did what, where, when, and to whom, as well as all kinds of assorted minutiae (aromas, sounds, visual details, thoughts, feelings etc.). Since most of these experiences are unique, however, there is little or no opportunity to organize procedural knowledge for such rituals according to quasi-theoretical, generalizable principles. It is only through subsequent experiences in the role of initiator that he will be able to pick out metonymical features and generate the sort of inductively driven principles characteristic of EI knowledge. This process of representational redescription is not, however, the same as that entailed in routinized rituals.

First, the initiate-turned-initiator is not on a path of converting implicit procedural knowledge into increasingly explicit representations. On the contrary, he starts with explicit representations of how the ritual is performed, and subsequent experiences of the initiatory process result in knowledge of a rather less explicit sort (EI), as yet unavailable to verbal report. He may only gradually become fully aware of the way imagery is consistently "clustered" and its presentation "sequenced" over a set of recurrent performances—a process that is, however, driven by the analogy-generating dynamics established at encoding (as suggested in the previous section). Second, the RR process is retarded. Since the frequency of imagistic practices is low, it may not be until quite late in life that the initiate's understanding becomes largely stateable (E3/4), as is characteristic of ritual experts and elders in most (if not all) documented cases. Third, the RR process in this case is not restricted to procedural schemas, but actively drives the production of exegetical knowledge. This is because rituals in the imagistic mode cannot be reproduced as automatic, habituated actions, but always require explicit processes of planning and implementation. Indeed, all recorded initiation rites entail advance planning and conscious coordination. Because procedural knowledge in such cases is also explicit knowledge, it forms part of a cross-system code by means of which exegesis is elaborated. Whereas routinized rituals can be (and often are) performed on autopilot, in the absence of any kind of reflexivity, imagistic practices must always be a locus of *conscious* thought.

These observations may help to explain the widespread lack (or relative paucity) of authoritative doctrinal discourse and exegesis with regard to imagistic practices. Unlike routinized rituals, imagistic practices do not present a vacuum for religious authorities to fill, nor do their elongated cycles of transmission facilitate the stable reproduction of an intricate doctrinal orthodoxy. On the other hand, a rich and revelatory religious experience is possible in the imagistic mode in the absence of authoritative dogma, since every participant is a potential exegete and, given time, a potential authority on religious matters. This explains why exegetical knowledge, with regard to imagistic practices, is highly restricted and available in its fullest form only to experienced experts. The fact that it may never be verbally transmitted, or is communicated piecemeal in highly opaque, cryptic allusions and mythological narratives, should not be construed as the absence of exegetical knowledge.

Ritual experiences that are surprising, personally consequential, and negatively valenced meet the conditions associated with FM effects. The encoding of FMs involves a frantic search for meaning and structure. Since the possible meanings of ritual actions are seemingly boundless, and since recall for these particular ritual episodes is long-lived and easily triggered, the imagistic mode entails extremely intense spontaneous exegetical reflection, based on principles of analogical reasoning. Low-frequency, high-arousal rituals set in motion a somewhat retarded process of RR, generating four main types of religious knowledge. First, participation in these rituals immediately produces explicit procedural knowledge in which the content of ritual actions is specified in episodic memory. Second, exegetical knowledge begins to develop (based on tentative and largely implicit associations between ritual acts or objects) on the grounds, for instance, that they elicit similar sensory or affective states or occur in the same structural positions within a sequence. Through long-term experience of periodic rites, knowledge of this sort is likely to become increasingly explicit as analogical links between ritual elements are strengthened through rehearsal. Third, there is a gradual development of explicit, internally generated exegetical knowledge based on explicit classification of ritual actions and objects according to analogic principles. This sort of knowledge, eventually stored in semantic memory, is likely to be available only to ritual experts and elders, whose extensive experience of periodic rites facilitates confident recognition of recurrent patterns and the formation of rich exegesis. Fourth, parts of the knowledge of elders or experts may be learned through verbal transmission. Not all climactic, periodic rituals give rise to the transmission of knowledge in this way and, even when they do, the knowledge may be highly restricted (for instance, available only to experienced persons who have already acquired knowledge of type 3).

Notes

1. See Foy 1992 (see also Horowitz and Reidbord 1992).

2. American Psychiatric Association's (1986) *Diagnostic and Statistical Manual of Mental Disorders* (DSM-IIIR), quoted in Conway (1995, 80).

3. For an overview of findings, see Baddeley (1997, chap. 15).

4. So marked are the differences in memory effects of singular versus repeated traumatic episodes that it has been suggested that they provide the foundations for distinguishable forms of pathology (Terr 1991).

Religious Enthusiasm and Its Limits   7

ONE OF THE MOST STRIKING CHARACTERISTICS of both doctrinal and imagistic modes of religiosity, as opposed to more cognitively optimal patterns of religious belief described in chapter 2, is the degree of passionate conviction their concepts evince. Notions of telepathy and love magic are no more or less intrinsically believable than notions of redemption and spiritual salvation. There is nothing to choose between these two sets of concepts with regard to relative degrees of inherent plausibility and absurdity. One set of concepts may be more complex and hard to acquire than the other, but that alone cannot explain why those concepts attract more fanatical commitment than the ragbag of supernatural beings, rituals, and folktales that cluster around the cognitive optimum position. Some people are prepared to die in the name of abstract theological or cosmological principles, whereas hardly anybody would lay down their lives to defend a belief in horoscopes and homeopathy. Why?

This chapter attempts to take us some way toward an answer to that question but, in so doing, must also explain why religious commitment sometimes flags. We know that at least in routinized religions, people can end up merely "going through the motions" or even dropping out. We also know that people can create their own versions of religion, so that the religion ends up looking less like the official, orthodox tradition and more like a bundle of homespun taboos, cures, stories, and prayers. These are the twin problems of the tedium effect and the cognitive optimum effect. Both have consequences for levels of religious enthusiasm, and both influence historical processes of religious transformation and renewal. We begin, though, with patterns of religious activity in which levels of motivation run high.

Religious Enthusiasm

As the appalling events of September 11, 2001, demonstrate, some people are willing to lay down their own lives and to take the lives of others in obedience to what they perceive as religious imperatives. In certain cases, such as the Christian crusades of the Middle Ages, violence is undertaken with offensive objectives in mind (e.g., to defeat the infidel). In other cases, such as contemporary Ulster loyalism, the rationale for sectarian violence is to defend a religious tradition that is perceived to be under threat of extinction or marginalization. More often than not, offence and defense are objectives pursued in tandem and may be hard to disentangle. And one thing that seems to be characteristic of many religiously fanatical coalitions is that they punish defectors among their own ranks in a manner that is both extreme and (where possible) public. At the same time, of course, there are decidedly nonviolent forms of religious fanaticism—for instance, passionate pacifism or asceticism in various Christian, Buddhist, and Hindu sects. How are we to explain all these things?

According to Pascal Boyer (2001a), two main strategies of explanation are commonplace. The first proposes that religious fanaticism is usually religiously motivated. This might suggest, for instance, that "fundamentalist extremism is simply an excessive form of religious adherence, a caricature of ordinary behaviour in the religious communities where it emerges" (Boyer 2001a, 292). A second view suggests, to the contrary, that religious extremism is altogether unrelated to religious thinking and in fact runs counter to its principles. The acts of violence committed by (at least some) religious fanatics are really a result of power struggles that would take place anyway (and that just happen to use religion as a cloak, to disguise what would otherwise be revealed as naked ambition and political maneuvering).

Boyer rejects the first argument on the grounds that it fails to explain the variability of religious fanaticism (some religious traditions are notably tolerant and nonviolent). He rejects the second on the grounds that the behavior of religious extremists is seldom strategically rational: "[T]he notion that fundamentalists are simply lusting after power fails to tell us why they seek it in that particularly dangerous, costly, and often ineffective way (Boyer 2001a, 293). Instead, Boyer offers a slightly refined version of the second explanation. Religious extremism, he suggests, is driven by the desire of coalition members to inflate the costs of defection, and it therefore arises mainly in conditions where existing deterrents for defection are perceived to be potentially ineffective. This is why, according to Boyer, religious fanaticism often appears to be a reaction against modernity. It is not, he argues, a reaction against modern technologies per se, but against the pluralistic environments of the modern world in which people are relatively free to abandon or exchange coalitional ties at minimal personal cost (Atran 2002). Thus: "Fundamentalist violence . . . seems to be an attempt to raise the stakes, that is, to discourage potential defectors by demonstrating that defection is actually going to be very costly, that people who adopt different norms may be persecuted or even killed" (Boyer 2001a, 295).

Boyer's argument might help to explain why religious violence is so often directed against transgressors within the coalition, rather than only against outsiders. Given that the deterrent principle appears beloved by reactionaries everywhere, this argument would also seem to explain the excessively public and spectacular nature of the punishments meted out to sinners. But there are also major limitations to Boyer's perspective on this matter.

First, religious violence is prevalent in a great many traditions where opportunities for changing allegiance are virtually nonexistent. If one considers, for instance, the extremely violent initiation systems of many small-scale, warlike societies around the world, these have often thrived in places where alternative coalitions were inaccessible and more liberal conditions of existence simply unknown. Second, although internally directed violence is *part* of what needs to be explained, it is far from being the whole story. We also need to explain patterns of systematic violence directed externally, examples of which are abundant among the world's religious traditions. Certainly, this cannot be adequately explained as a concomitant of defection-deterring measures within the coalition. Third, we are still left with the problem of explaining variable levels of religious fervor among different traditions. There may be some correlation between the level of risk that adherents will tolerate in defense of religious commitments on the one hand and the presence of viable alternative coalitional bonds on the other. If so, and it is by no means obvious, then I suspect it would be a weak correlation. It is certainly not enough to explain the variability at issue. The opportunities for defection are no greater for members of Protestant churches in Northern Ireland, for instance, than for those in England. And yet the blood-and-thunder brigades in Belfast readily whip themselves up into frenzies while Church of England vicars worry their heads about how to get "bums on pews." Levels of motivation in these two traditions, by almost any conceivable measure (including, at the simplest, church attendance figures), are massively different. And yet the opportunities for defection—excluding all religious incentives and sanctions (which we must, for the purposes of Boyer's deterrent argument, to avoid tautology)—are not subject to any obvious regional variation in the United Kingdom. "Alternative lifestyles," after all, are freely available to individuals in *all* parts of that liberal democracy. So why are religious leaders (and their followers) foaming at the mouth here, while over there we find vicars (and their flocks) politely withering on about whether gay bishops are a good or a bad thing, in the light of various possible lines of theological interpretation? To answer this question at least at a general level, we have to take seriously an argument that Boyer dismisses rather hastily—namely, that at least some of the causes of varying levels of religious intolerance and aggressivity may be found *within* religious systems themselves.

One way of exposing the basic mechanisms involved in religious extremism is to follow the time-honored tradition in social and cultural anthropology of examining how the mechanisms in question operate in relatively simple societies. One of the features typical of initiation systems in small-scale, nonliterate societies is that they involve extremely painful and traumatic ordeals. What is equally striking, however, is that most of these systems, at least prior to colonization, offered only one alternative to these ordeals. That alternative was certain death. In many Australian Aboriginal cults of initiation,[1] for instance, failure to comply exactly with the requirements of initiators resulted in execution (ordered and orchestrated by elders, although typically carried out by younger and more athletic men). Much the same story has been systematically reported in traditional societies all around the world. The point seems to be a very simple one: people can only be induced to endure traumatic ritual episodes if the costs of evasion or defection are even more extreme than those entailed by compliance. Explaining the participation of novices in these systems is not a problem: they are coerced into acquiescence at the point of a spear (or equivalent). What is rather more difficult to explain is why the elders (and other initiators) would insist on conducting these patently dangerous rituals. After all, these traditions place one of the group's most valuable assets—its offspring—at considerable risk. What kinds of parents, uncles, aunts, and so on, would stand by as their beloved children are degraded and injured? Or, worse, what kinds of family members would take part in these acts of ritualized child abuse?

The answer, of course, is that things are not what they seem. Societies that stage initiations of this sort have to take these risks—and kinsmen have to suffer the anguish of standing by while it happens—if everyone agrees that the survival of their world depends on it. And that is exactly what people in these societies believe. If the rituals were not performed, boys would not become men, or the rains would fail to come, or the crops would be visited by dreaded pestilence, or the sky would fall in. The range of terrible consequences that people sincerely claim would follow from failure to perform initiations correctly are many and varied. But they are almost always catastrophic. So the question is why those very people who would otherwise have the power to abandon their traditions of ritualized violence generally believe (and believe passionately) that they have no choice: the initiations *must* be conducted.

The theory of modes of religiosity accounts for this extraordinary depth of commitment (to otherwise apparently absurd conclusions) in terms of processes of revelation associated with imagistic mode dynamics. Elders believe in the efficacy of initiation rituals not out of some kind of perverse or sadistic inclination, nor simply as an elaborate ploy to consolidate their authority or to deter defection; they actually believe that the rituals have real effects, and they believe it because they have mysterious but profoundly compelling insights into how these rituals work. These insights do not come easily. They result from years of (initially tentative) reflection on the meanings of the rituals that they themselves first experienced as terrified initiates. As these insights unfold, it is as if layers of partial truths are successively unveiled until finally a kind of personally coherent cosmological vision takes form and begins to harden in the recesses of semantic knowledge. While these revelations take the form of mostly explicit understandings, they are communicable only in principle and not (for the most part) in practice due to the absence of suitable conditions in which they may be publicly inspected, reiterated, and learned by others. Such knowledge is therefore condemned to a fate of continual re-creation across each individual lifespan, for it cannot be passed on in any other way.

In the doctrinal mode, explicit religious meanings also play a role in motivating transmission, even though the absolute presuppositions of this religious knowledge may be as bizarre and arbitrary as that buried in quite personal and idiosyncratic imagistic revelations. In the doctrinal mode, though, levels of motivation depend far more heavily on the persuasiveness of verbally transmitted knowledge, which in turn depends on the timely use of rhetoric, emotive imagery, and implicational logic. Some evangelical Christian traditions specialize in the sharpening of these tools, often giving rise to rather extreme forms of religious commitment. On the whole, however, they are extreme only in the sense that they seem unusually dogmatic and rigid. Paradoxically, of course, this kind of rigidity can be ultraliberal. But whether or not it is devoted to sending people to hell or stuffing them with love and forgiveness, doctrinal transmission often seems to falter when it comes to serious risk taking. The reasons for this are probably quite complex.

To begin with, there is an important distinction to make between beliefs based on direct personal experience and beliefs based on verbal testimony (Harris 2000, chap. 5). Of course, there is a thin line between the two. Being persuaded of something is a matter of forming concepts and coming to own them as part of one's personal belief system. But a sense of revelation triggered by persuasion can never be entirely separated from its external sources. It remains something that came from someone else's mind, and (even when this content can be referred back to a higher source) we all know from a relatively early age that other people can be wrong. Although we might like to think that passionate religious leaders have (on numerous occasions) talked people into various kinds of extreme behavior (e.g., suicide missions)—and there is a significant literature in social psychology that focuses on the role of verbal persuasion in cult behavior—this seems to me rather implausible, or at any rate questionable. To achieve real fanaticism, it may be necessary to experience personally something that rather closely resembles the revelations of ageing initiators, as previously described (and set out in detail in chapter 5). Religious extremism and violence, I would suggest, is always at least partly the outcome of a somewhat personal and private journey.

Although spontaneous reflection on the nature and meaning of religious experience is one of the hallmarks of the imagistic mode and is not similarly essential to the reproduction of doctrinal dynamics, it undoubtedly features also among adherents to religious traditions dominated by the doctrinal mode. Within such traditions, for instance, processes of training may actively encourage (and reward) private rumination (usually on specified issues), even if the dominant effect of heavy repetition is to deaden much of the potential for independent thought. In addition, it is not uncommon for high-arousal, low-frequency religious experiences to figure rather prominently in otherwise routinized traditions. Miraculous healings, sudden conversions, visitations, possessions, and many other such epiphanic episodes not only are widespread in religions of all kinds but are clearly capable of driving processes of spontaneous exegetical reflection (SER), as set out in the previous chapter. But where these sorts of experiences occur in the context of a routinized tradition, the episodic memories they evince typically are contaminated by standard interpretive schemas. The narrative conventions adopted by evangelical Christians, for instance, when verbally rehearsing their conversion experiences (something they are often encouraged to do with considerable regularity), undoubtedly block access to the emotions and images initially encoded. The *experience*, in other words, is somewhat obscured by standardized *stories about* the experience. In addition, these special experiences (in traditions dominated by the doctrinal mode) are often solitary events. In some cases they occur when a person is alone; but even in a crowd, the person's moment of crisis seldom is felt to be shared by those around him or her, or at least not with the same intensity or consequentiality. Both these conditions can obstruct the establishment of full-blown imagistic dynamics, including the motivational effects they would otherwise evince.

People normally take extreme premeditated personal risks for the sake of non-kin only where levels of group cohesion are exceptionally high. The doctrinal mode in itself is probably not capable of generating group cohesion at such levels of intensity. Military groupings (including traditional warrior cults and paramilitary cells) invariably sustain traditions of extremely high-arousal and cognitively shocking rituals, and that is one of the main ways in which these groups sustain exceptionally high levels of in-group solidarity, even to the extent of being able to rely on fellow members to lay down their lives for the survival of the collectivity. These patterns, obviously, are characteristic of the imagistic mode, and we can also find them lurking in the background of *all* situations of sustained and large-scale religious violence.

When we think of the world's bleakest trouble spots (e.g., the Middle East, Central Africa, the Balkans, Northern Ireland, and parts of Southeast Asia), we may think that we are dealing with regions in which religious transmission is built solely around the doctrinal mode. Christians, Muslims, Sikhs, Hindus, and so on, are members of huge religions that undoubtedly incorporate full-blown doctrinal domains of operation. But I will hazard the following predictions. First, wherever trouble flares up, we will also find entrenched manifestations of the imagistic mode at work. Second, where evidence of the imagistic mode is lacking, so too is large-scale, religiously motivated violence.[2] Of course, proposing correlations of this sort is a risky business. Take for instance the correlation alleged by many liberal commentators between relative deprivation and civil unrest. This hypothesis has considerable intuitive appeal, and yet it is easy to identify large portions of humanity that have been subjected to appalling exploitation and long-term political domination but who have adopted strikingly peaceful or passivist forms of religion.[3] And, by the same token, some of the most violent and reactionary religious communities in the world have suffered only rather mild forms of economic and political injustice, at least if the "relative" part of "relative deprivation" is to mean anything.[4] What reasons do we have to think that the proposed correlation between imagistic mode operations and religious violence will turn out to be any stronger? The answer lies in imagistic dynamics themselves.

In an excellent survey of theories of warfare, R. Brian Ferguson (1990) observes that the link with religion has been astonishingly neglected. And yet:

> War involves, in an extreme form, virtually all of the circumstances [that] have been invoked to explain the genesis of religion and magic. It is a collective activity, closely linked to group solidarity and survival. It forces individuals to confront a hazardous unknown, beyond their rational-instrumental control. It poses "the question of meaning" repeatedly, as it leads to tragedy, injustice, and immorality. For all these reasons, war is a virtual magico-religious magnet. (1990, 46)

Note, however, that most of the traits that Ferguson holds to be common to both war and religion are really characteristic only of the imagistic mode of religiosity: intense cohesion or solidarity arising from group action; encounters with novel or unknown situations; extreme coercion; deep and extensive reflection on issues of meaning or exegesis. All these traits may be associated with ritual ordeals. And when one reads in any detail about religiously motivated atrocities in one's own society or others, the ritualized aspects of the violence described often stand out quite prominently. Victims, and in some cases perpetrators, are liable to experience long-term memory effects with regard to events of this sort, encouraging enduring patterns of rumination on their experiences—and there is a wealth of (admittedly anecdotal) evidence that would encourage this expectation in the form of autobiographical writings and accounts of clinical psychologists and counselors.[5] In many cases, the victims of religious attacks form intensely cohesive bonds in much the same manner as participants in high-arousal, low-frequency rituals. This cohesion may well be linked to cycles of orchestrated violent reprisal, as news reports from all over the world persistently seem to suggest. But is that where any similarity with imagistic practices ends? Remember that the traumatic ordeals of novices are not just experiences of coming under attack: they are experiences that carry meanings initially difficult to grasp but eventually blossoming into rather complex and highly motivating bodies of revelatory knowledge. Not all religiously motivated acts of violence trigger these effects, but we should not underestimate the capacity of *ritualized* violence to do precisely that.

Consider the following somewhat arbitrarily selected example from recent ethnographic research in Rwanda. In *Sacrifice As Terror* (1999), Christopher Taylor argues that the notorious genocide of 1994 cannot be understood purely in terms of the clashing interests of diverse coalitions. As the blurb on the book puts it: "political and historical analyses . . . fail to explain the forms that the violence took and the degree of passion that motivated it. Instead, Rwandan ritual and practices related to the body are revelatory in this regard." He illustrates this point in many ways, but here is a particularly short and graphic example:

> Among the accounts of Rwandan refugees that I interviewed in Kenya during the late spring and early summer of 1994, there was persistent mention of barriers and roadblocks. . . . One refugee who had made it to Kenya by the circuitous route of fleeing southward to Burundi told me that he and everyone else in his company had been forced to pay an unusual toll at one barrier. Each had been forced to bludgeon a captured Tutsi with a hammer before being allowed to move on. Some in the party had even been made to repeat their blows a second or third time for lack of initial enthusiasm. (1999, 131)

This horrific anecdote presents an instance of apparently spontaneous ritualization. Refugees, forced to participate in the killings of Tutsi captives, were placed in a position closely analogous to that of novices in initiation rituals. On the one hand, their participation was coerced, in that they would have faced death themselves if they had failed to comply. On the other hand, the acts required of them were not straightforwardly reducible to technical motivations—if the aim were simply to kill, then there would be no need to delegate and distribute the act of bludgeoning in the manner described. Indeed, the requirement that these blows be delivered with sufficient vigor is strongly reminiscent of Amazonian initiations described by Gustaaf Verswijver in which novices were required to deliver repeated blows to the corpses of slain enemies, long after they had actually died (1992, 177–179). Taylor argues, with regard to the Rwandan atrocities, that the hapless refugees were being forced to assume the role of sacrificers within the logic of locally prevailing ritual concepts (1999, 131–132). But, quite clearly, we are dealing here with a particularly abnormal and shocking ritual, one that would never be forgotten by the refugees who survived and that had considerable potential for driving subsequent processes of exegetical reflection. Taylor's central thesis is that experiences of this sort have revelatory effects that are highly motivating and feed into the long-term perpetuation of cycles of violence.

The imagistic mode of religiosity generates some of the most powerful and durable motivational states available to human groups, although convictions of comparable strength can be (and evidently are) generated by more individualized revelatory traumas. Although the causes of psychopathic behavior, for instance, are undoubtedly complex, clinical evidence suggests that experiences of being abused are causally connected to subsequent abusive behavior. Abusive individuals sometimes display idiosyncratic belief systems of an extraordinarily elaborate kind, of which it would be facile to interpret merely as post hoc rationalizations of immoral or criminal desires and behavior. Not only are such belief systems often far more complex than would be required for the purposes of self-justification, but they also seem to take shape long before the abusive behavior itself is manifested. There is a good case for the view that at least some forms of psychopathology develop in ways that rather closely parallel the emergence of imagistic revelations (Whitehouse 2001c). A marked difference, however, is that the imagistic mode is constructed around collective trauma and associated group cohesion. The lone psychopath may have the same kind of belief system as the religious fanatic. But what he or she normally lacks is the opportunity to create a fanatical religious coalition.

The dynamics of the doctrinal mode of religiosity are rather less robust and easily maintained than those of the imagistic mode. The most powerful outputs of the former take the appearance of dogmatic rigidity rather than true fanaticism (although the doctrinal mode can, of course, provide a home for psychopaths as well). As a set of dynamics operating at the population level, the doctrinal mode favors verbal testimony over independently derived convictions. And therein lies certain weaknesses, as we shall see.

The Limits of Religious Enthusiasm

Reliance on verbal testimony in a religious tradition carries certain costs. If doctrines are to be persuasive, then they must be reasonably comprehensive, coherent, and stable; but that requires routinization (for all the reasons I have set out in the preceding chapters). Continual repetition of verbal testimony is potentially boring and is thus capable of triggering the tedium effect (see chapter 4). But there are other problems for the doctrinal mode arising from the intrinsic complexity of the concepts in which it deals.

Cognitive psychologist Justin Barrett (1998, 1999, 2001a, 2001b, 2002a, 2002b, 2003) uses the term "theologically correct" (TC) discourse to refer to explicit, officially endorsed religious concepts, as distinct from the more natural, tacit concepts entailed in religious thinking (Barrett and Keil 1996; Barrett 1999). Barrett has shown that TC discourse only ever constitutes part of the story when it comes to the ways in which religious concepts and ritual procedures are represented and evaluated. Theologically correct thinking utilizes explicit schemas organized in semantic memory, whether taking the form of orthodox religious teachings (in the doctrinal mode) or the more idiosyncratic revelations that gradually take shape in the minds of ritual experts (in the imagistic mode). Lurking beneath this kind of religious knowledge, however, is a wealth of tacit assumptions and understandings—deriving from natural cognition—that persistently skews religious discourse in directions that are easier to process. Consider the following simple examples:

According to TC discourse in a number of religious traditions, the realm of the supernatural is not bound by ordinary constraints of time and space. For instance, other worldly time is often represented as nondurational, and a single god may be perfectly able to respond simultaneously to two separate problems in geographically distant locations. Nevertheless, Barrett and his collaborators have shown that when confronted with tasks that require the activation of tacit, online reasoning, religious adherents routinely abandon their TC concepts and envisage the gods as having to deal with problems in a sequential fashion (e.g., answering each prayer in turn, before dealing with the next).

To take another example, TC discourse in Christian traditions holds that God can respond to prayer by intervening in a number of different domains, including that of the physical and mechanical (e.g., by causing a flood), that of the psychological (e.g., by causing a person to perform a particular act or to adopt a particular belief), or that of the biological (e.g., by miraculously curing a disease). Nevertheless, Barrett (2002b) has presented evidence that at least some Christians (in this case a sample of American Protestants) make the tacit assumption that divine intervention would more naturally be focused on the psychological domain rather than on the physical or biological. Theologically correct discourse would suggest that any of the three sorts of intervention are equally feasible for an omnipotent being, and yet people's implicit, online reasoning would encourage them to envisage God as better placed to influence people's attitudes, feelings, and intentions, rather than to fix mechanical or biological problems. Barrett suggests that the bias toward requests for psychological intervention in petitionary prayer stems from tacit representations of God as occupying a distant but specific location (heaven) and thus as being subject to the same constraints that apply to ordinary people wishing to act at a distance. From early infancy, humans implicitly assume that both mechanical and biological effects cannot be brought about without physical contact (directly or indirectly), whereas we can certainly influence each other's psychological states at a distance. Natural cognition appears to envisage God in much the same way.

Although these are examples of TC discourse being reprocessed at an implicit level in ways that are highly intuitive, there is good evidence that a wide range of minimally counterintuitive concepts introduce similar biases (Barrett 1999). In chapters 2 and 3, we observed that the minimally counterintuitive concept of "ghost" will always be easier to learn and transmit than the much more elaborate TC concept of the "Holy Ghost." The same would be true of all patterns of mentation that are clustered around the cognitive optimum position—including, of course, simpler kinds of ritual procedures and meanings, taboos, myths, narratives, and doctrinal principles. Theologically correct versions would always be relatively difficult to acquire, but even having been acquired, people will invariably fall back on cognitively optimal versions in tacit, "online" processing.

Several scholars (Boyer 2001a, Barrett 1999, Pyysiäinen 2001) have noted that the mismatch between TC concepts and online reasoning is liable to affect patterns of religious transmission. Since the cognitive optimum position is a universal attractor position, it would not be surprising if we were to find a tendency in all religious traditions for TC concepts to migrate in the direction of more cognitively optimal versions. According to Boyer, this is precisely what we find: "Actual religious concepts always seem to stick out, as it were, to distort the official message or to add all sorts of officially incorrect interpretations. . . . People are never quite as 'theologically correct' as the guild would like them to be" (Pyysiäinen 2001, 282–283). Moreover, as Barrett (2002a) points out, the problem is not just found in religious traditions. *Any* cultural domain that deals in extremely hard-to-acquire concepts may be vulnerable to reformulation in cognitively simpler terms that can be deployed in practical situations. An obvious example would be the way in which people often resort to scientifically incorrect versions of evolutionary theory or astronomy when attempting to explain how giraffes come to have long necks or why the position of the sun changes during the day. In some cases, the more intuitive versions come to form widely held popular beliefs. In other cases, they are just makeshift simplifications that we know to be false. A biologist, for instance, may know that the category "tree" is not taxonomically separate from the category "plant," but that would not prevent him or her from reasoning in ways that operationalize such a distinction when planning the layout of his or her garden.

In doctrinal systems, as in science, the orthodoxy is perpetually vulnerable to reformulation as a set of simpler concepts. In part, this has to do with way official religious dogma is supposed to cohere. The glue that holds TC knowledge together is the "logic of question-and-answer" (Whitehouse 2000a, chap. 2). Originally described most comprehensively by the philosopher Robin Collingwood (1940), ostensibly as a means of analyzing histories of ideas, the method presents itself as a strikingly apposite descriptor of the logic utilized by doctrinal systems in the domain of religion. What this logic entails is that a set of absolute presuppositions (normally beyond all possibility of falsification) drives a series of rhetorical questions and orthodox answers that have been fixed by convention through their studious repetition (and also, usually, their codification in sacred texts). None of the standard answers presented by officialdom may be regarded as the only possible answers. On the contrary, all answers are the way they are only on the basis of the argument of authority. That is partly how religious rhetoric succeeds in persuading its audiences, but it also requires extensive mnemonic support in order to be preserved intact. If it is perverted by the cognitive optimum effect, there is no guarantee that anybody will be able to hold the system together. Religious authorities in the doctrinal mode can permanently *lose* much of their accumulated knowledge if they fail adequately to rehearse it.[6] As such, doctrinal religion is especially vulnerable to the cognitive optimum effect, and that is also why long-term stability in the doctrinal mode depends on effective policing. This is not such a simple matter as one might suppose.

The doctrinal mode must balance itself precariously between two opposing forces. On the one hand, risks of unintended innovation—for instance, in the direction of the cognitive optimum position—can be reduced only if repetition of the orthodoxy is sustained at a very high level. But this in turn can trigger the tedium effect. As well as its potentially negative implications for motivational levels, the tedium effect also increases the susceptibility of religious adherents to innovative recodification of the tradition's teachings (e.g., through the emergence of splinter groups operating in the imagistic mode). Boyer (2001a, 284) puts it like this:

> Religious guilds provide many contexts for acquiring consistent propositional messages through repetition and systematic teaching, but very few contexts where salient episodes . . . can be recruited as an aid to memory. A consequence emphasized by Whitehouse is that the guilds may gradually lose their influence because of what could be called a tedium-based decay function. That is, people become gradually more and more familiar with the doctrine, but this very familiarity removes much of the motivation for taking part in the guild's rituals and other activities. As a consequence, the more religious institutions favor the doctrinal mode of transmission, the more vulnerable they are to periodic outbursts of imagistic dissent.

On the other hand, however, if the religious authorities loosen their grip on the orthodoxy—for instance, by allowing a reduction in the extent and frequency of lay participation or by weakening the sanctions for unauthorized innovation—the door is left wide open for cognitive optimum effects to become entrenched. This too produces motivational problems. It is not that the cognitively optimal versions of religious orthodoxy are themselves at risk of dying out. On the contrary, their "naturalness" makes these beliefs and practices extraordinarily robust, all else being equal. But these practices are not capable of generating the same degree of neofanatical dogmatism and rigidity that doctrinal revelations characteristically produce. Any religious authorities who have retained their revelatory commitments would undoubtedly regard this as an appalling degeneration or dilution of whatever it is they happen to hold dear. Hence, these circumstances are liable to trigger patterns of religious reformation. Ilkka Pyysiäinen (2004) observes:

> It thus seems that loosening of the principle of agreement ("liberal theology") tends to have the effect of bringing about revivalist movements that emphasize a more rigorous reading of the doctrine as well as the necessity for a personally felt relationship with the doctrine. . . . By inversion of the argument, it could also be predicted that a too strict principle of agreement will tend to produce revivalist movements whose primary aim is to evoke personal, "ecstatic" experiences to ensure that the relevance of religion is not lost. We might thus analytically distinguish between two kinds of revivalist movements: those whose protest is directed against the dry routine of theological traditions, and those whose protest is primarily against a too loose interpretation of doctrine within the theological tradition. To the first category belong elements of religious revival aspiring towards heightened personal experience, i.e. various kinds of "ecstatic" phenomena. They are more imagistic in their orientation. To the latter category belong elements [that] primarily aim at restoring "the original doctrine." They are clearly doctrinal in their orientation.

The previous observations serve both to qualify and enrich certain aspects of the theory of religious transformation presented in my earlier work.

Previously, I described the historical profile for Melanesian movements, in very general terms, as consisting of long-term routinization in the doctrinal mode, punctuated by sporadic outbursts of localized cult activity based on imagistic-mode dynamics (Whitehouse 1995, 2000a). A key hypothesis was that levels of susceptibility to imagistic revelations correlated directly with the onset of the tedium effect, helping to account for the periodicity of cult outbursts. The account I presented of late medieval Christianity in Europe was somewhat different. Here, I suggested, modal dynamics operated differently within different sectors of the population. Full-blown doctrinal dynamics characterized the literate tradition, centered on the monasteries. By contrast, lay Christianities in the late Middle Ages incorporated most, but not all, of the features of the doctrinal mode. At least for large sectors of the laity, the motivating force of exegetical or theological knowledge reproduced in the monasteries was not fully accessible. So what motivated popular forms of Christianity among uneducated people? In an attempt to answer that question, I suggested that the folk traditions tended to cluster around various imagistic-mode dynamics, expressed in notably high-arousal rituals associated with "pilgrimages, carnivals, witch-hunts, folk religions, and agricultural festivals" (Whitehouse 2000a, 150). Both Protestant and Catholic Reformations were attempts to extend the motivational systems of the monasteries (albeit with revised theological content) to a much wider audience and, in the process, to suppress the imagistic mode in all its diverse manifestations. That project was never entirely successful, however. The more austere, iconoclastic, and highly routinized Protestant churches were vulnerable to the tedium effect, and thus to sporadic outbursts of imagistic splintering (i.e., in much the same way as I described among Melanesian religious movements in the twentieth century).

In *Bringing Ritual to Mind* (2002), Robert McCauley and Thomas Lawson present a series of criticisms of my account of modal dynamics of Christianity in the late Middle Ages. Their critique focuses more or less exclusively on the last move in my account of the history of Christianity—namely, the point at which I attempt to draw comparisons between post-Reformation traditions in Europe and new religious movements in Melanesia. McCauley and Lawson (2002, 202) frame their critique as follows: "We are not convinced that most splinter groups in most other religious systems—and especially in the history of Christianity since the Middle Ages—either arise from the same conditions or exhibit the same profile as the Melanesian cases that Whitehouse aims to group with them within the framework of his doctrinal mode." They then proceed to set out three main reasons for these doubts.

First, the causes of splintering in European traditions differ markedly from those identified in Melanesia. In particular, whereas the role of the tedium effect in the formation of Melanesian splinter groups seems to be quite apparent in the available evidence, the causes of splintering in European and American churches, from at least the eighteenth century onward seem to have more to do with squabbles over doctrine than with problems of lowered motivation (McCauley and Lawson 2002, 202–203). Moreover, the latter state of affairs seems to be prevalent in many of the other world religions as well:

> At the conceptual level, religious systems have splintered over everything from arguments about lines of descent from Muhammad (Islam) to disagreements over the

character of enlightenment (in Buddhism) to squabbles about the language in which the mass should be said (in Catholicism) to disputes about the possibilities of ice in August in the American South (in the Southern Baptist system). On the political front, breakaway groups have arisen over issues such as who is the head of the church in England, who is the most recent incarnation of the Dalai Lama, and whether members of a variety of Protestant denominations lived in the Confederate States of America. . . . By contrast with the Melanesian cases, splintering in these instances seems primarily to concern *content* rather than *codification*. (2002, 203)

Second, the *outcomes* of splintering caused by doctrinal disagreements are rather different from those that arise from the onset of the tedium effect. In the latter scenario, as illustrated by the Melanesian case studies, splinter-group members are generally welcomed back into the fold of the mainstream tradition whenever their ritual systems crash. This pattern of reassimilation is much less typical where splinter groups have formed on the basis of theological and political disputes. More commonly in such cases, splinter-group members are permanently excluded from the mainstream tradition. They may be subject to persecution (even annihilation) or self-destruction, but if such splinter groups survive at all, they must establish themselves as fully independent religious traditions, severing all links to the coalitions that spawned them.

Third, the *motivational* implications of splintering will be different in the two sets of cases. Since the Melanesian splinter groups described in *Arguments and Icons* (Whitehouse 2000a) merely recodified mainstream dogma, the reassimilation of members served to reinvigorate commitment to the mainstream tradition. Obviously, that would be impossible in cases where splinter-group members are permanently excommunicated. It follows that both mainstream *and* splinter-group traditions operating successfully in the latter circumstances must somehow establish adequate motivational states by *independent* means.

All these observations are well taken. Like McCauley and Lawson, Pyysiäinen (2004) proposes that we regard the "Melanesian profile" (oscillation between long-term routinization and sporadic imagistic outbursts triggered by the tedium effect) as just one possibility. Exactly how widespread that profile might be cross-culturally remains to be seen. Another possible profile with the general characteristics described by McCauley and Lawson would involve long-term patterns of splintering in the doctrinal mode occasioned by disputes over the orthodoxy or orthopraxy or both. Although there may be a number of different causes behind such a pattern, one of the most prominent of these is probably not the tedium effect but the cognitive optimum effect.

The doctrinal mode is vulnerable not only to overpolicing and excessive routinization (resulting in tedium), but also to underpolicing and the resulting mutation of complex religious knowledge into more easily transmitted forms, at least in popular or folk versions of the tradition. It seems to me that this naturalizing of doctrinal-mode concepts may affect not only doctrinal concepts per se but also the ways in which rituals and myths are processed and transmitted. In the case of rituals, it is possible that a significant reduction in the level of routinization or habituation, coupled with more liberal policing of authoritative exegesis, would bring about a situation in which tacit intuitive assumptions of the sort predicted by the ritual form hypothesis (see chapter 2) are likely to flourish. The following effects might then be predicted: (1) accentuation of any differences in levels of sensory pageantry obtaining between odd- and even-numbered rituals, (2) special emphasis on the more central rituals, (3) further proliferation of rites for reversing the effects of special-agent rituals, and (4) a closer correspondence between intuitions concerning repeatability and the actual practice. Meanwhile, in the domain of mythological transmission, one would expect to see a proliferation of nonstandard narrative forms rather than the endless rehearsal of the orthodox repertoire.

The cognitive optimum effect may be one of the major causes of religious renewals or reformations. Although these revitalizing projects may be officially sanctioned, more often than not reformers arouse the guardians of the old regime from their state of lethargy or inattention and all the weapons of policing the coalition are wheeled out. This would go some way toward accounting for the divisive consequences of this pattern of splintering noted by McCauley and Lawson.

Religious enthusiasm takes a wide variety of forms, ranging from stubborn adherence to dogma in the face of more plausible alternatives through to fanatical actions carried out without regard to the human costs. Some scholars think that these traits derive from patterns of human thought and social interaction that have little to do with specifically religious concepts. The latter are invoked to justify the stubbornness or aggression that people would exhibit anyway. By contrast, many observers of religion (whether adherents or outsiders) suspect that explicit religious knowledge really does drive people's feelings, judgments, and actions. People actually *are* motivated to kill or die for their religious beliefs, just as they may also feel compelled to perform great acts of compassion and charity at enormous personal cost. Which one of these two interpretations is correct? One possible answer, of course, is that they both contain important truths. Religious traditions are coalitions, after all, and coalitional thinking informs a great deal of human behavior, whether religious or otherwise. But religious revelations can also drive our behavior.

When we arrive at our deepest convictions through processes of direct, personal inference, they can shape and mold our attitudes and beliefs in a variety of ways. Low-frequency, high-arousal rituals promote intense cohesion, partly because of the sense people have of sharing common stock of memories. But the people who survive these ordeals *also* generally assume their common experiences give them access to deeper meanings that are unavailable to those who haven't similarly suffered. This kind of meaning only faintly resembles everyday kinds of knowledge available to outsiders. The sufferers think that they know something the rest of us simply could not begin to imagine (and would grotesquely misunderstand if we were to try to steal a peek). Therein lies another basis for coalitional thinking in the imagistic mode. Survivors of ritualistic ordeals not only share episodic memories for the ordeal itself but they *also* share (or think they share) a special kind of semantic knowledge arising out of the experience. That knowledge is felt to be more valuable than everyday knowledge, and it must remain the secret possession of those who have earned it at great personal cost. One day, though, it must be revealed to others so that the coalition and its valued knowledge can live on. This, unfortunately, requires more violence. The valued knowledge that must somehow be preserved may compel us to subject our children to agonizing initiations or to slay our enemies (or, more commonly, both). But when we try to explain *why* all this is so important, our capacities for expression often seem to fail us.

The doctrinal mode generates its convictions rather differently. Since verbal testimony is privileged over personal inspiration, much depends on the talents of gurus, messiahs, prophets, preachers, and priests. If they can formulate a message that is relevant and rhetorically compelling, they've got us. But not for long. The coherence and comprehensiveness of the message makes great demands on memory and so it is vulnerable to the effects of distortion and decay. Enter the religious police.

The difficulties faced by religious authorities are comparable to those confronting their secular counterparts (and whose existence they historically inspired). If they exercise their powers too oppressively, they stoke disaffection and revolt. If they are too liberal and permissive, they open the doors to theological thieves and vandals. In the history of routinized religion, we find a range of ways of responding to these problems. But the problems will never go away.

Notes

1. For a particularly lucid description of the powers of elders among the Aranda-speaking Aborigines of central Australia, see Strehlow 1965.

2. These two predictions are not essential to my main arguments, but are worth testing nonetheless, and might be added to the list of problems to be investigated by new research set out in chapter 9.

3. Consider, for instance, the forbearance quite commonly displayed by Roman Catholics in the face of appalling poverty and dictatorship in many parts of South America and Southeast Asia.

4. Consider, for instance, the aggressivity of Loyalist Protestant teaching in Northern Ireland despite a history of Protestant dominance in public institutions and commerce.

5. Of particular interest is the literature on trauma, memory, and rumination stimulated by Martin and Tesser's (1989) hypothesis that the interruption of subjectively valued goals encourages subsequent intrusive rehearsal of memories for the interruption event. Kent Harber and James Pennebaker (1992), for instance, suggest that this may help to account for certain aspects of the ruminative cycles associated with memories for traumatic experiences.

6. Cultural anthropologist Scott Atran has challenged my argument that part of what makes both scientific and doctrinal concepts hard to transmit and maintain is their logical integration. According to Atran (2002, 156–157):

> If liturgical doctrines were truly integrated through logical inference, then frequent repetition would seem superfluous. Once a logical procedure is known, inferences can be "automatically" generated and applied to indefinitely many new or old cases and situations. . . . One could imagine a group of mathematicians, scientists, or lawyers congregating to repeat some formula as mantra for the purposes of some social convention; however, no amount of repetition would make mathematics, science or law more "logically integrated," consistent or coherent. . . . In fact, Whitehouse's important observation about frequent repetition of liturgy arguably leads to a conclusion diametrically opposed to his own: People may need to repeat such rituals precisely because the ritual elements are not, and cannot be, logically integrated or independently induced from multiple experiences.

Nevertheless, I have never argued that the concepts of doctrinal systems can be automatically inferred on the basis of learned principles of deductive and inductive reasoning. Moreover, Atran's comments on the transmission of scientific knowledge seem to me highly implausible. There is far more to the training of "mathematicians, scientists, or lawyers" than the transmission of a set of "logical procedures" from which all their other expert knowledge somehow flows. A vast array of intrinsically hard-to-recall concepts have to be learned through the labors of continual rehearsal in classes and late-night study sessions. Although the methods of deductive and inductive reasoning are more prominent in the precise sciences than in religious orthodoxies, that observation is somewhat irrelevant to the fact that both kinds of knowledge are hard to acquire, demanding extensive reminding or consolidation in order to be successfully transmitted and maintained. Perhaps what really distinguishes doctrinal knowledge from other kinds of hard-to-acquire conceptual frameworks is that the excessive routinization of the former stunts the formation of *new* analogical connections and makes the activation of orthodox analogues seem to derive from sources external to the worshipper's mind (see introduction and chapter 6).

THEORETICAL AND EMPIRICAL CHALLENGES

III

Theoretical Challenges 8

IN *RETHINKING RELIGION* (1990), Robert N. McCauley and E. Thomas Lawson set out a competence theory of ritual, which proposed that the various forms taken by religious rituals are generated by the same basic cognitive principles and categories that all normal humans use for the construction and interpretation of every kind of action. More recently, in *Bringing Ritual to Mind* (McCauley and Lawson 2002), they have extended this model in such a way that bears directly and explicitly on the theory of modes of religiosity. The latter work advances "the ritual form hypothesis," a set of predictions concerning the relationships among memory, frequency, and sensory pageantry in the transmission of rituals.

Both the theory of ritual competence and the ritual form hypothesis were summarized at some length in chapter 2 because they hold out the promise of predicting people's intuitive judgments concerning the structure, repeatability, reversibility, efficacy, and sensory tonus of religious rituals. It is important to emphasize, however, that we are talking here about intuitive, largely implicit, cognitive processes rather than (necessarily) people's reflective and explicit ideas about rituals. As noted at various points in this book, much current scholarship in the cognitive science of religion tends to assume that explicit religious thinking consists largely of (more or less elaborated) post hoc rationalizations of ideas, attitudes, and behaviors that people would have adopted in any case. The theory advanced in this book seeks to modify that view. The substantial mnemonic supports for the transmission and elaboration of religion —associated with doctrinal and imagistic modes of religiosity—allow the development of highly salient and motivationally powerful bodies of explicit religious knowledge, especially relating to the nature and meaning of ritual.

Until recently, this particular aspect of the modes theory had not been challenged directly by a competing theory of the causes and implications of varying frequency and arousal in the domain of ritual. But in *Bringing Ritual to Mind* such a challenge is systematically laid out. In that volume, McCauley and Lawson (2002) argue that implicit judgments concerning the properties of rituals determine their forms and social consequences not only in cognitively optimal kinds of ritual transmission (an argument with which I largely concur in chapter 2) but in religious ritual transmission per se. In other words, they present their "ritual form hypothesis" not merely as a complement to the theory of modes of religiosity but largely as an *alternative* to it. The challenge is therefore a serious one, and this chapter attempts to respond to some of the key issues it raises.

McCauley and Lawson's starting point is that the cognitive claims underpinning the theory of modes of religiosity are incomplete and would need to be augmented by an understanding of the way rituals are formally conceptualized. Specifically, they claim, the bifurcation of ritual types into low-frequency and high-arousal versus high-frequency and low-arousal profiles is at least partly a consequence of the different formal properties of rituals. The challenge is boldly advanced: "Our aim is no less than delineating the cognitive architecture of *Homo religiosus*—not merely to understand well-known historic patterns in religious systems better but also to *explain* them" (2002, 8). Moreover, they argue strenuously and repeatedly (2002, 124, 125, 139, 178, 180) for the superiority of their account over that supplied by the modes theory, at least with regard to the somewhat limited range of cases on which, by their reckoning, the predictions of the two theories would appear to conflict. In addition, their work is characterized by an exemplary concern with scientific theory building and empirical substantiation. For these reasons (and as we already saw in chapter 2, there are others), it is necessary to take their model seriously and to examine its claims in detail.

The Challenges

As indicated in chapter 2, McCauley and Lawson argue that considerations of ritual form are sufficient to predict which rituals will be accompanied by elevated levels of arousal and sensory pageantry and which will not. Special agent rituals are performed once only, from the viewpoint of those in the patient position, and are likely to be relatively low frequency in the society as a whole. In keeping with the predictions of the theory of modes of religiosity, such rites may depend for their survival on the activation of episodic memory, which (as we have seen in chapter 6) in turn may require elevated arousal. In developing this aspect of the ritual form hypothesis, McCauley and Lawson draw heavily on what they refer to as the "Whitehouse ritual frequency hypothesis" (or "frequency hypothesis," for short): "The frequency hypothesis . . . holds, in short, that the amount of sensory stimulation (and resulting emotional excitement) a ritual incorporates is inversely proportional to its performance frequency" (McCauley and Lawson 2002, 6).

According to McCauley and Lawson, the frequency hypothesis is on the right track, and in large part this is because of the mnemonic demands placed on ritual transmission, identified by the theory of modes of religiosity. That is to say, the survival of low-frequency rituals normally depends substantially on the activation of episodic memory, which in turn requires heightened arousal (cf. Whitehouse 1992 and McCauley and Lawson 2002, chap. 2). Conversely, rituals that are very frequently repeated are unable to sustain comparable levels of arousal (even if that were attempted) due to habituation (cf. Whitehouse 1992 and McCauley and Lawson 2002, chap. 2). In addition, McCauley and Lawson emphasize that elevated arousal is also important in establishing the motivational states necessary for subsequent transmission (2002, 43–44).

Thus far, we would appear to be in agreement. We shall presently see, however, that the consensus does not run as deep as all that. Our intuitions concerning the role of memory and motivation in the transmission of low-frequency, high-arousal rituals actually turn out to be rather different. But first it is necessary to deal with a rather more obvious point of theoretical divergence. This concerns the nature and causes of what McCauley and Lawson call "sensory pageantry," and this is also the point at which their ritual form hypothesis decisively comes into play.

According to McCauley and Lawson, the relative frequency of rituals may regulate sensory pageantry by ensuring the minimum levels needed for the production of mnemonic and motivational effects (without which the ritual would not be transmitted). But, they argue, that still leaves unanswered the question of what causes variations in the frequency of ritual performances in the first place. The answer, they maintain, is provided by considerations of ritual form. Recall that odd-numbered (special agent) rituals (see chapter 2) must have very low performance frequencies since the human patients of these rituals can only undergo them once (at least in theory). By contrast, even-numbered (special instrument or special patient) rituals are repeatable and thus prone to higher performance frequencies.

One of the major claims of the ritual form hypothesis, then, is that it identifies the hitherto unrecognized cause of divergent patterns of transmissive frequency in ritual systems. The theory of modes of religiosity had already more or less accurately described the tendency of ritual systems to bifurcate, such that their activities cluster around either low-frequency and high-arousal rituals (with the associated social morphological consequences that characterize the imagistic mode) or high-frequency, low-arousal rituals (giving rise to the features of the doctrinal mode) or both, but within distinct domains of operation. But according to McCauley and Lawson, the theory of modes of religiosity is at a loss to explain this bifurcation, since it does not specify the causes of divergent performance frequencies. Thus, frequency, they maintain, is the unexplained independent variable in the modes theory, which the ritual form hypothesis can now explain. What causes a ritual to be infrequent is the relative proximity of "culturally postulated superhuman agents" (CPS agents) to the ritual's agent slot, and what causes a ritual to be frequent is the relative proximity of CPS agents to the ritual's patient or instrument slot.

In order to make these claims, McCauley and Lawson (2002) are obliged to refine their account of some of the key elements and variables that figure in our respective theories. These refinements dramatically increase the (otherwise seemingly narrow) gap between the predictions of the modes theory and those of the ritual form hypothesis.

First, since McCauley and Lawson's account of ritual form requires the presence of representations of CPS agents, their theory is explicitly confined to religious rituals (stipulated as rituals in which CPS agents are assumed to play some role). Unlike the theory of modes of religiosity, the ritual form hypothesis does not claim to be applicable to rituals in which CPS agents are absent in the action representation system. Indeed, it *could not* apply to such rituals since all its predictive claims rest on assumptions about the nature of CPS agent involvement.[1]

Second, the ritual form hypothesis introduces an explanation for elevated sensory pageantry in low-frequency rituals *additional* to that provided by the theory of modes of religiosity. Since, on McCauley and Lawson's view, low-frequency rituals are normally also special agent rituals, they are ones that effect irreversible changes in their patients. It makes some intuitive sense to suppose that big events like these require relatively impressive fanfare. Moreover, since the changes in question are set in motion by the presumed intervention of CPS agents, this adds a certain weightiness to the events at hand. Turning up the emotional volume might help to impress on participants that the god is really behind all of this (McCauley and Lawson 2002, 43–444, 112–113, 122–123). For these reasons, McCauley and Lawson regard elevated sensory pageantry not only as an outcome of mnemonic and motivational considerations, but also (and perhaps even more directly) as a result of the way special agent rituals are conceptualized as actions.

Third, according to the ritual form hypothesis, the sensory pageantry occasioned by low-frequency rituals will normally only be higher relative to more frequent rituals within the same community. McCauley and Lawson are obliged to introduce this caveat because they argue that all low-frequency religious rituals fall into the special agent category—and yet we know that special agent rituals in some varieties of Christianity, for instance, elicit overwhelmingly lower levels of sensory pageantry than certain of the widely distributed special patient or instrument rituals that famously inhabit non-Western traditions. Thus, for McCauley and Lawson, we can predict that Lutheran special agent rituals (e.g., baptisms, weddings, funerals, and ordinations) will incorporate markedly higher levels of sensory stimulation than Lutheran special patient or special instrument rituals (e.g., Holy Communion and blessings), but that the former will not necessarily entail higher sensory pageantry than the even-numbered rituals of all other Christian traditions. This, too, constitutes an important point of contrast with the theory of modes of religiosity, which proposes an inverse correlation between levels of frequency and arousal *across* religious traditions.

These three points of contrast between the ritual form hypothesis and the modes theory are explicitly noted in McCauley and Lawson's book (2002). Moreover, they argue that every point at which their theory diverges from mine affords them an embarrassment of riches (both theoretically and empirically). At the end of chapter 3, they declare:

> In the next two chapters we shall compare the merits of the ritual form and ritual frequency hypotheses. We shall examine especially closely their abilities to account for the events in Dadul and Maranagi on which Whitehouse has reported. We shall argue that the ritual form hypothesis provides not only a consistently superior explanation of this specific set of cases but a far more penetrating causal account of much larger patterns that hold both within and among religious ritual systems across cultures and through time.

The following sections of this chapter attempt to penetrate more deeply the main differences between McCauley and Lawson's theoretical framework and my own. Not all these differences are recognized or acknowledged in *Bringing Ritual to Mind*, but each of them has major theoretical ramifications affecting the credibility of our respective arguments.

Form and Frequency

According to McCauley and Lawson, all the interconnected variables with which the theory of modes of religiosity concerns itself are ultimately reducible to one, which stands at the beginning of a series of additional causal chains (and relations of mutual reinforcement). This variable is frequency. And thus the entire theory of modes of religiosity stands or falls on the frequency hypothesis. This cardinal hypothesis is depicted by McCauley and Lawson in diagrammatical form (see figure 8.1).

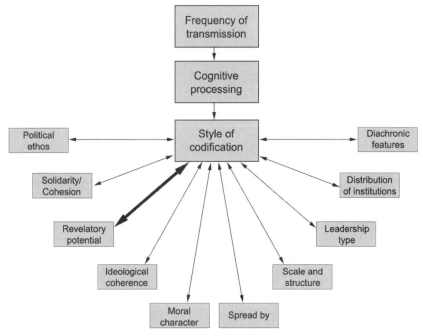

Figure 8.1.   Direction of Influence among Whitehouse's Thirteen Variables (McCauley and Lawson 2002, 106)

The frequency hypothesis, as depicted here, has a number of problems. For now, let us consider a problem that McCauley and Lawson themselves identify, namely, the inability of the model to account for variations in transmissive frequency. The solution, according to McCauley and Lawson, is supplied by the ritual form hypothesis. In the case of special agent rituals, the argument runs as follows: given that the measure of frequency adopted for such rituals is the number of times each person participates in the patient role, frequency is bound to be extremely low (barring failures and subsequent ritual reversals, each person participates as a patient one time, and one time only). But what about McCauley and Lawson's even-numbered rituals (special patient and special instrument types)? At best, considerations of ritual form only stipulate that rituals of this sort *can be* repeated. Nothing in the logic of this framework could serve to explain why they are in fact repeated. What is more, a great many rituals of this type are repeated with such a high degree of frequency that (if these were not institutionalized, socially required forms of behavior) we might almost be tempted to describe them as *compulsively* repetitious.

As early as chapter 2 (2002, 43), McCauley and Lawson advance the claim that considerations of ritual form *will explain* the bifurcation of ritual systems into those based on very rare (or one-off) performances per individual patient versus those based on highly repetitious or routinized activities. They later reiterate the promise that this claim will be demonstrated or at least the basis for it clarified (2002, 113). Finally, in their penultimate chapter, McCauley and Lawson confront the matter head on, as follows:

> The cognitive principles of our ritual competence theory—to which the ritual form hypothesis appeals—*explain* the *relative* performance frequencies for all religious rituals. They explain the relative performance frequencies for the two broad categories the theory supplies for exhaustively classifying religious rituals, viz., odd-numbered, special agent rituals on the one hand and even-numbered, special patient and special instrument rituals on the other. At this general level at least, the cognitive representation of ritual form is the variable that most significantly influences these comparative performance frequencies. But since rituals' performance frequencies are the crucial underlying variable driving the ritual frequency hypothesis, the pivotal role *ritual form* plays in determining rituals' performance frequencies indicates that the ritual form hypothesis gets at a more fundamental causal variable. Consequently, it possesses greater theoretical depth than either the ritual frequency hypothesis or Whitehouse's overarching theory of religious modes. (2002, 126, italics in original)

This conclusion, however, still does not explain how the ritual form hypothesis might account for the excessively high performance frequencies that typify routinized religious traditions the world over. In order to account for routinization, McCauley and Lawson's theory would seem to fall back on mnemonic considerations: frequent repetition is an adaptation to the risks of memory failure. A major problem with that argument, however, is the fact that the rituals in question are often far more repetitive than mnemonic considerations would require. In fact, McCauley and Lawson run into a double problem on this front.

On the one hand, they restrict themselves to the problem of explaining how ritual *procedures* are transmitted, rather than how *ritual meanings* are reproduced and transformed (this issue is discussed further when we examine the relationship between ritual and exegesis later in this chapter). Many rituals, as bundles of procedures, are remarkably easy to learn and recall. We even have some experimental evidence, if evidence were needed at all, that people pick up and remember ritual procedures far more easily than complex theological concepts (see chapter 4). So the degree of routinization found in many ritual systems is far in excess of what McCauley and Lawson's argument would be capable of predicting. On the other hand, and following from the first problem, McCauley and Lawson are unable to explain how routinized religions that lack special agent rituals can possibly thrive and expand (we shall presently see that they can and do). The point to emphasize at this juncture, though, is very simple: ritual form cannot, as McCauley and Lawson claim, drive frequency.

In view of this, it should come as little surprise that the ethnographic record is replete with examples of low-frequency, even-numbered (i.e., special patient or instrument) rituals. These range from annual rituals (e.g., linked to agricultural cycles and calendrical celebrations) through to even less frequently performed rites (e.g., linked to reproductive or long-term astronomical cycles).[2] Thus, it is not just that ritual form fails to explain frequency at a purely theoretical level; it also fails to predict levels of ritual frequency *in practice*.[3]

Selectionalism or Mechanistic Causation?

In many ways, McCauley and Lawson's ritual form hypothesis (2002) is a hybrid of two rather different strategies of explanation: the selectionist account proposed by the theory of modes of religiosity and the mechanistic arguments inspired by their theory of ritual competence. Some of the thornier implications of the resulting amalgamation are easiest to spot by perusing their three-dimensional model of the space of ritual possibilities.

The spherical objects adorning this diagram (figure 8.2) represent the two main types of rituals that become established within religious traditions, at least

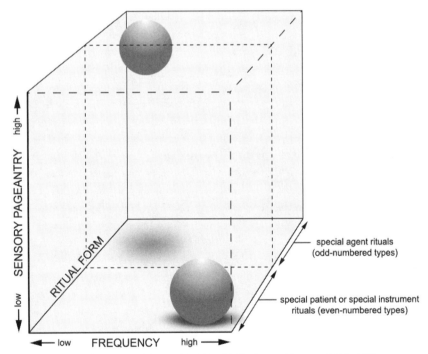

Figure 8.2.   Ritual Form as a Discrete Variable (McCauley and Lawson 2002, 139)

according to McCauley and Lawson. The ball in the bottom foreground represents high-frequency, low-sensory pageantry, even-numbered rituals; the one hovering in the background represents low-frequency, high-sensory pageantry, odd-numbered rituals. The crunch question is, of course: How do the balls come to occupy these contrasting positions in the space of all possible rituals?

The selectionist part of McCauley and Lawson's response to this question is broadly consistent with the theory of modes of religiosity and concerns the relationship between frequency and arousal. Crudely, rituals that fall into one or the other of these two attractor positions have a selective advantage over those that do not. A low-frequency, low-arousal ritual runs the risk of extinction due to lowered motivation (and possibly also memory failure due to distortion or loss).[4] A high-frequency, high-arousal ritual has no chance of survival at all, and its fate lies in three possible transformations. It could persist at its existing frequency level, in which case habituation would drive it toward the low-arousal attractor position. It could persist in its high-arousal form, but that would require a massive reduction in its frequency. Or it could simply become extinct. McCauley and Lawson acknowledge the appeal of a selectionist account of this situation and explicitly ground their own model in the epidemiological approach pioneered by Dan Sperber (cf. Sperber 1996 and McCauley and Lawson 2002, 44–45).

The mechanistic strategy of McCauley and Lawson's theory resides in the one parameter of variation in their model that differs from the other two by virtue of being a simple opposition rather than a continuum of possibilities. According to McCauley and Lawson's theory, all religious rituals are either even- or odd-numbered (this is represented in figure 8.2 by the depth dimension of their cube). There are no shades between these two possibilities. To cope with the representational problems arising from this, McCauley and Lawson bisect their box with a dotted line. But they include some arrows, presumably so that their third dimension would at least *appear to be* commensurate with the two continua proposed by the frequency hypothesis. The arrows, however, apparently have no purpose other than to hide the discrepancy, for one simply could not have a "high degree of special agent-ness" in a ritual and a lower degree of it. But the problem remains. The fact is that considerations of ritual form concern a different kind of variation in the properties of rituals than that postulated by the frequency hypothesis. And consequently, the ritual form hypothesis is a very different kind of argument: namely; a functionalist one.

Consider the following string of assertions:

> Rituals employ countless *means* of arousing participants' emotions. . . . Of course, sensory pageantry is only a *means to an end*. . . . [We shall] focus throughout on what we have been calling sensory pageantry, i.e., on the stimulation of participants'

various sense modalities *in order to* arouse their emotions. (McCauley and Lawson 2002, 102–103, my italics)

> If a ritual establishes a super-permanent arrangement, it must convince participants that something profound is going on. . . . The comparatively high emotion such rituals instigate *helps to persuade* at least some of the participants involved not only that they have undergone fundamental changes but also that the CPS agent . . . [is] vitally important to them. (2002, 122–123, my italics)

In these passages, and a number of others, McCauley and Lawson appear to be saying that the *function* of sensory pageantry is to arouse emotions and, later, that the *function* of emotional arousal is to mark suitably the effects of divine intervention, via special agent rituals. This is no longer a matter simply of selectional advantage or disadvantage (although it could have implications for selectionist stories as well). At least part of what McCauley and Lawson are saying is that people will actively (if unconsciously) manipulate their rituals so as to ensure that they correspond more closely to the model presented in figure 8.2. This is an important point of contrast with the exclusively selectionist argument proposed by the theory of modes of religiosity, which maintains that people may be very satisfied with rituals that crop up in all kinds of strange positions in McCauley and Lawson's cubic space, but (despite the intuitive suitability of the latter *as rituals*) not all these rituals survive and flourish because of their lack of fitness as (clusters of) cultural representations.

McCauley and Lawson do not recognize this fundamental difference between the modes theory and the arguments they are advancing in its stead, and some of the problems they identify with the frequency hypothesis stem from that misunderstanding. If, as they suggest, people somehow sense that one particular kind of ritual should be high in arousal and low in frequency, whereas another should be low in arousal and high in frequency, then this would indeed raise the problem of explaining how they arrive at these extraordinary intuitions. But there is no compelling reason to suppose that such intuitions determine the frequency of religious rituals in general. An alternative explanation for the bifurcation in McCauley and Lawson's space of ritual possibilities (Whitehouse 1992, 1995, 2000a) looks to the differential challenges placed on human memory and motivational levels by a spectrum of possible (and actual) transmissive episodes. Out of these innumerable episodes, the fittest patterns of religious thought and action emerge triumphant. But that process of selection is not reducible to any single variable, such as transmissive frequency.

Arousal, Memory, and Motivation

According to McCauley and Lawson, the high arousal occasioned by low-frequency rituals has two main effects: First, it serves to arrest the attention of participants, a fact that McCauley and Lawson stress would play a role in motivating subsequent transmission. Second, it enhances recall for ritual procedures—information that would otherwise be vulnerable to memory decay or distortion or both. These arguments also assume that special agent rituals elicit higher levels of sensory pageantry (and therefore arousal), at least relative to special patient or instrument rituals within the same tradition.

The latter assumption, and hence the arguments that follow from it, raises a great many empirical problems. For instance, the Baining of New Britain in Papua New Guinea traditionally performed a number of low-frequency rituals that involved extremely high levels of arousal, including the Mali *awan* (described at length in Whitehouse 1995)—a rarely performed and typically violent ritual that would not seem to fit the special agent ritual profile.[5] By contrast, Baining weddings (which undoubtedly constituted bona fide special agent rituals) evinced remarkably low levels of sensory pageantry and arousal, comprising merely a series of moralistic speeches from elders and the ceremonial exchange between bride and groom of a split taro tuber. Quite clearly, levels of sensory pageantry associated with special agent rituals (such as weddings) are *not necessarily higher* than for even-numbered rituals in the same tradition.

Obviously, this observation has implications for McCauley and Lawson's argument that special agent rituals *require* elevated sensory pageantry *in order* to convince people that the changes effected by the intervention of CPS agents are real and permanent. The main problem here is that, while such a post hoc rationale might be advanced (in *some* cultures, in relation to *some* rituals), it is hardly an adequate explanation for patterns of ritualized sensory stimulation more generally. To return to the example of Baining weddings, the change of status (both spiritually and socially) that this low-key ceremony was believed to effect, was regarded as both permanent and supernaturally sanctioned. Moreover, rates of divorce in Baining societies were traditionally very much lower than in contemporary North America and Europe, even though in the latter societies weddings tend to entail rather higher levels of sensory pageantry than most special patient or instrument rituals.[6] In short, stimulation of the senses or emotions is not connected to motivational states in any simple and straightforward fashion. Some special agent rituals simply are not concerned with generating revelatory religious knowledge capable of motivating subsequent transmission. The effects of wedding ceremonies, in particular, often have more to do with the recalibration of social relations (between bride and groom, but also among a wider range of kin and affines) than with the propagation of religious meanings. The subsequent stability of changes affected by such rituals consequently does not depend in any significant way on features of the rituals themselves. To put it more concretely, weddings conducted at St. Paul's Cathedral amidst a blaze of fanfare do not necessarily evince greater commitment to the effects of the ritual than weddings performed in a little hut where two pieces of an everyday vegetable are peremptorily swapped.

Consider, finally, McCauley and Lawson's claim that sensory pageantry or arousal is needed to enhance recall for rarely performed rituals (2002). It is undeniably the case that people often have detailed autobiographical memories for their own weddings, confirmations, ordinations, and so on. The question is whether this is necessary for the ritual procedure to be accurately recalled and passed on. This is questionable. Recall for ritual *procedures*, even one-off procedures, is generally rather impressive in humans. Moreover, people may even remember rituals that triggered major changes in their own social statuses *without* any exceptional sensory pageantry. If some rarely performed rituals involve extremely high levels of arousal, then the explanation for this probably lies elsewhere.

The view advanced in chapter 6 and developed further in chapter 7 is that elevated arousal mainly contributes to motivational states through its role in triggering spontaneous exegetical reflection (SER). But that would certainly not be the case for special agent rituals per se, or even for only a particular category of special agent rituals. That is to say, although some low-frequency, high-arousal rituals that operate within the imagistic mode of religiosity also conform to the special agent type, many do not. Of those that do, it is easy to find examples of special agent rituals that belong fairly and squarely in a doctrinal mode of operation (e.g., Christian weddings and baptisms), and consequently derive their motivational force from a verbally transmitted corpus of beliefs. Not only that, but these kinds of special agent rituals are using the modal theory measure (which operates *across* traditions), very much lower in levels of arousal than the kinds of shocking ordeals that typify a truly imagistic mode of religiosity. And, on top of that, many special agent rituals are not really low frequency at all, even by McCauley and Lawson's measures, because they freely cannibalize more routinized rituals (a syndrome that McCauley refers to as "compositionality").

If these problems present a challenge to the ritual form hypothesis, those associated with high-frequency, low-arousal rituals are very much more serious. As noted previously, McCauley and Lawson have no means of accounting for people's motivations to perform rituals of this type, and consequently, they make the questionable prediction (discussed in a later section) that traditions based on rituals of this sort have poor survival chances in the absence of adequate doses of more high-arousal forms of ritual activity (which, for them, means having a decent set of special agent rituals to complement the set of more tedious, even-numbered rituals).[7] This problem with McCauley and Lawson's model stems primarily from the fact that theirs is a theory only of ritual transmission. Ritual exegesis and processes of revelation are not of concern to them.

Procedural versus Exegetical Knowledge in the Domain of Ritual

From the very beginning of *Bringing Ritual to Mind* (2002), McCauley and Lawson are very clear about the fact that their concern is with the transmission of procedural knowledge pertaining to rituals and not with the transmission of ritual or religious meanings more generally. They justify this strategy on the grounds that much of what passes as religious thinking has no causal significance regarding ritual systems but is merely a kind of epiphenomenal side effect of the real business of ritual transmission. Consider McCauley and Lawson's following comments on the profusion of exegetical religious knowledge in many ritual traditions: "Rituals often occasion an astonishingly wide range of interpretations. . . . While the meanings associated with rituals may vary, such variability typically has no effect on the stability of the ritual actions' underlying forms. . . . Not only do other things matter besides meanings, for some explanatory purposes meanings hardly matter at all" (2002, 9–10).

Herein lies another crucial difference between McCauley and Lawson's theory and the modes theory. The former assumes not only that implicit and intuitive forms of cognition furnish the most decisive mechanisms biasing cultural selection, but that explicit cultural knowledge in all its wondrous diversity is a mere side effect rather than a cause of patterns of cultural (e.g., religious and ritual) transmission. This view could not be squared with the theory of modes of religiosity, but it also proves untenable on McCauley and Lawson's own account of how ritual form considerations affect the stability of ritual traditions (as we shall see presently).

According to the modes theory, explicit religious knowledge is crucially important in *motivating* transmission. In the case of some (otherwise potentially tedious and uninspiring) rituals, people are willing to lay down their lives to preserve and defend them, and therefore the question is surely not whether but *how* explicit religious beliefs come to have such high levels of motivational force. The theory of modes of religiosity not only specifies the conditions necessary for the transmission of knowledge of this kind, but in so doing, it accounts for something McCauley and Lawson's model crucially cannot—the routinization of many kinds of rituals. As we've seen, McCauley and Lawson have no means of explaining extremely frequent rituals and ultimately fall back on the claim that this aids accurate recall for ritual procedures. But, as we've also noted, transmissive frequency is much higher than would be needed merely to reproduce knowledge for *ritual procedures*. The modes theory, by contrast, maintains that these very high transmissive frequencies are adaptations to demands placed on memory not by rituals as such, but by persuasive bodies of doctrinal knowledge and the maintenance of these in a stable, credible, and centrally legitimated (i.e., orthodox) form. The way in which this occurs turns out to be rather complex, enlisting not only semantic memory for explicit teachings but also implicit or procedural knowledge for rituals (which helps to suppress rates of exegetical—and more generally—doctrinal innovation).

McCauley and Lawson also underplay the possibility of causally significant explicit religious knowledge deriving from low-frequency, high-arousal rituals. On their view, the difficulties often faced by ethnographers in gathering explicit exegesis with regard to such rituals may well reflect its absence. But whether this is the case or not, there is no space in their model for imagistic revelations that have causal efficacy with regard to ritual transmission. For the modes theory, by contrast, processes of spontaneous exegetical reflection deriving from low-frequency, high-arousal rituals are crucial to the construction of religious knowledge in the imagistic mode and highly consequential in motivating subsequent transmission (ritual performances).

Historical Transformations

As we saw in the last chapter, McCauley and Lawson endorse some—but not all—of the claims of the modes theory with regard to patterns of historical transformation in religious systems. Consider the observation, made at the very end of *Bringing Ritual to Mind*, that "some religions have existed that have had no special patient or special instrument rituals" (2002, 212). This is a puzzling statement because McCauley and Lawson emphasize throughout their book that tacit, intuitive knowledge *drives* patterns of ritual innovation and transmission in much the same way everywhere. For instance, in chapter 4 (2002), they maintain that relations between religious adherents and their god(s) must always be a two-way street. The traffic could never flow in one direction for any appreciable length of time because odd-numbered rituals are intrinsically no more or less salient cognitively than even-numbered ones. As they put it: "The theory of mind and the general social intelligence underlying participants' presumptions about the relations between human agents and CPS agents so underdetermines the production of both sorts of ritual types that what can happen will" (2002, 143). And yet, in startling contrast to this statement, it seems to be suggested on the last page of their book that even-numbered rituals may not have taken hold during most of the time that fully modern humans have roamed the planet.

> Diamond's and Boyer's views on the history of culture and Donald's, Boyer's, and Whitehouse's views of the natural history of human cognition all suggest that

some religions have existed that have had no special patient or special instrument rituals. This suggests that *special agent rituals must play a more fundamental role in the transmission and persistence of religion than do special patient and special instrument rituals.* (2002, 212, emphasis in original)

The claim that I have previously advanced (Whitehouse 2000a) is not that special agent rituals preceded those of special patient or instrument in human prehistory or but that the *imagistic mode* was established long before the *doctrinal mode.* The imagistic mode incorporates both odd- and even-numbered rituals. In fact, ritual form is not the independent variable determining levels of sensory pageantry and arousal (we have already established that it does not determine frequency either). Only when these points are acknowledged can the really important insights of the ritual form hypothesis be rescued and accorded the significance they deserve (as I hope to have done in chapter 2 of this book).

This chapter has examined closely the proposals advanced by McCauley and Lawson's "ritual form hypothesis" (2002), which differs from the theory of modes of religiosity in a number of ways. First, the ritual form hypothesis treats frequency as the unexplained independent variable driving doctrinal- and imagistic-mode dynamics. Second, it replaces the modes theory's arguments about memory and motivation with a rather different set of proposals about the impact of people's tacit intuitions about the well-formedness of rituals. The latter, McCauley and Lawson claim, have specific consequences for levels of sensory pageantry, affecting both motivational states and memory for ritual procedures in ways that differ markedly from the predictions of the modes theory. As a result of this move, McCauley and Lawson's theory is concerned only with relative levels of sensory pageantry within (and not across) religious traditions. Third, the ritual form hypothesis accords no role to exegetical meanings in motivating ritual action. Fourth, it offers an alternative theory of the causes of varying patterns of religious stability and transformation over time.

In the end, the differences between the theory of modes of religiosity and the ritual form hypothesis would seem to loom larger than any similarities. Nevertheless, these approaches *do* have many basic goals in common. Both are seeking to provide a cognitive explanation for divergent patterns of ritual transmission and to show how these patterns might account for the varied profiles of religious systems both ethnographically and historically. The question is, which (if either) of these two approaches gets it right? My preferred conclusion would be that both theories are on the right tracks. But certain elements of the ritual form hypothesis would need to be jettisoned, if we are to keep the stock rolling. The arguments advanced by McCauley and Lawson are most persuasive when taken as a set of (highly sophisticated) predictions with regard to people's tacit, intuitive judgments concerning religious rituals. These judgments exercise an especially prominent influence over the transmission of rituals clustered around the cognitive optimum position, as indicated in chapter 2. But the very same judgments can be overridden by officially sanctioned teachings and suppressed by habituation in conditions of extreme routinization (as is characteristic of the doctrinal mode). And where elaborate and highly motivating explicit reflection on the nature and meaning of rituals is fostered (as occurs in both modes, but especially the imagistic), the resulting patterns of ritual innovation are similarly remote from what we might predict on the basis of implicit intuitive thinking. In sum, the ritual form hypothesis potentially *complements* the theory of modes of religiosity, and vice versa.

Notes

1. For rather different reasons, praying, chanting, the singing of hymns, and various other actions that many of us might assume to be "religious rituals" are also excluded from McCauley and Lawson's theory (2002, 13–14).

2. The classic surveys of Sir James Frazer (1922) and Arnold Van Gennep (1960) furnish abundant examples, but a brief perusal of ethnographic cases provided by any standard contemporary textbook on the anthropology of religion would equally suffice. In seeking clear instances of low-frequency, even-numbered rituals, the literature on ritual inversion (or "rituals of conflict") provides a particularly rich starting point (see the excellent survey by Edward Norbeck 1963).

3. It is worth noting also that ritual form considerations specify remarkably *unstable* features of ritual, as compared with the durability of the ritual procedures and cycles themselves. Examples abound of rituals that have historically rather rigid features in terms of their action elements, sequences, and frequencies, and yet slip very easily between the odd- and even-numbered categories. Take, for instance, the low-frequency, high-arousal ritual known as Yangis, performed among the Yafar people of the Sepik region of Papua New Guinea (Juillerat 1992). This ritual forms the core of a religious tradition that exhibits all the key elements of the imagistic mode, and yet there is a great deal of slippage here in terms of ritual form considerations. On occasions when most junior participants are performing it for the first time, this ritual constitutes their initiation in the mysteries of the Yafar fertility cult. It is thus a special agent ritual. But when all the performers of Yangis consist of men who have participated at least once in the past, it would appear to take the form of a special patient ritual (by McCauley and Lawson's criteria), concerned with the periodic renewal of natural fertility by supernatural means, and to follow rather closely the logic of a sacrificial rite. But whether or not the ritual is performed in the special agent or special patient modality, the procedures it involves would not seem to be affected. It is often unsafe to assume that a given ritual can be classified as odd- or even-numbered: some rituals, it would seem, can be both at different times.

4. Motivational issues are dealt with very differently in McCauley and Lawson's account, as compared with mine, but this matter is addressed in the proceeding.

5. Although performed as part of an initiation complex, the *awan* were also performed sporadically by initiated men to celebrate public achievements and to carry out beatings and homicides.

6. It is probably fair to say that the predictions of the ritual form hypothesis, at least with regard to levels of sensory pageantry, fits rather well with the evidence from *most* variants of Christianity. But not all. Consider the case of Pentacostalism, which seems quite deliberately to raise levels of sensory stimulation relative to its special agent rituals. On the face of it, this would also seem to pose a problem for the modes theory, which predicts an inverse correlation between frequency and arousal. But there is a crucial distinction to make between sensory pageantry and arousal. Weekly services in evangelical Christian churches may involve high levels of sensory pageantry, but this does not mean that arousal levels remain high over a period of regular, long-term participation. On the contrary, the modes theory would predict declining levels of measurable arousal among adherents. Conversely, some very high-arousal rituals in Melanesia involve quite ordinary levels of sensory pageantry. A good example would be ritual acts that involve eating (an everyday sensory experience) but in which the menu consists of very special kinds of "foods" (e.g., human flesh), the consumption of which evinces strong emotions. Nevertheless, even if McCauley and Lawson were to revise their claim by arguing that ritual form considerations predict levels of *arousal* rather than levels of sensory pageantry, their argument would still run into serious empirical problems, as noted here.

7. Consider the case of ISCKON (the Hare Krishna movement), which spread with remarkable rapidity first in the United States and subsequently all around the world since its foundation nearly forty years ago. This flourishing religious tradition is based very heavily upon highly repetitive forms of ritual, exegetical, and doctrinal transmission (Ketola 2002). And yet, in terms of McCauley and Lawson's model, it is a profoundly unbalanced system, based almost exclusively around even-numbered rituals. Such "special agent" rituals as may be found in the movement would seem to elicit levels of arousal that are lower (and at least no higher) than any of the various aspects of daily worship. Cases such as these may be explained much more productively with reference to selectional mechanisms operating on a number of variables simultaneously, summarized in the following chapter.

Empirical Challenges　　9

MANY OF THE SPECIFIC HYPOTHESES advanced in previous chapters could easily have been obscured or separated by a torrent of arguments, evidence, speculation, and rhetoric. This chapter attempts to sort out some of the wheat from the chaff by highlighting the main predictions of the theory of modes of religiosity and indicating, if only in a preliminary fashion, the kinds of evidence needed to test them.

Predictions

The key predictions of the theory of modes of religiosity can be broken down into a limited range of scenarios for ritual transmission that can only have four kinds of outcomes: doctrinal effects (see figure 4.2, chapter 4), imagistic effects (see figure 4.3, chapter 4), survival without doctrinal or imagistic effects, and extinction of the practices in question. These key predictions may be summarized in the form of a series of flow charts (figures 9.1–9.4).[1] The starting point, with regard to each set of predictions, is the combination of arousal level (high or low) and modality of codification (doctrinal or nondoctrinal), allowing four possible combinations (low arousal or doctrinal, low arousal or nondoctrinal; high arousal or doctrinal; high arousal or nondoctrinal).[2] The consequences of any one combination depend on transmissive frequency (high or low). The range of predicted scenarios may be enumerated as follows.

    I. Predictions arising from the low-arousal and doctrinal condition.
        According to the theory presented in this book, all the various
        sociopolitical features associated with the doctrinal mode of religiosity
        (diffuse cohesion, dynamic leadership, inclusivity, efficient dissemination,

large-scale membership, high degree of uniformity, and centralized structure) will invariably be associated with high-frequency, low-arousal rituals and (if only within elite sectors of the tradition) conceptually complex, verbally transmitted doctrine. In other words, the latter traits furnish necessary conditions for the occurrence of the former. That core prediction is, of course, potentially falsifiable. Is there an example of a religious tradition somewhere in the world, in the past or in the present, that has all those sociopolitical characteristics and yet has no repertoire of high-frequency/low-arousal rituals and complex teachings? As far as I know, no such tradition exists or has ever existed. That prediction may seem to be relatively safe (at least until a counterexample is produced). A more risky prediction would present necessary conditions as sufficient conditions, by suggesting that low-arousal/doctrinal rituals, if repeated frequently, will invariably give rise to the complete suite of features that comprises the doctrinal mode of religiosity. Nevertheless, the "modes" theory as presently constituted does not supply adequate grounds for such a prediction, even if it were to be empirically supported. At best, it suggests that high-frequency/low-arousal/doctrinal rituals will *typically* give rise to full-blown doctrinal-mode dynamics, because such a pattern of transmission affords fertile opportunities for the formation of religious authorities and expansionary orthodoxies. Nevertheless, there may be external factors in a particular situation—ranging from natural barriers to population contact and communication through to politically motivated restrictions—that could prevent these opportunities from being realized. Note also that the "safer" hypothesis (certain psychological conditions are *necessary* for the establishment of certain sociopolitical ones) does not preclude the presence of other traits wholly unconnected to that particular story. One could imagine, or indeed expect, that some (perhaps all) members of a doctrinal orthodoxy might experience rare moments of ecstasy or trauma in the contexts of normally quite routine ritual activities, or that some people will be more prone to innovative religious thinking than others (despite a common experience of routinization). The traits associated with the doctrinal mode do not exhaust all possible aspects of interior experience or sociopolitical morphology in routinized religious traditions. What the theory does predict, however, is that doctrinal-mode characteristics will tend to coalesce as distributed traits when certain psychological mechanisms are activated in concert across a given population, and that the sociopolitical features identified by the model cannot occur if these psychological mechanisms are *not* activated.

If high-frequency/low-arousal/doctrinal rituals do indeed give rise to the doctrinal mode of religiosity, that is not necessarily the end of the line for possible patterns of historical transformation. As discussed in chapter 7, excessive routinization and control can render this mode of transmission vulnerable to the "tedium effect" and lowered motivation. This could spell disaster for the religious tradition, resulting in its extinction. It is also possible, however, that the tradition will undergo a reformation led by "charismatic" leaders or will be rejuvenated by sporadic outbursts of imagistic splintering (see figure 9.1).

What would happen, though, if the level of ritual frequency were significantly reduced? The model predicts that the doctrinal mode would be unable to survive in these conditions. This does not necessarily mean that the *rituals* would be eliminated (although that is one possible outcome). Figure 9.1 sets out three immediate consequences of reduced frequency for low-arousal/doctrinal rituals.

First, assuming that these are quite elaborate rituals and the frequency level is very low, procedural knowledge might be stored in texts or by other methods of recording (pictures, drawings, film or video, audio tapes, etc.). External mnemonic support might be needed for the performance of rituals in which nobody participates for years at a time, especially if the rituals involve complex choreography or elaborate standardized speech acts. Alternatively, the rarely performed rituals might be composed of many more frequently performed rites that are tacked together and referred to collectively as constituting a separate ritual in its own right ("compositionality"). Either way, such rituals may be thin on the ground, but when they do occur they would offer little in the way of either intuitive appeal or revelatory potential and may be prone to extinction. My prediction would be that such rituals will only ever occur in the context of a wider religious tradition and that their elimination would have no discernible consequences for doctrinal or imagistic dynamics (since the practices neither enhance nor inhibit those dynamics). Second, an alternative consequence of reduced frequency in the case of low-arousal or doctrinal rituals would be forgetting or garbling of the religious teachings ("doctrinal distortion"). Distortions are likely to produce, cumulatively, more cognitively optimal versions of the orthodoxy (see chapter 2), which in turn would lead to some remnants of the ritual tradition surviving without doctrinal-mode effects. Third, the process of decay and distortion arising from these very same circumstances might trigger processes of religious renewal and reform (see chapter 7). If the reformed tradition is to succeed in the long run,

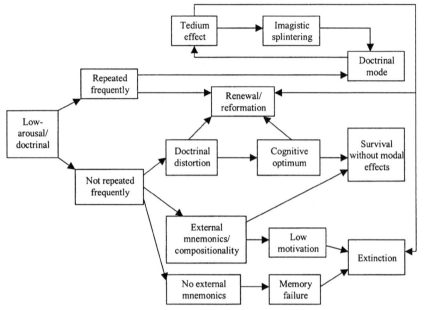

Figure 9.1.   Consequences of the Low-Arousal/Doctrinal Condition

routinization would need to be reestablished in turn allowing full-blown doctrinal-mode practices to be restored.

2. Predictions arising from the low-arousal/nondoctrinal condition.

The main prediction with regard to low-arousal/nondoctrinal rituals is that they are not capable in themselves of sustaining the modes dynamics described in this book. If a given tradition were based exclusively on low-arousal rituals in the absence of any corpus of conceptually complex teachings, then such a tradition would not exhibit the numerous features of social morphology associated with either doctrinal or imagistic modes of religiosity. That, too, is a falsifiable prediction. Is there, or has there ever been, a tradition of religious revelation that incorporates only low-arousal rituals, that lacks any elaborate ideology, and yet that is *either* widespread, centralized, and hierarchical *or* localized, uncentralized, and intensely cohesive? According to the modes theory, such a tradition should not exist. Of course, as in the unusual case of low-frequency/low-arousal/doctrinal rituals supported by external mnemonics or compositionality (see point 1) or both, there is no reason why low-arousal and nondoctrinal rituals should not occur *as part* of a wider tradition in which the conditions for

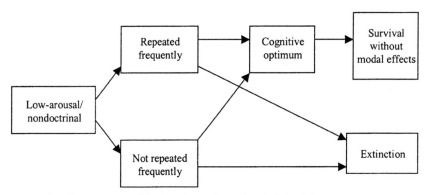

Figure 9.2.   Consequences of the Low-Arousal/Nondoctrinal Condition

modal dynamics are established on quite different ritual foundations. Indeed, low-arousal/nondoctrinal rituals may be particularly common in lay religiosity in which access to doctrinal revelations is largely restricted to elites. But these nonrevelatory rituals would need to assume cognitively optimal forms in order to survive.

The general prediction is that when low-arousal/nondoctrinal rituals occur in isolation from bona fide modes dynamics, they can survive only if the concepts necessary to reproduce them are sufficiently simple and intrinsically compelling to be learned, remembered, and transmitted without the creation/activation of any kind of expert knowledge. In other words, these rituals and the exegesis (if any) that they inspire would have to be clustered around the cognitive optimum position (as described at length in chapter 2). This would be the case regardless of the rate of transmissive frequency. If the rituals failed to achieve cognitive optimality, then the prediction is that they would not be successfully transmitted and so would suffer extinction. Falsification of this hypothesis would be provided if instances could be found of low-arousal/nondoctrinal rituals that lack intuitive procedural/exegetical characteristics. Although freestanding rituals of that kind are theoretically possible, I doubt if such cases actually occur.

3. Predictions arising from the high-arousal/doctrinal condition.

Let us now consider rituals that are emotionally or sensually stimulating, frequently performed, and closely connected to complex, verbally transmitted teachings. Since elevated arousal is known to impair processing of verbal information, one possible consequence of such rituals is that people will forget or garble the teachings associated with them. If, as a consequence, the verbal information is not transmitted intact, two possible consequences might follow: One would be a reduction in the frequency of ritual performances that, if carried far enough, could set the stage for the establishment of imagistic-mode dynamics (i.e., based on low-frequency/high-arousal rituals). The other possibility is that high-frequency transmission is maintained, in which case levels of arousal would be predicted to drop (see chapter 7). Since the verbally transmitted corpus has been lost, we would now have high-frequency/low-arousal/nondoctrinal rituals, doomed to the fates predicted earlier (figure 9.2)—that is, the rituals either would have to develop more cognitively optimal attributes or they would suffer extinction. If, however, the high-arousal, doctrinal rituals were to survive at their original high levels of frequency, then a process of arousal-accommodation would occur, resulting in high-frequency/low-arousal/doctrinal rituals, thus providing the standard foundations for a full-blown doctrinal mode of religiosity. (Many of the evangelical and charismatic Christian traditions seem to operate in that way.)

The other major alternative for high-arousal rituals associated with complex teachings is that the rituals are not repeated frequently. In that case, the verbally transmitted information will be impossible to recall, and we will be left with low-frequency/high-arousal rituals, and thus a basis

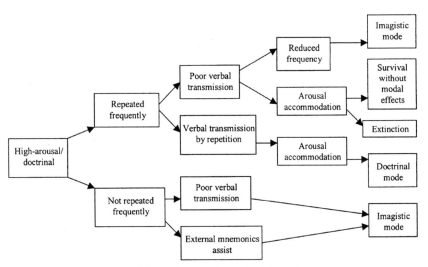

Figure 9.3.   Consequences of the High-Arousal/Doctrinal Condition

for imagistic-mode dynamics to come into operation. It is also possible, however, that the verbally transmitted information will be supported by external mnemonics (e.g., a written record) and so would survive intact. Nevertheless, external storage would have little palpable effect on the cognitive dynamics of the imagistic mode. Intricate texts, for instance, may be read aloud on ritual occasions, but because the rituals are still high-arousal, the information will be poorly encoded, and because the rituals are low frequency, the information will be poorly recalled. What remains would still be, at its core, an imagistic mode of religiosity in which revelations are constructed independently rather than being expressions of an orthodox body of teachings.

4. Predictions arising from the low-arousal/nondoctrinal condition.

Of the available permutations, low-arousal/nondoctrinal rituals produce the simplest possible scenario that could occur. If highly arousing rituals that are not associated with complex verbal teachings were to be frequently performed, then arousal levels would drop due to accommodation. This would produce the kind of high-frequency/low-arousal/nondoctrinal rituals depicted in figures 9.2 and 9.3. As in those cases, the rituals would either have to assume cognitively optimal forms or would simply disappear due to lack of motivation or tedium. If, on the other hand, the high-arousal/nondoctrinal rituals were also subject to low performance frequencies, then they would provide a basis for imagistic-mode dynamics to flourish.

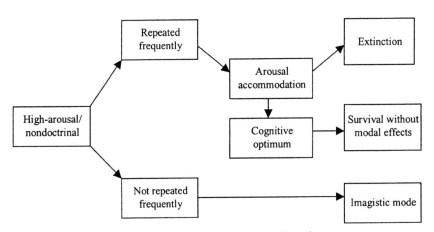

Figure 9.4.   Consequences of the High-Arousal/Nondoctrinal Condition

Evidence Needed from Ethnography, Historiography, and Archaeology

Some of the predictions outlined previously are clearly only possible to test adequately with reference to data on a wide range of religious traditions, past and present. If the broad thrust of the theory of modes of religiosity is correct, then its specific hypotheses concerning the underlying *cognitive causes* of religious experience and social morphology should be applicable not only to Christianity or to the "great religions" or to even the multitude of religious traditions from which contemporary versions of the latter descend, but rather the theory should apply to *all* religions, whether or not near and familiar or distant and exotic. To test that claim requires a wealth of information from social and cultural anthropology, historiography, and archaeology.

Perhaps the most fundamental question to ask of scholars in these fields is whether there is any compelling counterevidence for the claim that the sociopolitical features of doctrinal and imagistic modes are accompanied by the sets of psychological features that respectively are said to drive them. Can we say that most large-scale, inclusive, expansionary, diffusely cohesive, ideological homogeneous, centralized religious traditions also incorporate high-frequency, low-arousal rituals and sustain a body of conceptually complex religious teachings that are subject to routinized verbal transmission? Can we also say that most small-scale or localized, exclusive, intensely cohesive, ideologically heterogeneous, noncentralized religious traditions also incorporate low-frequency, high-arousal rituals and sustain conceptually complex religious knowledge that is internally generated rather than explicitly taught? If so, then what is the approximate ratio of "confirming" to "disconfirming" cases? That is, how much of the data are captured by the model? And in cases that do not fit the predictions of the modes theory, what alternative dynamics are in evidence with regard to processes of memory, codification, transmission, and social morphology? Are some of these dynamics explainable in terms of *interacting* modes of religiosity? In short, what scope is there for further development of the theory?

Beyond the modes dynamics themselves, there is also the question of what kinds of factors *outside* the ambit of the theory might serve to inhibit or enhance the predicted connections between the psychological and sociopolitical variables it addresses. For instance, can we identify any general patterns in the way natural catastrophes, invasion, colonization, demographic change, or migration affect the operations of doctrinal and imagistic modes or their interaction? What kinds of consequences might follow from repressive state policies that drive religious activity underground, perhaps influencing patterns of transmissive frequency, public rehearsal, policing of the orthodoxy, availability of texts, and so on?

Certain "negative" predictions of the theory also raise empirical questions. Modes of religiosity, it is claimed, could not be sustained by certain kinds of rituals. That is, if all the rituals performed by a given population were (1) low-frequency/low-arousal and/or (2) low-frequency/doctrinal and/or (3) low-arousal/nondoctrinal, then the prediction would be that the sociopolitical features associated with doctrinal and imagistic modes simply could not be sustained. Or, at least, if those features had somehow been generated by other means (though it is hard to imagine what), then the presence or absence of rituals in that population would have no material consequences for the social morphology. The rituals could proliferate or vanish altogether, and the political system would persist regardless. Moreover, the negative predictions of the theory go further by proposing circumstances in which rituals, if they were ever to occur, should rapidly disappear, barring certain very specific adaptations. For instance, the model predicts that low-arousal/nondoctrinal rituals should suffer extinction unless they comprise cognitively optimal traits. Meanwhile, low-frequency/doctrinal rituals should become extinct unless supported by external mnemonics.

All the previous predictions are capable, at least in principle, of being tested and developed in the light of ethnographic, historiographical, and archaeological data. Some of the theory's claims, however, might be more easily investigated within narrower disciplinary boundaries. Obviously, anthropologists are particularly well placed to investigate these topics in natural settings. Some aspects of memory and analogical reasoning may require forms of direct observation because the relevant evidence cannot survive in the material record. Ethnographic research may prove especially important in examining the relationship between explicit religious concepts and behavior, an area of crucial importance in testing the theory's claims about the motivating force of revelatory knowledge. Archaeologists are clearly in the best position to address questions surrounding the origins of modes of religiosity and the role of literacy in the independent invention of the doctrinal mode. Meanwhile, historians may be especially well equipped to decipher patterns of long-term doctrinal–imagistic oscillations or transformations and, in particular, to address such questions as whether unintended doctrinal distortion always favors cognitively optimal versions, whether imagistic splintering in the doctrinal mode is generally linked to the tedium effect, and whether doctrinal distortion is a major trigger for patterns of reformation and renewal.

The benefit of testing out theories in this way is not simply that we are then better able to describe and structure our data on religion. It would enable us also to fill the gaps in our knowledge of religions past with increasingly plausible and detailed hypotheses. And in the case of contemporary religions, we stand to gain more systematic comparative bodies of knowledge with the prospect not only of explaining the dynamics of religions we know about, but perhaps even of predicting future trajectories more accurately.

Evidence Needed from the Cognitive Sciences

Most of the psychological research on which this book relies is concerned with the study of learning, memory, and reasoning in nonreligious contexts. We know, for instance, with some degree of certainty, that verbal repetition is needed for aural learning of complex concepts, that repetition of particular tasks leads to implicit procedural knowledge, that the sharing of traumatic experiences promotes cohesion, that high-arousal/low-frequency/personally consequential episodes trigger flashbulb memories (FM), and that deep structural learning of a problem-solving task increases our creative ability to solve new problems of a similar kind, even if, superficially, the problems may seem very remote. It has not yet been specifically shown that the same applies to complex religious concepts, to repetition of ritual tasks, to sharing of traumatic ritual episodes, to recall for rites of terror, or to patterns of religious problem solving. One reason why these topics have not been investigated is that, on the whole, the cognitive operations entailed in religious thinking are exactly the same as those involved in any other kinds of thinking. This would certainly seem to be true of the way perception, intuitive cognition, learning, and memory operate. Nevertheless, we have also considered the possibility that ritual actions differ from non-ritual actions in ways that may have important ramifications for cognitive processing.

At the beginning of this book, it was suggested that rituals, like works of art, are irreducible to any set of technical motivations. But unlike paintings and sculptures, rituals are also irreducible to the intentional states of those who produce or perform them. This constitutes a violation of the intuitive expectations delivered by "theory of mind" mechanisms (see chapter 2). Barring certain pathologies, people continually try to read the intentions of other animate beings, especially other humans. Although they do so with varying degrees of success (for people often misread each other's signals), they nevertheless do it as automatically, unconsciously, and effortlessly as they would recognize a voice or respond to their own names. Yet ritual actions confound this most basic of cognitive mechanisms insofar as they foreclose the possibility of inferring anything about the actors' intentions. Catholics do not cross themselves for any transparent reason. They do it because this is something you do in certain situations, and because this is what people like themselves are presumed to have done for a long time. The intentions behind ritual actions do not lie buried in the particular actor, and so our mind-reading mechanisms either engage in a frustrated search for intentional meaning or, if taxed too heavily, give up altogether. What we do not really know with any certainty is how this state of affairs has an impact on the way people remember and reason about rituals. The hypotheses advanced in this book provide some (hopefully plausible) speculations on the basis of existing research, but there is a lot more we need to know.

To begin with, if we think of rituals as capable of being interpreted in a great variety of ways, then we need to know whether that potentiality is realized to a greater or lesser extent depending on the way rituals are remembered. One of the main predictions of the modes theory is that the volume and elaborateness of spontaneous exegetical reflection (SER) will correlate inversely with frequency of repetition. In other words, as the processing of ritual procedures becomes increasingly implicit, SER is reduced. If that proves to be the case, transmissive frequency is probably not the only variable regulating the rate and volume of SER. First-timers involved in a ritual should generate higher levels of SER than experienced participants. Nevertheless, the exegesis proffered by novices might be simple (cognitively optimal) and fleeting (subject to rapid decay). Whereas, in another case, one-time experience of a particular ritual could set off processes of SER that become extremely elaborate, complex, and enduring, with long-term consequences for religious experience and motivation. The latter scenario, I have suggested, is linked to the activation of vivid episodic memory for ritual episodes, which requires not only low-frequency exposure but *also* very high arousal and personal consequentiality ratings. This in turn would seem to have consequences for subsequent primes and cues and also for the elaboration of systematized exegesis based on analogical reasoning. To test these hypotheses, it would be necessary to run standard FM studies on participants in high-arousal rituals (e.g., rites of initiation), to develop new tests of analogical reasoning on tasks relating to ritual exegesis, to design experiments that control for the priming effects of ritual participation, and so on. In other words, a major program of new psychological research is needed, focusing specifically on the domain of ritual action and exegetical thinking.

In talking about ritual actions, it is important to bear in mind that speech is often a heavily ritualized kind of action, at least in conditions of routinization. We know relatively little about the psychological effects of high-frequency verbal reiteration on processes of analogical thinking. As noted previously, one of the predictions advanced in this book is that ritual repetition of all kinds serves to reduce the rate and volume of SER. But verbal repetition may give rise to very distinctive ways of conceptualizing propositional content. Because the inferences driven by mind reading mechanisms are thwarted by ritualization, the contents of doctrinal propositions are not implicitly attributed to particular speakers (priests, gurus, teachers, etc.) but are seen as emanating from some intuitively unknowable source (even if they are explicitly attributed to some higher power, such as God). As such, ritualized speech generates patterns of analogical reasoning in which source–target pairings appear to be stipulated in advance rather than creatively generated. What looks like dogmatism to the outsider, and spiritual purity or piety to the insider, may actually be an outcome of the way routinized ritual transmission interferes with normal patterns of creative analogical thinking. All these claims are also amenable, at least in principle, to empirical investigation.

This chapter has divided the evidence needed to test the theory of modes of religiosity into two major kinds: ethnographic/historiographical/archaeological on the one hand and cognitive on the other. The reasons for that division of labor are not necessarily as obvious as they may seem. The work of social and cultural anthropologists, historians, and archaeologists is as much concerned with the study of human minds as is the work of cognitive psychologists. Or to put it slightly differently, we are all psychologists of a sort. Although anthropologists may claim to study culture, historians to study history, and archaeologists to study physical remains, what we are all *really* studying are humans and, more specifically, the way humans think, feel, and behave. At a very general level, however, there is a genuine distinction to draw between those who describe themselves as cognitive psychologists and the rest of us. It is not that we study ontologically distinct categories of things, since all attempts to distinguish between the nature of sociocultural and mental phenomena as different orders of reality must ultimately founder (Sperber 1996). It is rather that we tend to study two different aspects of the same thing. By and large, psychologists (at least, the experimentalists) study aspects of mentation that are inaccessible to verbal report—that is, *unconscious* aspects. In order to access those dimensions of cognitive processing, people have to be studied in a controlled fashion so that the scientist can assert with confidence that particular regularities in behavior are really caused by the implicit mechanisms proposed in their hypotheses. This sort of guile and cunning is not required in order to access people's explicit concepts: all you need to do is ask them.

This, however, might seem rather unfair to those of us who are not (institutionally recognized as) psychologists. We *also* need to deploy rather cunning methods of inquiry, but of a different kind. Anthropologists are well aware that not all explicit knowledge is readily accessible—certainly it cannot all be accessed "simply" by asking people. What ethnographers are told is influenced by all kinds of variables, including what is being asked and how, the contexts in which questions are raised, the informants' present assumptions and strategies, and so on. Observation, participation, informal discussion, structured interviews, and a range of other techniques of investigation may illuminate different facets of people's knowledge, but it is almost always just a part of their explicit knowledge that we are able to access in any detail. Historians and archaeologists face rather different challenges of data gathering, since their main objective is to understand the mental states of peoples who have left behind enduring material traces of their activities. In the case of historians, it is of course largely textual traces that provide clues about what their authors thought and also what others around them may have been thinking. Although some archaeologists rely heavily on fragmented evidence of ancient inscribing practices, many depend entirely on inferences about the uses of surviving artifacts that had little or no deliberate communicative function. Still, for historians and archaeologists, as for anthropologists, the principal object of study is usually the explicit knowledge of humans, whether contemporary, freshly expired, or ancient.

Over a number of years, I have debated with one of my historian friends whether he has, as he claims, gained a more intimate knowledge of the Irish Republican leader Ernie O'Malley (based on secondary sources)[3] than I was able to muster as a fieldworker (encountering people in the flesh). Although O'Malley died before his biographer was born, the latter has been able to make a strong case for the view that competent historians, given adequate documentation, can enter more deeply the minds of their subjects than anthropologists in the field. In all likelihood, we shall never resolve this debate satisfactorily because the truth is that we have learned different things about the people we have studied. But what we have both learned is similar in one very important respect—we have learned primarily about the explicit concepts of our human subjects. Insofar as we may make inferences about the unconscious motives driving their behavior, all is speculation and intuition. For cognitive psychologists, it is a different matter. They can tell us something hard and factual about processes of implicit thinking and their impacts on behavior.

The theory of modes of religiosity attempts to combine these two kinds of knowledge in its approach to understanding the nature and causes of religion. This is primarily what makes it different from most other cognitive theories of religion currently available. The latter are interested mainly in the way implicit intuitive knowledge guides and shapes the formation and transmission of concepts of supernatural agency, ritual form, and mythology. Nevertheless, I have argued that religion is also a domain of human thought and action that typically struggles *against* the constraints of intuitive cognition. These views are complementary rather than conflicting at a general level, if not in all the details. Explicit knowledge, as argued at length in chapter 5, cannot exist independently of implicit processing—these are two sides of the same coin. Moreover, certain of the claims of the modes theory (most obviously my hypotheses concerning the cognitive optimum effect) hinge substantially on an acceptance of the main claims of the religion-is-natural camp. Still, any theory that seeks to take into account both sides of the coin—what we know that we know as well as what we are unaware of knowing—*must* be able to traverse the boundaries of cognitive psychology and seek assistance from anthropologists, linguists, sociologists, historians, philosophers, classicists, archaeologists, and others. These scholars often know much more about certain aspects of the human psyche than those who profess to study only that and nothing else.

Notes

1. These figures are based on a series of flow charts originally produced by Justin Barrett (reproduced in Whitehouse 2002c) to describe concisely the main claims advanced in *Arguments and Icons* (Whitehouse 2000a).

2. The shorthand "doctrinal/nondoctrinal," in this context, is intended to refer to the presence/absence of conceptually complex, verbally transmitted religious teachings (including ritual exegesis, parables, eschatology—in fact, *all* teachings of a given tradition, and not merely doctrine, as more usually construed). This shorthand usage is also to be distinguished from the notion of a "doctrinal mode" that refers to a suite of features (see chapter 3), of which "doctrine" (both in the usual sense and the special sense indicated in the preceding) constitutes just one aspect among many.

3. Compare the richly informative and penetrating study of character in Richard English's *Ernie O'Malley: IRA Intellectual* (1998) with my best attempts at individual biography in *Inside the Cult* (Whitehouse 1995).

Epilogue: Cumulative Theory Building in the Cognitive Science of Religion

COGNITIVE APPROACHES to the study of religion may offer discipline-specific benefits to a wide range of students of religious traditions: for anthropologists and sociologists, opportunities to build generalizing theories as well as to refine the techniques of ethnographic enquiry (Whitehouse 2001a); for historians and archaeologists, the possibility of filling in gaps in our knowledge of the past (Martin 2004); for psychologists, the opportunity to enrich and extend existing models of motivation, coalition-formation, cognitive development, and so on (Boyer 2001a); and for biologists, the capacity to understand more fully the two-way street between culture and cognitive evolution (Plotkin 2001). Nevertheless, while all these merits (and there are undoubtedly others) may be apparent to the scientifically inclined, they are not always obvious to scholars working in arts and humanities subjects who may doubt the feasibility, if not the value, of cumulative theory building. Since the involvement of such scholars is indispensable to the project at hand, this is an issue that needs to be addressed.

In general, the study of religion has tended to resist progress, or at least to display a certain skepticism toward the possibility of steady advancement. In my own discipline of social and cultural anthropology, older perspectives on religion generally merit reference primarily as instances of intellectual folly. One example would be the idea—widely touted among late-nineteenth-century scholars—that religious systems evolve (e.g., from polytheism to monotheism). Another would be the idea that religious institutions have social functions, such that they contribute to the stable reproduction of the societies in which they occur. Although there may be some truth in both of these hypotheses, few anthropologists today would take them very seriously. Then again, while most humanities disciplines have their traitors' gates festooned with the heads of currently discredited ancestors, academic genealogies and histories are also being continually rewritten. Unsung heroes are suddenly remembered and celebrated, villains reinvented as saints, figures of veneration toppled, and unlikely alliances forged among their descendants. Very little of this could be described as progress, even if it is sometimes presented that way to undergraduate classes.

In the natural sciences, by contrast, a significant building process has long been underway. When Isaac Newton said that he stood "on the shoulders of giants," he may have been ironically deriding the stature of a deformed (and debauched) adversary, but, still, the metaphor as commonly used today captures something of the cumulative nature of scientific knowledge. Whereas the hard sciences have genuine *paradigms*—bodies of ideas that closely converge on the basis of overwhelming empirical support—the humanities and social sciences tend to have only *agendas*, the truth and value of which is seldom agreed upon partly because what would count as empirical support is uncertain, hotly disputed, or irrelevant. If the history of the natural sciences may be characterized by rare shifts of paradigm, the history of the social sciences is punctuated by much more frequent shifts of agenda—a pattern that Roy D'Andrade (1995) appositely describes as "agenda hopping." Claudia Strauss and Naomi Quinn (1997) have spelled out the disadvantages of this situation for the discipline of social and cultural anthropology, but their comments have some relevance for trends in the humanities and social sciences more generally. They write:

> Too much anthropological debate these days seems akin to forms of urban renewal in which whole neighbourhoods are razed. The new critics seem to believe that efforts to create better structures require complete elimination of the old. Instead, we need a less destructive form of intervention that conserves what is good in the old while not mindlessly preserving its blind alleys, or crumbling edifices. (Strauss and Quinn 1997, 12–13)

If, following Strauss and Quinn, we were to imagine human knowledge as a city, its ancient centrum would be gloriously decorated by the grand and durable architecture of the natural sciences. Its skyline would be dominated by the office blocks of ever-advancing technologies (inspired by those sciences). And scattered across suburbia, we would find the humanities and social science districts, the crumbling nineteenth-century facades of its high streets bedecked in the banners of deconstructionism, hermeneutics, and interpretivism, and its bookshop windows dazzlingly illuminated by this season's titles. Regular demolition of twentieth-century dwellings would excite little sorrow, and few of the new constructions would be expected to endure either.

Nevertheless, the study of religion *can* leave a legacy for the future, it *can* generate truly *cumulative* forms of knowledge, but this requires a different kind of approach to theory building. We need approaches that are willing to salvage old materials, where appropriate, and that are based on wide cooperation among neighboring building projects rather than on the kind of competitive aesthetics popular in many humanities disciplines today, which so often privileges critical originality over theoretical precision and empirical productivity. This book seeks to contribute to building projects of the collaborative, borrowing kind.

As John Peel (2004) cogently argues, the modes theory resembles, and has been explicitly shaped by, the ideas of Charles Darwin, Robertson-Smith, Max Weber, Émile Durkheim, Ruth Benedict, Fredrik Barth, Victor Turner, Robin Horton, and many other luminaries. David Shankland (2004) has also demonstrated the relevance of Ernest Gellner's work and, through him, that of Karl Popper, Émile Durkheim, and David Hume (Laidlaw 2004). Fredrik Barth (2002), Jack Goody (2004), and Maurice Bloch (2004) have meanwhile explored some of the impacts of their own ideas on the modes theory. The effects of such work on the development of my ideas have been profound, but it has not been a matter of picking and choosing as the fancy dictates. There is an underlying unity to this preceding scholarship, and that is what I have sought to build on. Still, if the modes theory is partly a mosaic of pieces constructed from the fragments of older and greater theories, those bits and pieces have not been arbitrarily gathered. Older and greater they may be, but they are not without flaws.

In particular, some of the most influential social theory of the last hundred years has been plagued by faulty ontological assumptions (Sperber 1996). Theories of religion have often rested on the reification of belief systems as agent-like forces capable of acting on institutions and causing them to take particular forms. Such is the line of thinking that pervaded Durkheim's notion of "collective representations"—developed and extended by generations of subsequent scholars. Essentialized institutions are figments of peculiarly human imaginations—the same imaginations that lead some of us to suppose that specific kinds of agency lurk behind misfortune (e.g., witches, sorcerers) or dwell in features of the landscape (e.g., dreamtime ancestors, nymphs, and dryads). Like anthropomorphized gods and fairies, social institutions are not real agents—they do not exist outside human mentation and interaction, and they certainly do not intend things or, otherwise, cause things to happen.

And so our appeals to the great scholarship of our ancestors must be selective. To the extent that these forebears recognized and disentangled many aspects of a fundamental divergence in patterns of religious thinking and association, the theory of modes of religiosity merely builds on and around existing foundations. But this theory is also the outcome of collective efforts in a rather different sense. It is not merely premised on long-established findings but is being actively and continually created through collaboration among scholars in the here-and-now. That process likewise involves some dismantling as well as construction. And it is, of necessity, a cross-disciplinary project.

One of the central arguments of this book has been that the causes of religion reside not only in mechanisms of human thinking but in the contexts of their activation, and that the psychological processes by means of which religions are produced, transmitted, and transformed take simultaneously implicit and consciously knowable forms. For these reasons (and there are others, as we have seen), the task of explaining religion cannot fall solely to psychologists and biologists. It must also enlist the skills and knowledge of ethnographers, historians, archaeologists, and classicists—indeed, all scholars who, from one perspective or another, are engaged in the study of religion.

The predictions of the theory of modes of religiosity, summarized in the last chapter, are explicitly directed at a range of specialists. But it is not enough to pose questions; we must also be proactive in our pursuit of the answers. Having reached this conclusion some years ago, several of us formed a research group determined to build networks of collaborators to test some of my hypotheses. That group was composed of psychologist Justin L. Barrett, anthropologist James Laidlaw, philosopher Robert N. McCauley, historian Luther H. Martin, and myself. Together, we secured funding from the British Academy and the Templeton Foundation to host a series of conferences on the modes theory, and thereby to gather and discuss the inputs of specialists in the study of religion from a wide range of disciplines. The results of these intensive collaborative efforts will be published in three subsequent volumes by AltaMira Press that seek to test and develop the theory of modes of religiosity using ethnographic, historiographical or archaeological, and psychological evidence, respectively (Whitehouse and Laidlaw 2004, Whitehouse and Martin 2004, Whitehouse and McCauley, forthcoming). This volume merely sets the stage. The full story is yet to come.

References

Allen, M. R. 1967. *Male Cults and Secret Initiations in Melanesia.* Melbourne: Melbourne University Press.

American Psychiatric Association. 1986. *Diagnostic and Statistical Manual of Mental Disorders (DSM-IIIR).* 3rd ed. Washington, D.C.: American Psychiatric Association.

Anderson, John. R. 1983. *The Architecture of Cognition.* Boston, Mass.: Harvard University Press.

Aronson, E., and J. Mills. 1959. "The Effect of Severity of Initiation on Liking for a Group." *Journal of Abnormal and Social Psychology* 59: 177–181.

Asad, Talal. 1993 *Genealogies of Religion: Discipline and Reasons of Power in Christianity and Islam.* Baltimore, Md.: Johns Hopkins University Press.

Astuti, Rita. 2001. "Are We All Natural Dualists? A Cognitive Development Approach." *The Journal of the Royal Anthropological Institute* 7: 429–448.

Atran, Scott. 2002. *In Gods We Trust.* New York: Oxford University Press.

Aunger, Robert. 2000. *Darwinizing Culture: The Status of Memetics as a Science.* Oxford: Oxford University Press

Baddeley, Alan. 1997. *Human Memory: Theory and Practice.* Rev. ed. Hove, UK: Psychology Press.

Baron-Cohen, Simon. 1995. *Mindblindness: An Essay on Autism and Theory of Mind.* Cambridge, Mass.: MIT Press.

Barrett, Justin L. 1998. "Cognitive Constraints on Hindu Concepts of the Divine." *Journal for the Scientific Study of Religion* 37: 608–619.

———. 1999. "Theological Correctness: Cognitive Constraint and the Study of Religion." *Method and Theory in the Study of Religion* 11: 325–339.

———. 2000. "Exploring the Natural Foundations of Religion." *Trends in Cognitive Sciences* 4: 29–34.

———. 2001a. "Do Children Experience God Like Adults? Retracing the Development of God Concepts." In *Religion in Mind: Cognitive Perspectives on Religious Experience,* ed. J. Andresen. Cambridge: Cambridge University Press.

———. 2001b. "How Ordinary Cognition Informs Petitionary Prayer." *Journal of Cognition & Culture* 1: 259–269.

————. 2002a. "Smart Gods, Dumb Gods, and the Role of Social Cognition in Structuring Ritual Intuitions." *Journal of Cognition & Culture* 2: 183–193.

————. 2002b. "Dumb Gods, Petitionary Prayer, and the Cognitive Science of Religion." In *Current Approaches in the Cognitive Study of Religion,* ed. Veikko Anttonen and Ilkka Pyysiäinen. London: Continuum.

————. 2003. "Bringing Data to Mind: Empirical Claims of Lawson and McCauley's Theory of Religious Ritual." In *Religion as a Human Sacrifice: A Festschrift in Honor of E. Thomas Lawson,* ed. Brian C. Wilson and Timothy Light. Leiden, The Netherlands: Brill.

————. 2004. *Why Would Anyone Believe in God?* Walnut Creek, Calif.: AltaMira Press.

Barrett, Justin L., and Frank C. Keil. 1996. "Anthropomorphism and God Concepts: Conceptualizing a Non-natural Entity." *Cognitive Psychology* 31: 219–247.

Barrett, Justin L., and E. Thomas Lawson. 2001. "Ritual Intuitions: Cognitive Contributions to Judgments of Ritual Efficacy." *Journal of Cognition and Culture* 1: 183–201.

Barth, Fredrik. 1975. *Ritual and Knowledge among the Baktaman of New Guinea.* New Haven, Conn.: Yale University Press.

————. 1987. *Cosmologies in the Making: A Generative Approach to Cultural Variation in Inner New Guinea.* Cambridge: Cambridge University Press.

————. 1990. "The Guru and the Conjurer: Transactions in Knowledge and the Shaping of Culture in Southeast Asia and Melanesia." *Man,* n.s., 25: 640–653.

————. 2002. "Review of *Arguments and Icons.*" *Journal of Ritual Studies* 16: 14–17.

Bateson, Gregory. 1936. *Naven.* Stanford, Calif.: Stanford University Press.

Benedict, Ruth. 1935. *Patterns of Culture.* London: Routledge and Kegan Paul.

Blackmore, Susan J. 1999. *The Meme Machine.* Oxford: Oxford University Press.

Bloch, Maurice. 1998. *How We Think They Think: Anthropological Approaches to Cognition, Memory, and Literacy.* Boulder, Colo.: Westview Press.

————. 2004. "Ritual and Deference." In *The New Comparative Ethnography of Religion: Anthropological Debates on Modes of Religiosity,* ed. Harvey Whitehouse and James A. Laidlaw. Walnut Creek, Calif.: AltaMira Press.

Bonnemère, Pascale. 1996. *Le Pandanus Rouge: Corps, Différence des Sexes et Parenté Chez les Ankave-Anga (Papouasie-Nouvelle-Guinee).* Paris: CNRS Éditions.

Boyd, Robert, and Peter J. Richerson. 2000. "Memes: Universal Acid or Better Mousetrap." In *Darwinizing Culture: The Status of Memetics as a Science,* ed. Robert Aunger. Oxford: Oxford University Press.

Boyer, Pascal. 1990. *Tradition as Truth and Communication.* Cambridge: Cambridge University Press.

————. 1992. "Explaining Religious Ideas: Outline of a Cognitive Approach." *Numen* 39: 27–57.

————. 1993. "Pseudo-Natural Kinds." In *Cognitive Aspects of Religious Symbolism,* ed. Pascal Boyer. Cambridge: Cambridge University Press.

————. 1994a. "Cognitive Constraints on Cultural Representations: Natural Ontologies and Religious Ideas." In *Mapping the Mind: Domain-Specificity in Cognition and Culture,* ed. Lawrence A. Hirschfeld and Susan Gellman. Cambridge: Cambridge University Press.

————. 1994b. *The Naturalness of Religious Ideas: A Cognitive Theory of Religion.* Berkeley/Los Angeles: University of California Press.

———. 1996. "What Makes Anthropomorphism Natural: Intuitive Ontology and Cultural Representations." *The Journal of the Royal Anthropological Institute*, n.s., 2: 1–15.

———. 2001a *Religion Explained: The Evolutionary Origins of Religious Thought*. New York: Basic Books.

———. 2001b. "Cultural Inheritance Tracks and Cognitive Predispositions: The Example of Religious Concepts." In *The Debated Mind: Evolutionary Psychology versus Ethnography*, ed. Harvey Whitehouse. Oxford: Berg.

———. 2002. "Review of *Arguments and Icons*." *Journal of Ritual Studies* 16: 8–13.

Boyer, Pascal, and Charles Ramble. 2001. "Cognitive Templates for Religious Concepts: Cross-Cultural Evidence for Recall of Counter-Intuitive Representations." *Cognitive Science* 25: 535–564.

Brown, Roger, and James Kulik. 1977. "Flashbulb Memories." *Cognition* 5: 73–99.

Bynon, Theodora. 1977. *Historical Linguistics*. Cambridge: Cambridge University Press.

Chidester, David. 1996. *Savage Systems: Colonialism and Comparative Religion in Southern Africa*. Charlottesville: University of Virginia Press.

Chomsky, Noam. 1986. *Knowledge of Language: Its Nature, Origins, and Use*. New York: Praeger.

Christianson, Sven-Ake. 1992. "Emotional Stress and Eyewitness Memory: A Critical Review." *Psychological Bulletin* 112: 284–309.

Christianson, Sven-Ake, and Lars Goran Nilsson. 1989. "Hysterical Amnesia: A Case of Aversively Motivated Isolation of Memory." In *Aversion, Avoidance, and Anxiety: Perspectives on Aversively Motivated Behavior*, ed. J. Archer and L. G. Nilsson. Hillsdale, N.J.: Lawrence Erlbaum Associates.

Cohen, Gillian. 1989. *Memory in the Real World*. Hove, UK: Lawrence Erlbaum Associates.

Cohen, Neil J., and Larry R. Squire. 1980. "Preserving Learning and Retention of Pattern Learning Skill in Amnesia: Dissociation of Knowing How and Knowing That." *Science* 210: 207–210.

Collingwood, Robin G. 1940. *An Essay on Metaphysics*. Oxford: Clarendon Press.

Collinson, P. 1997. "From Iconoclasm to Iconophobia: The Cultural Impact of the Second English Reformation." In *The Impact of the English Reformation 1500–1640*, ed. P. Marshall. London: Arnold.

Conway, Martin A. 1995. *Flashbulb Memories*. Hillsdale, N.J.: Lawrence Erlbaum Associates.

Conway, Martin. A., S. J. Anderson, F. S. Larsen, C. M. Donnelly, M. A. McDaniel, A. G. R. McClelland, R. E. Rawles, and R. H. Logie. 1994. "The Formation of Flashbulb Memories." *Memory and Cognition* 22: 326–343.

D'Andrade, Roy G. 1995. *The Development of Cognitive Anthropology*. Cambridge: Cambridge University Press.

Dawkins, Richard. 1982. *The Extended Phenotype*. Oxford: Oxford University Press.

Diamond, Jared M. 1998. Guns, Germs, and Steel: A Short History of Everybody for the Last 13,000 Years. London: Vintage.

Dorson, Richard M., ed. 1972. *African Folklore*. Bloomington: Indiana University Press.

Dunbar, Kevin. 2001. "The Analogical Paradox: Why Analogy Is So Easy in Naturalistic Settings Yet So Difficult in the Psychological Laboratory." In *The Analogical Mind: Perspectives from Cognitive Science*, ed. Keith J. Holyoak, Dedre Genter, and Boicho N. Kokinov. Cambridge, Mass.: MIT Press.

Edelman, Gerald. 1992. *Bright Air, Brilliant Fire: On the Matter of the Mind.* London: Penguin.

English, Richard. 1998. *Ernie O'Malley: IRA Intellectual.* Oxford: Oxford University Press.

Evans-Pritchard, Edward E. 1937. *Witchcraft, Oracles, and Magic among the Azande.* Oxford: Oxford University Press.

Fazio, R. H. 1990. "Multiple Processes by Which Attitudes Guide Behavior: The MODE Model as an Integrative Framework." In *Advances in Experimental Social Psychology*, ed. M. P. Zanna. San Diego, Calif.: Academic Press.

Ferguson, R. Brian. 1990. "Explaining War." In *The Anthropology of War*, ed. J. Haas. Cambridge: Cambridge University Press.

Festinger, L. 1957. *A Theory of Cognitive Dissonance.* Stanford, Calif.: Stanford University Press.

Fisher, Simon E., Fareneh Vargha-Khadem, Kate E. Watkins, Anthony P. Monaco, and Marcus E. Pembrey. 1998. "Localization of a Gene Implicated in a Severe Speech and Language Disorder." *Nature Genetics* 18: 168–170.

Fiske, Alan P., and Nick Haslam. 1997. "Is Obsessive-Compulsive Disorder a Pathology of the Human Disposition to Perform Socially Meaningful Rituals? Evidence of Similar Content." *Journal of Nervous and Mental Disease* 185: 211–222.

Fitzgerald, Timothy. 2000. *The Ideology of Religious Studies.* Oxford: Oxford University Press.

Foy, D. W. 1992. *Treating PTSD.* New York: Guilford Press.

Frazer, James. 1922. *The Golden Bough.* London: Macmillan.

Freud, Sigmund. 1913. *The Interpretation of Dreams.* Translated with an introduction by A. A. Brill. London: George Allen.

Gelman, Rochel. 1990. "First Principles Organize Attention and Learning about Relevant Data: Number and the Animate-Inanimate Distinction as Examples." *Cognitive Science* 14: 79–106.

Gelman, Susan A. 1988. "The Development of Induction within Natural Kind and Artifact Categories." *Cognitive Psychology* 20: 65–95.

Gelman, Susan A., Gail M. Gottfried, and John Coley. 1994. "Essentialist Beliefs in Children: The Acquisition of Concepts and Theories." In *Mapping the Mind: Domain Specificity in Cognition and Culture*, ed. Lawrence A. Hirschfeld and Susan A. Gelman. Cambridge: Cambridge University Press.

Gell, Alfred. 1975. *Metamorphosis of the Cassowaries: Umeda Society, Language, and Ritual.* London: Athlone Press.

Gellner, Ernest. 1969. "A Pendulum Swing Theory of Islam." In *Sociology of Religion: Selected Readings*, ed. R. Robertson. Harmondsworth, UK: Penguin Education.

Gibson, Thomas. 1986. *Sacrifice and Sharing in the Philippine Highlands.* London: Athlone Press.

Gick, Mary, and Keith J. Holyoak. 1980. "Analogical Problem Solving." *Cognitive Psychology* 12: 306–355.

Gold, P. E. 1992. "A Proposed Neurobiological Basis for Regulating Memory Storage for Significant Events." In *Affect and Accuracy in Recall: Studies of "Flashbulb" Memories*, ed. E. Winograd and U. Neisser. New York: Cambridge University Press.

Goody, Jack. 1968. "Introduction." In *Literacy in Traditional Societies*, ed. Jack Goody. Cambridge: Cambridge University Press.

———. 1986. *The Logic of Writing and the Organization of Society.* Cambridge: Cambridge University Press.

———. 2004. "Is Image to Doctrine as Speech to Writing? Modes of Communication and the Origins of Religion." In *The New Comparative Ethnography of Religion: Anthropological Debates on Modes of Religiosity*, ed. Harvey Whitehouse and James A. Laidlaw. Walnut Creek, Calif.: AltaMira Press.

Graf, Peter, and Daniel L. Schachter. 1985. "Implicit and Explicit Memory for New Associations in Normal and Amnesic Subjects." *Journal of Experimental Psychology, Learning, Memory, and Cognition* 11: 501–518.

Graf, Peter, Larry R. Squire, and George Mandler. 1984. "The Information That Amnesic Patients Do Not Forget." *Journal of Experimental Psychology: Learning, Memory, and Cognition* 10: 164–78.

Griaule, Marcel. 1975. *Conversations with Ogotemmeli: An Introduction to Dogon Religious Ideas*. London: Oxford University Press of the International African Institute.

Guthrie, Stewart. 1993. *Faces in the Clouds: A New Theory of Religion*. Oxford: Oxford University Press.

———. 2002. "Gods, Abominable Snowmen, and Chiquita Banana: Why Do We Generate the Humanlike Beings of Religion?" Presented at the International Conference on Minds and Gods: The Cognitive Science of Religion, Ann Arbor, Michigan.

Harber, Kent D., and James W. Pennebaker. 1992. "Overcoming Traumatic Memories." In *The Handbook of Emotion and Memory: Research and Theory*, ed. Sven-Ake Christianson. Hillsdale, N.J.: Lawrence Erlbaum Associates.

Harding, Susan. 1987. "Convicted by the Holy Spirit: The Rhetoric of Fundamental Baptist Conversion." *American Ethnnologist* 14: 167–181.

Harris, Paul. 2000. *The Work of the Imagination*. Oxford: Blackwell.

Herdt, Gilbert H. 1981. *Guardians of the Flutes: Idioms of Masculinity*. New York: Columbia University Press.

———. ed. 1982. *Rituals of Manhood: Male Initiation in Papua New Guinea*. Berkeley: University of California Press.

Herrenschmidt, O. 1982. "Sacrifice: Symbolic or Effective?" In *Between Belief and Transgression: Structuralist Essays in Religion, History, and Myth*, ed. Michel Isard and Pierre Smith. Chicago: University of Chicago Press.

Hinde, Robert. 1999. *Why Gods Persist*. London: Routledge.

Hirschfeld, Lawrence A. 1996. *Race in the Making: Cognition, Culture, and the Child's Construction of Human Kinds*. Cambridge, Mass.: MIT Press.

Holyoak, Keith J., Dedre Gentner, and Boicho N. Kokinov. 2001. "Introduction: The Place of Analogy in Cognition." In *The Analogical Mind: Perspectives from Cognitive Science*, ed. Keith J. Holyoak, Dedre Gentner, and Boicho N. Kokinov. Cambridge, Mass.: MIT Press.

Horowitz, M. J., and S. P. Reidbord. 1992. "Memory, Emotion, and Response to Trauma." In *The Handbook of Emotion and Memory: Research and Theory*, ed. Sven-Ake Christianson. Hillsdale, N.J.: Lawrence Erlbaum Associates.

Houseman, Michael. 2002. "Review of *Arguments and Icons*." *Journal of Ritual Studies* 16: 18–22.

Humphrey, Caroline, and James A. Laidlaw. 1994. *The Archetypal Actions of Ritual: A Theory of Ritual Illustrated by the Jain Rite of Worship*. Oxford: Oxford University Press.

Hutchins, Edwin. 1995. *Cognition in the Wild.* Cambridge, Mass.: MIT Press.

Jacobs, J. 1887. "Experiments on 'Prehension.'" *Mind* 12: 75–79.

James, William 1890. *Principles of Psychology.* New York: Holt.

Johnson, Karen. 2004. "Primary Emergence of the Doctrinal Mode of Religiosity in Prehistoric Southwestern Iran." In *Theorizing Religions Past: Archaeology, History, and Cognition*, ed. Harvey Whitehouse and Luther H. Martin. Walnut Creek, Calif.: AltaMira Press.

Juillerat, Bernard, ed. 1992. *Shooting the Sun: Ritual and Meaning in West Sepik.* Washington, D.C.: Smithsonian Institution Press.

Karmiloff-Smith, Annette. 1992. *Beyond Modularity: A Developmental Perspective on Cognitive Science.* Cambridge, Mass.: MIT Press.

Keesing, Roger M. 1981. *Cultural Anthropology: A Contemporary Perspective.* 2nd ed. London: Holt, Rinehart, and Winston.

Ketola, Kimmo. 2002. *An Indian Guru and His Western Disciples: Representation and Communication of Charisma in the Hare Krishna Movement.* PhD dissertation, Department of Comparative Religion, University of Helsinki.

Kokinov, Boicho N. 1990. "Associative, Memory-Based Reasoning: Some Experimental Results." In *Proceedings of the Twelfth Annual Conference of the Cognitive Science Society.* Hillsdale, N.J.: Lawrence Erlbaum Associates.

———. 1994. "The Context-Sensitive Cognitive Architecture DUAL." In *Proceedings of the Sixteenth Annual Conference of the Cognitive Science Society.* Hillsdale, N.J.: Lawrence Erlbaum Associates.

Kokinov, Boicho N., and M. Yoveva. 1996. "Context Effects on Problem Solving." In *Proceedings of the Eighteenth Annual Conference of the Cognitive Science Society.* Hillsdale, N.J.: Lawrence Erlbaum Associates.

Laidlaw, James A. 2004. "Embedded Modes of Religiosity in Indic Renouncer Religions." In *The New Comparative Ethnography of Religion: Anthropological Debates on Modes of Religiosity*, ed. Harvey Whitehouse and James A. Laidlaw. Walnut Creek, Calif.: AltaMira Press.

Lawson, E. Thomas, and Robert N. McCauley. 1990. *Rethinking Religion.* Cambridge: Cambridge University Press.

———. 1993. "Crisis of Conscience, Riddle of Identity: Making Space for a Cognitive Approach to Religious Phenomena." *Journal of the American Academy of Religion* 61: 201–223.

Leach, Edmund R. 1954. *Political Systems of Highland Burma.* London: G. Bell & Son.

LeDoux, Joseph E. 1992. "Emotion and Memory: Anatomical Systems Underlying Indelible Neural Traces." In *The Handbook of Emotion and Memory: Research and Theory*, ed. Sven-Ake Christianson. Hillsdale, N.J.: Lawrence Erlbaum Associates.

LeRoy, John. 1985. *Kewa Tales.* Vancouver: University of British Columbia Press.

Leslie, Alan M. 1994. "Pretending and Believing: Issues in the Theory of ToMM." *Cognition* 50: 211–238.

Lewis, Gilbert. 1980. *Day of Shining Red: An Essay on Understanding Ritual.* Cambridge: Cambridge University Press.

Lewis, Ioan M. 1971. *Ecstatic Religion: A Study of Shamanism and Spirit Possession.* London: Routledge.

Lewis-Williams, J. David. 1997. "Agency, Art, and Altered Consciousness: A Motif in French (Quercy) Upper Paleolithic Parietal Art." *Antiquity* 71: 810–830.

Livingston, R. B. 1967. "Brain Circuitry Relating to Complex Behavior." In *The Neurosciences: A Study Program*, ed. G. C. Quarton, T. Melnechuck, and F. O. Schmitt. New York: Rockefeller University Press.

Lowie, R. 1924. *Primitive Religion*. New York: Boni and Liveright.

McCauley, Robert N. 2001. "Ritual, Memory, and Emotion: Comparing Two Cognitive Hypotheses." In *Religion in Mind: Cognitive Perspectives on Religious Belief, Ritual, and Experience*, ed. Jensine Andresen. Cambridge: Cambridge University Press.

McCauley, Robert N., and E. Thomas Lawson. 2002. *Bringing Ritual to Mind*. New York: Cambridge University Press.

McCutcheon, Russell. 2001. *Critics Not Caretakers: Redescribing the Public Study of Religion*. Albany: State University of New York Press.

Malley, Brian. 2004. "The Doctrinal Mode and Evangelical Christianity in the United States." In *Ritual and Memory: Toward a Comparative Anthropology of Religion*, ed. Harvey Whitehouse and James A. Laidlaw. Walnut Creek, Calif.: AltaMira Press.

Malley, Brian, and Justin L. Barrett. Forthcoming. "Does Myth Inform Ritual: A Test of the Lawson–McCauley Hypothesis." *Journal of Ritual Studies*.

Mandler, J., and P. Bauer. 1989. "The Cradle of Categorization: Is the Basic Level Basic?" *Cognitive Development* 4: 247–264.

Martin, L., and A. Tesser. 1989. "Toward a Motivational and Structural Theory of Ruminative Thought." In *Unintended Thought*, ed. J. S. Uleman and J. A. Bargh. New York: Guilford.

Martin, Luther H. 2004. "Introduction." In *Theorizing Religions Past: Archaeology, History, and Cognition*, ed. Harvey Whitehouse and Luther H. Martin. Walnut Creek, Calif.: AltaMira Press.

Meggitt, M. J. 1962. *Desert People: A Study of the Walbiri Aborigines of Central Australia*. Sydney, Australia: Angus and Robertson.

Meltzoff, Andrew, and Keith M. Moore. 1994. "Imitation, Memory, and the Representation of Persons." *Infant Behavior and Development* 17: 83–99.

Mills, J., and P. Mintz. 1972. "Effect of Unexplained Arousal on Affiliation." *Journal of Personality and Social Psychology* 24: 11–13.

Mishkin, Mortimer, and Tim Appenzellar. 1987. "The Anatomy of Memory." *Scientific American* 256: 62–71.

Mithen, Steven J. 1996. *The Prehistory of the Mind*. London: Thames and Hudson.

———. 2004. "From Ohalo to Çatalhöyük: The Development of Religiosity during the Early Prehistory of Western Asia, 20,000–7,000 BC." In *Theorizing Religions Past: Archaeology, History, and Cognition*, ed. Harvy Whitehouse and Luther H. Martin. Walnut Creek, Calif.: AltaMira Press.

Myers, David. 1998. *Psychology*. 5th ed. New York: Worth Publishers.

Neisser, Ulric. 1982. "Snapshots or Benchmarks?" In *Memory Observed: Remembering in Natural Contexts*, ed. Ulric Neisser. San Francisco: W. H. Freeman.

Neisser, Ulric, Eugene Winograd, and M. S. Weldon. 1991. "Remembering the Earthquake: 'What I Experienced' vs. 'How I Heard the News.'" Paper presented to the Psychonomic Society, San Francisco, Calif.

Norbeck, Edward. 1963. "African Rituals of Conflict." *American Anthropologist* 65:1254–1277.

Peel, John D. Y. 2004. "Modes of Religiosity and Dichotomous Theories of Religion." In *The New Comparative Ethnography of Religion: Anthropological Debates on Modes of Religiosity*, ed. Harvey Whitehouse and James A. Laidlaw. Walnut Creek, Calif.: AltaMira Press.

Pfeiffer, John E. 1982. *The Creative Explosion: An Inquiry into the Origins of Art and Religion.* New York: Harper & Row.

Piaget, Jean. 1962. *Play, Dreams, and Imitation,* London: Routledge and Kegan Paul. (Orig. pub. 1945.)

Pillemer, David B. 1984. "Flashbulb Memories of the Assassination Attempt on Ronald Reagan." *Cognition* 16: 63–80.

Pillemer, David B., E. D. Rinehart, and S. H. White. 1986. "Memories of Life Transitions: The First Year in College." *Human Learning* 5: 109–123.

Pillemer, David B., E. D. Koff, E. D. Rinehart, and J. Rierdan, J. 1987. "Flashbulb Memories of Menarche and Adult Menstrual Distress." *Journal of Adolescence* 10: 187, 199.

Pinker, Steven. 1994. *The Language Instinct.* London: Allen Lane.

Plotkin, Henry. 2001. "Some Elements of a Science of Culture." In *The Debated Mind: Evolutionary Psychology versus Ethnography*, ed. Harvey Whitehouse. Oxford: Berg.

Poole, F. J. P. 1982. "The Ritual Forging of Identity: Aspects of Person and Self in Bimin-Kuskusmin Male Initiation." In *Rituals of Manhood: Male Initiation in Papua New Guinea*, ed. G. H. Herdt. Berkeley: University of California Press.

Powell, M. C. and R. H. Fazio. 1984. "Attitude Accessibility as a Function of Repeated Attitudinal Expression." *Personality and Social Psychology Bulletin* 10: 139–148.

Pyysiäinen, Ilkka. 2001. *How Religion Works: Towards a New Cognitive Science of Religion.* Leiden, The Netherlands: Brill.

———. 2004. "Corrupt Doctrine and Doctrinal Revival: On the Nature and Limits of the Modes Theory." In *Theorizing Religions Past: Archaeology, History, and Cognition*, ed. Harvey Whitehouse and Luther H. Martin. Walnut Creek, Calif.: AltaMira Press.

Redfield, Robert. 1955. *The Little Community: Viewpoints for the Study of a Human Whole.* Chicago: University of Chicago Press.

Reichel-Dolmatoff, Gerardo. 1971. *The Sexual and Religious Symbolism of the Tukano Indians.* Chicago: University of Chicago Press

Roediger, Henry L. 1990. "Implicit Memory: Retention without Remembering." *American Psychologist* 45: 1043–1056.

Roediger, Henry L., and Teresa A. Blaxton. 1987. "Retrieval Modes Produce Dissociations in Memory for Surface Information." In *Memory and Cognitive Processes: The Ebbinghaus Centennial Conference*, ed. D. S. Gorfein and R. R. Hoffman. Hillsdale, N.J.: Lawrence Erlbaum Associates.

Saler, Benson. 2002. "Finding Wayú Religion." Paper presented to the British Academy Networks Conference on Modes of Religiosity, University of Vermont, Burlington.

Schachter, Daniel L. 1987. "Implicit Memory: History and Current Status." *Journal of Experimental Psychology: Learning, Memory, and Cognition* 13: 501–518.

Schwartz, Theodore. 1962. "The Paliau Movement in the Admiralty Islands, 1946–1954." *Anthropological Papers of the American Museum of Natural History* 49: 210–421.

Shankland, David. 2004. "Modes of Religiosity and the Legacy of Ernest Gellner." In *The New Comparative Ethnography of Religion: Anthropological Debates on Modes of Religiosity*, ed. Harvey Whitehouse and James A. Laidlaw. Walnut Creek, Calif.: AltaMira Press.

Sjöblom, Tom. 2000. *Early Irish Taboos: As Study in Cognitive History*. Helsinki, Finland: University of Helsinki, Department of Comparative Religion.

Smith, Jonathan Z. 1998. "Religion, Religions, Religious." In *Critical Terms for Religious Studies*, ed. Mark C. Taylor. Chicago: University of Chicago Press.

Spelke, Elizabeth S. 1990. "Principles of Object Perception." *Cognitive Science* 14: 29–56.

Sperber, Dan. 1975. *Rethinking Symbolism*. Cambridge: Cambridge University Press.

———. 1985. "Anthropology and Psychology: Towards an Epidemiology of Representations." *Man*, n.s., 20: 73–89.

———. 1996. *Explaining Culture: A Naturalistic Approach*. London: Blackwells.

———. 2000. "An Objection to the Memetic Approach to Culture." In *Darwinizing Culture: The Status of Memetics as a Science*, ed. Robert Aunger. Oxford: Oxford University Press.

Sperber, Dan, and Dierdre Wilson. 1986. *Relevance: Communication and Cognition*. Cambridge, Mass: Harvard University Press.

Squire, Larry R. 1992. "Memory and the Hippocampus: A Synthesis from Findings with Rat, Monkeys, and Humans." *Psychological Review* 99: 195–231.

Strauss, Claudia, and Naomi Quinn. 1997. *A Cognitive Theory of Cultural Meaning*. Cambridge: Cambridge University Press.

Strehlow, T. G. H. 1965. "Culture, Social Structure, and Environment in Aboriginal Central Australia." In *Aboriginal Man in Australia: Essays in Honour of Emeritus Professor A. P. Elkin*, ed. Ronald M. Berndt and Catherine H. Berndt. Sydney, Australia: Angus and Robertson

Taylor, Christopher C. 1999. *Sacrifice as Terror: The Rwandan Genocide of 1994*. Oxford: Berg.

Terr, Lenore C. 1979. "Children of Chowchilla: A Study of Psychic Trauma." *Psychoanalytic Study of the Child* 34: 547–623.

———. 1983. "Chowchilla Revisited: The Effects of Psychical Trauma Four Years after a School Bus Kidnapping." *American Journal of Psychiatry* 140: 1543–1550.

———. 1991. "Childhood Traumas: An Outline and Overview." *American Journal of Psychiatry* 148: 10–19.

Thagard, Paul, and Cameron Shelley. 2001. "Emotional Analogies and Analogical Inference." In *The Analogical Mind: Perspectives from Cognitive Science*, ed. Keith J. Holyoak, Dedre Gentner, and Boicho N. Kokinov. Cambridge, Mass: MIT Press.

Tulving, E. 1972. "Episodic and Semantic Memory." In *Organization of Memory*, ed. E. Tulving and W. Donaldson. New York: Academic Press.

Turnbull, Colin. 1962. *The Forest People: A Study of the Pygmies of the Congo*. New York: Simon and Schuster.

Turner, Mark. 1996. *The Literary Mind: The Origins of Thought and Language*. Oxford: Oxford University Press.

Turner, Victor W. 1974. *Dramas, Fields, and Metaphors: Symbolic Action in Human Society*. Ithaca, N.Y.: Cornell University Press.

Tuzin, Donald F. 1980. *The Voice of the Tambaran: Truth and Illusion in Ilahita Arapesh Religion*. Berkeley: University of California Press.

Tylor, Edward B. 1871. *Primitive Culture*. London: Murray.

Van Gennep, Arnold. 1960. *The Rites of Passage*. Chicago: University of Chicago Press. (Orig. pub. 1909.)

Verswijver, Gustaaf 1992. *The Club-Fighters of the Amazon: Warfare among the Kaiapo Indians of Central Brazil*. Gent, Belgium: Rijksuniversiteit te Gent.

Weber, Max. 1930. *The Protestant Ethic and the Spirit of Capitalism*. London: George Allen and Unwin.

———. 1947. *The Theory of Social and Economic Organization*. Oxford: Oxford University Press.

Werbner, Richard P., ed. 1977. *Regional Cults*. London: Academic Press.

Werner, Alice. 1968. *Myths and Legends of the Bantu*. London: Frank Cass.

Whitehouse, Harvey. 1992. "Memorable Religions: Transmission, Codification, and Change in Divergent Melanesian Contexts." *Man*, n.s., 27: 777–797.

———. 1994. "Strong Words and Forceful Winds: Religious Experience and Political Process in Melanesia." *Oceania* 65: 40–58.

———. 1995. *Inside the Cult: Religious Innovation and Transmission in Papua New Guinea*. Oxford: Oxford University Press.

———. 1996a. "Rites of Terror: Emotion, Metaphor, and Memory in Melanesian Initiation Cults." *Journal of the Royal Anthropological Institute*, n.s., 4: 703–715.

———. 1996b. "Jungles and Computers: Neuronal Group Selection and the Epidemiology of Representations." *Journal of the Royal Anthropological Institute*, n.s., 1: 99–116.

———. 1996c. "Apparitions, Orations, and Rings: Experience of Spirits in Dadul." In *Spirits in Culture and Mind*, ed. J. M. Mageo and A. Howard. London: Routledge.

———. 1996d. "From Possession to Apotheosis: Transformation and Disguise in the Leadership of a Cargo Movement." In *Leadership and Change in the Western Pacific*, ed. Richard Feinberg and Karen Ann Watson-Gegeo. London: Athlone Press.

———. 1998. "From Mission to Movement: The Impact of Christianity on Patterns of Political Association in Papua New Guinea." *Journal of the Royal Anthropological Institute*, n.s., 4: 43–63.

———. 2000a. *Arguments and Icons: Divergent Modes of Religiosity*. Oxford: Oxford University Press.

———. 2000b. "Cultural Cognition and Psychopathology: Anthropological Perspectives." In *Cultural Cognition and Psychopathology*, ed. J. Schumaker and T. Ward. Westport, Conn.: Greenwood.

———. ed. 2001a. *The Debated Mind: Evolutionary Psychology versus Ethnography*. Oxford: Berg.

———. 2001b. "Transmissive Frequency, Ritual, and Exegesis." *Journal of Cognition and Culture* 2: 167–181.

————. 2001c. "Cultural Cognition and Psychopathology: Anthropological Perspectives."
In *Cultural Cognition and Psychopathology*, ed. John F. Schumaker and Tony Ward. London:
Praeger.

————. 2002a. "Implicit and Explicit Knowledge in the Domain of Ritual." In *Current Approaches in the Cognitive Study of Religion*, ed. Veikko Anttonen and Ilkka Pyysiäinen. London: Continuum.

————. 2002b. "Religious Reflexivity and Transmissive Frequency." *Social Anthropology/
Anthropologie Sociale* 10: 91–103.

————. 2002c. "Conjectures, Refutations, and Verification: Towards a Testable Theory of
Modes of Religiosity." *Journal of Ritual Studies* 16 (2): 44–59.

Whitehouse, Harvey, and James A. Laidlaw, eds. 2004. *The New Comparative Ethnography of
Religion: Anthropological Debates on Modes of Religiosity*. Walnut Creek, Calif.: AltaMira Press.

Whitehouse, Harvey, and Luther H. Martin, eds. 2004. *Theorizing Religions Past: Archaeology,
History, and Cognition*, Walnut Creek, Calif.: AltaMira Press.

Whitehouse, Harvey, and Robert N. McCauley. Forthcoming. *Cognition and Religion: Explaining Divergent Modes of Religiosity*. Walnut Creek, Calif.: AltaMira Press.

Wiebe, Donald. 2000. The Politics of Religious Studies. New York: Palgrave Macmillan.

Williams, Francis E. 1928. *Orokaiva Magic*. London: Humphrey Milford.

Winograd, Eugene, and William A. Killinger. 1983. "Relating Age at Encoding in Early
Childhood to Adult Recall: Development of Flashbulb Memories." *Journal of Experimental Psychology: General* 112: 413–422.

Woodburn, James. 1982. "Egalitarian Societies." *Man*, n.s., 17: 431–451.

Wright, Daniel B., and George D. Gaskell. 1992. "The Construction and Function of
Vivid Memories." In *Theoretical Perspectives on Autobiographical Memory*, ed. M. A. Conway, D.
C. Rubin. H. Spinnler, and W. A. Wagenaar. Dordrecht, The Netherlands: Kluwer Academic Publishers.

Yuille, John C., and Judith L. Cutshall. 1986. "A Case Study of Eyewitness Memory of a
Crime." *Journal of Applied Psychology* 71: 291–301.

Index

About the Author

Harvey Whitehouse is professor of anthropology and director of postgraduate studies in the faculty of humanities at Queen's University, Belfast. A specialist in Melanesian religion, he carried out two years of field research on a cargo cult in New Britain, Papua New Guinea, in the late eighties. In recent years, he has focused his energies on the development of collaborative programs of research on cognition and culture. He is currently the principal grant holder of a British Academy Networks project on modes of religiosity and in 2003 was appointed to a British Academy Research Readership. He is also coeditor, with Luther H. Martin, of the AltaMira Cognitive Science of Religion series. His previous books include *Inside the Cult: Religious Innovation and Transmission in Papua New Guinea*, *Arguments and Icons: Divergent Modes of Religiosity*, and *The Debated Mind: Evolutionary Psychology versus Ethnography*.